Cooking Light

PICK FRESH

COOKBOOK

ISBN-13: 978-0-8487-3915-7
ISBN-10: 0-8487-3915-9
Library of Congress Control Number: 2012949215

Printed in the United States of America
First Printing 2013

Be sure to check with your health-care provider before making any changes in your diet.

Oxmoor House

Editorial Director: Leah McLaughlin
Creative Director: Felicity Keane
Brand Manager: Michelle Turner Aycock
Senior Editor: Andrea C. Kirkland, MS, RD
Managing Editor: Rebecca Benton

Cooking Light Pick Fresh Cookbook

Editor: Rachel Quinlivan West, RD
Art Director: Claire Cormany
Senior Designer: Shay McNamee
Assistant Designer: Allison Sperando Potter
Director, Test Kitchen: Elizabeth Tyler Austin
Assistant Directors, Test Kitchen: Julie Christopher, Julie Gunter
Recipe Developers and Testers: Wendy Ball, RD; Victoria E. Cox; Tamara Goldis; Stefanie Maloney; Callie Nash; Karen Rankin; Leah Van Deren
Recipe Editor: Alyson Moreland Haynes
Food Stylists: Margaret Monroe Dickey, Catherine Crowell Steele
Photography Director: Jim Bathie
Senior Photographer: Helene Dujardin
Senior Photo Stylist: Kay E. Clarke
Photo Stylist: Mindi Shapiro Levine
Assistant Photo Stylist: Mary Louise Menendez
Production Managers: Theresa Beste-Farley, Tamara Nall Wilder

Contributors

Garden Editor: Mary Beth Burner Shaddix
Garden Writer: Linda Askey
Project Editor: Lacie Pinyan
Copy Editors: Jacqueline Giovanelli, Kate Johnson
Proofreader: Dolores Hydock
Indexer: Mary Ann Laurens
Interns: Morgan Bolling, Susan Kemp, Sara Lyon, Staley McIlwain, Emily Robinson, Maria Sanders
Food Stylist: Charlotte Autry
Photographers: Johnny Autry, Iain Bagwell, Rod. D. Brodman, Beau Gustafson

Time Home Entertainment Inc.

Publisher: Jim Childs
VP, Strategy & Business Development: Steven Sandonato
Executive Director, Marketing Services: Carol Pittard
Executive Director, Retail & Special Sales: Tom Mifsud
Director, Bookazine Development & Marketing: Laura Adam
Executive Publishing Director: Joy Butts
Associate Publishing Director: Megan Pearlman
Finance Director: Glenn Buonocore
Associate General Counsel: Helen Wan

Cooking Light®

Editor: Scott Mowbray
Creative Director: Carla Frank
Executive Managing Editor: Phillip Rhodes
Executive Editor, Food: Ann Taylor Pittman
Special Publications Editor: Mary Simpson Creel, MS, RD
Senior Food Editors: Timothy Q. Cebula, Julianna Grimes
Senior Editor: Cindy Hatcher
Assistant Editor, Nutrition: Sidney Fry, MS, RD
Assistant Editors: Kimberly Holland, Phoebe Wu
Test Kitchen Director: Vanessa T. Pruett
Assistant Test Kitchen Director: Tiffany Vickers Davis
Recipe Testers and Developers: Robin Bashinsky, Adam Hickman, Deb Wise
Art Directors: Fernande Bondarenko, Shawna Kalish
Senior Deputy Art Director: Rachel Cardina Lasserre
Senior Designer: Anna Bird
Designer: Hagen Stegall
Assistant Designer: Nicole Gerrity
Photo Director: Kristen Schaefer
Assistant Photo Editor: Amy Delaune
Senior Photographer: Randy Mayor
Senior Prop Stylist: Cindy Barr
Chief Food Stylist: Kellie Gerber Kelley
Food Styling Assistant: Blakeslee Wright
Production Director: Liz Rhoades
Production Editor: Hazel R. Eddins
Assistant Production Editor: Josh Rutledge
Copy Chief: Maria Parker Hopkins
Assistant Copy Chief: Susan Roberts
Research Editor: Michelle Gibson Daniels
Administrative Coordinator: Carol D. Johnson
Cookinglight.com Editor: Allison Long Lowery
Associate Editor/Producer: Mallory Daugherty Brasseale

To order additional publications, call **1-800-765-6400** or **1-800-491-0551**. To search, savor, and share thousands of recipes, visit **myrecipes.com**

Front flap: Roast Pork Tenderloin with Plum Barbecue Sauce, page 55
Back cover: Roasted Butternut Squash Risotto with Sugared Walnuts, page 209; Lemony Snap Peas, page 166; Fresh Cherry Gallette, page 27
Back flap: Prosciutto, Fresh Fig, and Manchego Sandwiches, page 36

Cooking Light®

PICK FRESH

COOKBOOK

Creating irresistible dishes from the best seasonal produce

Oxmoor House®

Strawberry-Buttermilk Sherbet, page 63

Spaghetti with Tomato Sauce, page 202

Spicy Basil-Beef Salad, page 215

Gardening Guide, page 250

CONTENTS

WELCOME

Since I first joined *Cooking Light* years ago, I've done an about-face on food and gardening. During my 10 wonderful years in the magazine's marketing department, I talked about food, researched food, traveled to great food events, and ate at wonderful restaurants with famous chefs...but I had a full suitcase and an empty refrigerator. Childhood memories of picking fresh berries on our farm left me wanting a taste of that again.

So I decided to give up suits in favor of rubber boots. I marched into a retail nursery, wanting to start with the basics and learn everything about plants, while getting certified as a master gardener. Little did I know when I told the handsome manager who skeptically eyed my resume, "I want to grow my own food. I want to start seeds. I want to tear up my lawn to plant a veggie garden," that we'd soon be married and working together on his nursery and farm.

Today our life at Maple Valley is what you'd imagine: exhausting and exhilarating. Our vegetable garden feeds us—and the recipe-testing needs of the *Cooking Light* Test Kitchen staff. We pick lettuces for lunch salads and plant fig trees for future preserves. David and I pore over colorful tomato descriptions and swear with a vengeance that we will *not* grow 92 varieties again this year—and then promptly plant 120! Has our love of food encouraged us to garden and enjoy so many varieties and flavors? Or has our love of gardening and basket-bursting harvests directed what's on our dinner table?

However you come into this book, from a love of recipes or an interest in growing the ingredients, we show you how to choose, grow, store, and prepare 50 of the garden's most popular harvests. We also give detailed recipes for season-to-season garden plans that can be mixed to match your taste buds.

Grow your own tomatoes on your patio. Get dewy squash blossoms from your local farmers' market. Try your hand at a raised-bed garden, or interplant a few veggies in your landscape. Starting with fresh ingredients makes even the most simple meal stunning. You get a taste of satisfaction, better nutrition, and a little bit of sunshine, all in one amazing bite.

Mary Beth Burner Shaddix
Cooking Light Gardener

FRUITS

There is no match for just-picked seasonal fruits. Naturally sweet and naturally good for you, these jewels belong on every table.

APPLES

Fall is the prime season to sample the wonderfully diverse array of apples.

SEASON: Midsummer until frost, peaking in fall

CHOOSING: Select fruit that is not bruised or cut—any injury causes the quality of the fruit to decline rapidly. Buy only what you can easily keep in your refrigerator.

STORING: Though you may be tempted to display apples in a fruit bowl, resist the urge. Store them in a plastic bag in the refrigerator. Apples emit ethylene, a gas that hastens ripening; the bag will help prevent them from accelerating the ripening of other produce. The storage time for apples varies from a couple of weeks to six months: Early, summer apples are best eaten immediately, while later-ripening varieties hold longer.

GROWING: With a reputation for tricky maintenance, apples are not for everyone, but the unique flavors of local, homegrown apples outweigh the effort. It takes several years for a young tree to start fruiting, so buy a nursery tree that is two or three years old. If you have room, get at least two varieties—some are better for eating fresh, while others are best for cooking or desserts—since cross-pollination among trees increases production.

Dwarf and semidwarf trees are ideal for home landscapes, producing a remarkable amount of fruit for the space they require—a single dwarf tree can bear a hundred pounds of apples or more. Catalogs and nurseries now list selections that are great for container or patio gardening, too. For the best varieties and maintenance schedules for your area, contact your local Cooperative Extension office. Apples should be chosen based on your climate as well as disease tolerance, so recommendations vary widely. Two varieties that don't require very cold or long winters are Fuji and Pink Lady, while others denote the best home base in their names, such as Arkansas Black.

Shrimp Tacos with Green Apple Salsa

Hands-on time: 37 min.   Total time: 49 min.

Tart Granny Smith slices take the bite out of the sweet heat from the shrimp. This is easy for a weeknight meal but also unique for weekend entertaining. As you look for apples in the fall markets, also seek locally grown black beans, such as Cherokee Trail of Tears, to simmer slowly for a side.

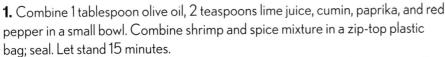

1½ tablespoons olive oil, divided	⅓ cup sliced green onions
4 teaspoons fresh lime juice, divided	½ teaspoon grated lime rind
¼ teaspoon ground cumin	¼ teaspoon salt, divided
¼ teaspoon hot smoked paprika	1 Granny Smith apple, thinly sliced
¼ teaspoon ground red pepper	1 minced seeded jalapeño pepper
1 pound medium shrimp, peeled and deveined	8 (6-inch) corn tortillas
	1 ounce crumbled queso fresco (about ¼ cup)

1. Combine 1 tablespoon olive oil, 2 teaspoons lime juice, cumin, paprika, and red pepper in a small bowl. Combine shrimp and spice mixture in a zip-top plastic bag; seal. Let stand 15 minutes.

2. Combine 1½ teaspoons oil, 2 teaspoons juice, onions, rind, ⅛ teaspoon salt, apple, and jalapeño; toss to combine.

3. Remove shrimp from bag; discard marinade. Heat a grill pan over medium-high heat. Sprinkle shrimp with ⅛ teaspoon salt. Arrange half of shrimp in pan; grill 2 minutes on each side or until done. Remove from pan; keep warm. Repeat procedure with remaining shrimp. Toast tortillas in grill pan or over a gas stovetop, if desired. Place 2 tortillas on each of 4 plates; divide shrimp evenly among tortillas. Divide salsa evenly among tacos; top evenly with queso fresco. Serves 4 (serving size: 2 tacos).

CALORIES 259; FAT 9.4g (sat 1.6g, mono 5.3g, poly 1.7g); PROTEIN 21.2g; CARB 24.3g; FIBER 3g; CHOL 170mg; IRON 3mg; SODIUM 364mg; CALC 87mg

Warming Tortillas

There are many ways to warm a stack of tortillas—you can microwave them with a damp paper towel or heat them in a dry skillet or grill pan, for example. But our favorite way is to take advantage of a gas stovetop, which adds a tasty charred flavor. Place one tortilla on each burner, directly over the flames. After the first side gets slightly blackened (about 5 seconds), carefully turn the tortillas with tongs to toast the other side. As soon as they're done, wrap tortillas in a kitchen towel to keep warm. Repeat procedure with remaining tortillas.

Apple, Goat Cheese, and Pecan Pizza

Hands-on time: 10 min.   Total time: 18 min.

How about a salad with that pizza? Or rather, on top of the pizza. This combination turns traditional pizza on its head by layering thin slices of crisp Fuji apple with tangy goat cheese, and then topping them with a tossed arugula salad after baking.

1   (1-pound) six-grain pizza crust
Cooking spray
3   cups thinly sliced Fuji apple (about 8 ounces)
4   ounces crumbled goat cheese (about 1 cup)
2   teaspoons chopped fresh thyme

1   tablespoon extra-virgin olive oil
2   teaspoons Dijon mustard
1½   teaspoons honey
1   teaspoon fresh lemon juice
2   cups baby arugula
3   tablespoons chopped pecans, toasted

1. Preheat oven to 450°.
2. Place pizza crust on a baking sheet coated with cooking spray. Arrange apple slices evenly over pizza crust; top evenly with cheese. Sprinkle thyme evenly over cheese. Bake at 450° for 8 minutes or until cheese melts. Combine oil and next 3 ingredients (through lemon juice) in a medium bowl, stirring with a whisk. Add arugula; toss gently to coat. Sprinkle pecans evenly over pizza; top with arugula mixture. Cut pizza into 6 wedges. Serves 6 (serving size: 1 wedge).

CALORIES 316; FAT 11.2g (sat 4.4g, mono 4.3g, poly 1.1g); PROTEIN 11.3g; CARB 43.2g; FIBER 3g; CHOL 15mg; IRON 0.7mg; SODIUM 419mg; CALC 77mg

Celery-Apple Salad

Hands-on time: 8 min.   Total time: 8 min.

Simple sometimes means the best and the boldest. This fresh apple and celery salad is certainly the crunchiest.

2   tablespoons extra-virgin olive oil
2   tablespoons fresh lemon juice
¼   teaspoon kosher salt
¼   teaspoon black pepper
2   cups thinly sliced Honey Crisp apple

2   cups sliced celery
½   cup loosely packed fresh flat-leaf parsley
⅓   cup sliced red onion

1. Combine first 4 ingredients in a large bowl. Add apple and remaining ingredients; toss to combine. Serves 6 (serving size: ⅔ cup).

CALORIES 62; FAT 4.6g (sat 0.7g, mono 3.3g, poly 0.5g); PROTEIN 0.5g; CARB 5.2g; FIBER 1.1g; CHOL 0mg; IRON 0.4mg; SODIUM 110mg; CALC 24mg

Apple, Goat Cheese,
and Pecan Pizza

BLACKBERRIES

Fat, juicy blackberries are highly sought in summer.
Tart and sweet, they belong in your basket.

SEASON: Because these tender berries are rarely shipped long distances, the season is usually dictated by local harvests. They ripen in May along the Gulf Coast, in June and July in the central states, and in August and September in the Pacific Northwest.

CHOOSING: If you are shopping at a farmers' market, you can usually taste a berry before you buy. They should be sweet and plump, without any unripe redness.

STORING: If you don't eat all the berries on your way home from the market, cover them loosely by placing the container in a produce bag without sealing it. Keep them in the refrigerator, and try to use them within a few days.

GROWING: Have memories of thorny afternoons picking wild berries? Well, modern varieties of blackberries aren't quite so prickly. They're three to four times the size of those wild berries, and many of the plants are thornless.

Blackberries need full sun, rich soil, and good drainage; a trellis or hedgerow area is also helpful for easier management. Prepare the soil before planting by tilling in a generous amount of compost or other source of organic matter. You'll need to choose a variety that suits your location, as fruiting plants need a certain amount of winter cold (known as "chill hours") to break dormancy and perform well. Consult your local Cooperative Extension office for recommendations. Options today include not only thornless varieties, such as Arapaho or Navaho, but also late-bearing varieties that gardeners deem "cold-hardy" for those in climates at risk for late frosts.

Properly managed, a blackberry plant can provide 10 to 15 pounds of berries. Plan to harvest daily during berry season to enjoy one of the tastiest and healthiest snack foods you can find.

Blackberry Curd Tart

Hands-on time: 51 min.   Total time: 3 hr. 34 min.

4.5 ounces all-purpose flour (about 1 cup)
⅓ cup powdered sugar
¼ cup almonds, toasted and finely ground
⅜ teaspoon salt, divided
8 tablespoons chilled butter, divided
Baking spray with flour

3 cups fresh blackberries
1¾ cups granulated sugar, divided
¼ cup fresh lemon juice
2 tablespoons cornstarch
2 large egg yolks
¼ teaspoon cream of tartar
3 large egg whites
⅓ cup water

Elevate your summer dessert beyond the berry cobbler. This lemony blackberry curd is a Test Kitchen favorite. The meringue is worth every step, and you can make the curd a day ahead for convenience.

1. Preheat oven to 350°.
2. Weigh or lightly spoon flour into a dry measuring cup; level with a knife. Place flour, powdered sugar, almonds, and ⅛ teaspoon salt in a food processor; pulse to combine. Cut 7 tablespoons butter into small pieces. Add to flour mixture; pulse just until mixture resembles coarse meal. Press in bottom and up sides of a 9-inch round removable-bottom tart pan coated with baking spray. Bake at 350° for 30 minutes or until golden. Cool on a wire rack.
3. Combine berries, ¾ cup granulated sugar, and juice in a saucepan over medium-high heat; bring to a boil. Reduce heat, and simmer 6 minutes. Place mixture in a blender; let stand 5 minutes. Blend until smooth. Strain mixture through a cheesecloth-lined sieve into a medium bowl, pressing on solids. Discard solids. Wipe pan clean; return mixture to pan. Combine cornstarch and egg yolks, stirring until smooth. Stir yolk mixture into berry mixture; bring to a boil over medium-low heat. Cook 1 minute, stirring constantly. Remove from heat; stir in ⅛ teaspoon salt and 1 tablespoon butter. Scrape mixture into a bowl; cover surface directly with plastic wrap. Chill.
4. Combine ⅛ teaspoon salt, cream of tartar, and egg whites in a large bowl; beat with a mixer at high speed until soft peaks form. Combine 1 cup granulated sugar and ⅓ cup water in a saucepan; bring to a boil. Cook, without stirring, until a candy thermometer registers 250°. Gradually pour hot sugar syrup in a thin stream over egg whites, beating at medium speed, and then at high speed until stiff peaks form.
5. Preheat broiler.
6. Spoon curd over crust; top with meringue. Broil 2 minutes or until golden. Serves 12 (serving size: 1 slice).

CALORIES 285; FAT 10.2g (sat 5.3g, mono 3.3g, poly 0.9g); PROTEIN 3.7g; CARB 46.6g; FIBER 2.5g; CHOL 55mg; IRON 0.9mg; SODIUM 90mg; CALC 27mg

Blackberry-Merlot
Granita

Blackberry-Merlot Granita

Hands-on time: 8 min.   Total time: 5 hr. 23 min.

4	cups fresh blackberries	½	cup merlot
¾	cup water	1	tablespoon lemon juice
½	cup sugar	1	(3-inch) cinnamon stick

1. Combine all ingredients in a medium saucepan over medium heat; bring to a boil, stirring occasionally. Remove from heat; let stand 15 minutes.

2. Strain mixture through a fine sieve over a bowl, reserving soaking liquid (do not press berries or mixture will be cloudy). Reserve berries for another use; discard cinnamon stick. Pour mixture into an 8-inch square glass or ceramic baking dish. Cover and freeze until partially frozen (about 2 hours). Scrape mixture with a fork, crushing any lumps. Freeze 3 hours or until completely frozen, scraping with a fork every hour. Remove from freezer; scrape entire mixture with a fork until fluffy. Serves 4 (serving size: ½ cup).

CALORIES 130; FAT 0.1g (sat 0g, mono 0g, poly 0.1g); PROTEIN 0.2g; CARB 27.8g; FIBER 0.8g; CHOL 0mg; IRON 0.6mg; SODIUM 1mg; CALC 7mg

Few things top tasting a ripe, juicy blackberry in the height of summer. This granita grants you two uses: the cooked berry juices that flavor the icy granita and strained berries that can be served with angel food cake or ice cream another day.

Blackberry Margaritas

Hands-on time: 30 min.   Total time: 30 min.

1½	tablespoons sugar	1	cup 100% agave blanco tequila
½	teaspoon kosher salt	⅔	cup fresh lime juice
1	lime	½	cup Grand Marnier (orange-flavored liqueur)
1¼	cups water		
½	cup sugar	12	ounces fresh blackberries

1. Combine 1½ tablespoons sugar and salt in a dish. Cut lime into 9 wedges; rub rims of 8 glasses with 1 lime wedge. Dip rims of glasses in salt mixture.

2. Combine 1¼ cups water and ½ cup sugar in a microwave-safe glass measuring cup. Microwave at HIGH 2½ minutes, stirring to dissolve sugar; cool. Place syrup, tequila, lime juice, Grand Marnier, and blackberries in a blender; process until smooth. Strain mixture through a cheesecloth-lined sieve over a pitcher; discard solids. Serve over ice. Garnish with 8 lime wedges. Serves 8 (serving size: about ½ cup margarita and 1 lime wedge).

CALORIES 179; FAT 0.2g (sat 0g, mono 0g, poly 0.1g); PROTEIN 0.5g; CARB 23.1g; FIBER 1.6g; CHOL 0mg; IRON 0.2mg; SODIUM 121mg; CALC 11mg

Combine ripe blackberries, simple syrup, Grand Marnier, and fresh lime juice for a perfectly puckering and sweet margarita. Carefully strain out berry seeds to enjoy the incredible color and flavor. Your guests will toast you for this one.

BLUEBERRIES

The subtle sweetness of these deep-blue berries takes center stage when eaten by the fistful but also marries beautifully with other flavors.

SEASON: Growing from Florida to Maine and west to Washington, blueberries vary greatly in type. Ripening times range from spring to late summer. Although they are shipped and sold fresh in groceries, local markets are always best and reasonably priced.

CHOOSING: Look for plump berries that are dark blue with a light blue frosting. Green or pink berries are not ripe, except for the pink varieties. Many farms market their berries to customers who enjoy picking their own, so you can also look for U-pick operations in your area.

STORING: Do not wash blueberries before storing them. Place them in a plastic or perforated produce bag in the vegetable bin of your refrigerator. They will be good for 7 to 10 days.

GROWING: Because most regions have blueberry varieties that are well adapted, many people are able to make blueberry shrubs part of their home landscape design.

Plants lose their leaves in winter, but only after a wonderful display of fall color, making them a multi-season asset that produces spring flowers, summer fruit, and fall foliage.

Blueberries thrive in acidic soil that's loose, well drained, and rich in organic matter such as compost. Much like your beloved rhododendrons, holly, or azaleas, a few fruits such as blueberries thrive when grown in soil with a pH less than 7. Learn more about soil requirements and raising or lowering the pH on page 254. They also need a full-sun location. Select a variety that's suited for your area of the country. Sunshine Blue, Chippewa, Polaris, and Northsky are compact blueberry plants for small gardens and containers. For the best in-ground varieties, consult your local Cooperative Extension. For berry picking all summer, plant early, mid-, and late-season varieties for continual harvest. It's important to plant two or three varieties to ensure good pollination and fruitful harvests.

"Royal Blueberry" Gazpacho with Lemon and Mint

Hands-on time: 12 min. Total time: 2 hr. 37 min.

This twist on gazpacho is an unexpected first course, a new idea for brunch, or a great summer dessert. It is interesting enough just topped with grated lemon zest and snippets of fresh mint, or with flake salt or finely diced honeydew and cantaloupe for drama and texture. Diced strawberries and a dollop of Greek yogurt would also be nice.

1	pound dark purple seedless grapes	2	teaspoons grated lemon rind
12	ounces fresh blueberries	2	tablespoons fresh lemon juice
½	cup white grape juice	¼	teaspoon salt
2	tablespoons honey		Small mint leaves (optional)
			Additional grated lemon rind (optional)

1. Remove stems from fruit. Rinse and pat dry with paper towels. Place fruit in a 4-quart saucepan over medium-high heat. Add grape juice and honey; bring to a boil. Reduce heat to medium; simmer 15 minutes, stirring occasionally. Remove from heat; let stand 10 minutes. Place blueberry mixture in a food processor; process until almost smooth. Strain; discard solids. Chill 2 hours.
2. Stir in rind, juice, and salt. Ladle about ½ cup into each of 5 chilled bowls; garnish with mint and additional lemon rind, if desired. Serves 5.

CALORIES 142; FAT 0.4g (sat 0.1g, mono 0g, poly 0.2g); PROTEIN 1.3g; CARB 37.2g; FIBER 2.7g; CHOL 0mg; IRON 0.6mg; SODIUM 124mg; CALC 18mg

Plant the Perfect Berry

Choosing the right blueberry shrubs for your region's climate and ensuring you have those that ripen at points throughout the season may require the help of your local garden center or Cooperative Extension office. Here are a few early, mid-, and late-season options:

For warm or Southern climates: Rabbiteye blueberries

Early: Alapaha, Climax, Premier, Titan

Mid: Brightwell, Tifblue, Powderblue

Late: Baldwin, Centurion, Ochlockonee

For cooler-to-warm zones: Southern highbush

Early: Emerald, Jewel, Misty, Star, Suziblue, Palmetto, O'Neal

Mid: Camellia, Jubilee, Lenoir, Magnolia

Late: Southmoon

For cool climates: Northern highbush

Early: Duke, Earliblue, Reka

Mid: Legacy, Bluecrop, Blueray

Late: Elliott, Jersey

Blueberry Crisp

Hands-on time: 20 min.   Total time: 50 min.

Spend your time in the garden or at the farmers' market instead of in the kitchen today: This crisp offers a quick reward with little effort. Crisps are a traditional favorite for highlighting fresh berries, and this lighter version may become your new tradition.

Cooking spray
4   teaspoons cornstarch, divided
2   tablespoons brown sugar
½   teaspoon vanilla extract
1   pound fresh blueberries
2.25 ounces all-purpose flour
      (about ½ cup)
½   cup packed brown sugar

¼   cup old-fashioned rolled oats
3   tablespoons chopped walnuts
2   tablespoons cornmeal
½   teaspoon salt
¼   teaspoon ground cinnamon
¼   cup chilled butter, cut into small
      pieces

1. Preheat oven to 375°.
2. Coat an 8-inch square glass or ceramic baking dish with cooking spray. Sprinkle 2 teaspoons cornstarch evenly in dish.
3. Combine 2 teaspoons cornstarch, 2 tablespoons brown sugar, vanilla, and blueberries in a large bowl; toss. Place in prepared baking dish.
4. Weigh or lightly spoon flour into a dry measuring cup; level with a knife. Place flour and next 6 ingredients (through cinnamon) in a food processor; pulse twice to combine. Add butter; pulse 5 times or until mixture resembles coarse meal. Spoon topping evenly over blueberries, packing down lightly. Bake at 375° for 30 minutes or until filling is bubbly and topping is golden. Serves 8 (serving size: about ½ cup).

CALORIES 217; FAT 8.1g (sat 3.9g, mono 1.8g, poly 1.7g); PROTEIN 2.2g; CARB 35.9g; FIBER 2.4g; CHOL 15mg; IRON 0.9mg; SODIUM 195mg; CALC 25mg

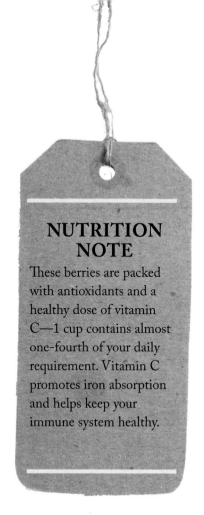

NUTRITION NOTE

These berries are packed with antioxidants and a healthy dose of vitamin C—1 cup contains almost one-fourth of your daily requirement. Vitamin C promotes iron absorption and helps keep your immune system healthy.

CHERRIES

Sweet or tart, fresh cherries are firm but surprisingly syrupy and juicy.

SEASON: The season varies from May to August depending on location.

CHOOSING: When shopping local fresh markets, always sample sweet cherries before buying. Sweetness just needs to be tasted. Tart cherries are smaller, a little softer, and acidic rather than sweet. Sweet, deep-crimson Bing and peachy-colored Rainier are the most abundant varieties, though you might find yellow or inky purple ones, too. If you live in an area where sour cherries are available, most certainly use those, though you'll need to balance the tang with some sweetness. Select cherries that are large, firm, glossy, and plump. Avoid fruit that is misshapen, cracked, or injured. Those with the stems attached will last longer.

STORING: Place unwashed cherries in a plastic or per-forated produce bag in your refrigerator. They should last about two weeks. Wash them just before eating.

GROWING: Growing cherries is rewarding, but it does require some year-round attention. Cherry trees are small to medium-sized and thrive where summers are short and winter is long and consistently cold. Choose a loca-tion that receives full sun and is not a cold pocket where late-spring freezes will settle. Planting on a slope is ideal so the cold air will move farther down the hill.

Tart cherry varieties pollinate themselves, so you only need one tree. Try Montmorency, Balaton, Meteor, or North Star. Sweet cherries, however, aren't as simple. You'll need more than one tree and both need to bloom at the same time. Rainier, Kristin, Schmidt, Lapins, Sweet-heart, Hedelfingen, Hudson, and Ulster are a few options. It's a good idea to get advice from a garden center or your local Cooperative Extension office for help selecting the right variety, as well as pruning and maintenance sug-gestions. A bonus before your bounty? Gorgeous spring blooms!

Salad with Cherries, Goat Cheese, and Pistachios

Hands-on time: 15 min.   Total time: 15 min.

The cherries offer a sweet, juicy burst that complements the peppery greens. This salad shows off the color of Rainier cherries beautifully, but any variety will do. If you don't want to splurge on an extra tool to pit them, here's a tip: Hold the cherry centered atop a small-mouthed bottle (such as beer or soda) and quickly poke a chopstick through the center to push the pit out the other side. Voilà!

4	cups arugula
2	cups baby spinach leaves
1/3	cup thinly vertically sliced red onion
1 1/2	tablespoons fresh lemon juice
1/2	teaspoon Dijon mustard
1/2	teaspoon honey
1/4	teaspoon salt
1/4	teaspoon freshly ground black pepper

1	small garlic clove, minced
2	tablespoons extra-virgin olive oil
1	cup pitted halved fresh Rainier cherries
1	ounce crumbled goat cheese (about 1/4 cup)
1/4	cup salted dry-roasted pistachios

1. Combine first 3 ingredients in a large bowl.
2. Combine juice and next 5 ingredients (through garlic) in a medium bowl, stirring with a whisk. Gradually add oil, stirring constantly with a whisk. Drizzle dressing over salad, and toss gently to coat. Arrange 1 1/2 cups salad on each of 4 plates. Top each serving with 1/4 cup cherries, 1 tablespoon cheese, and 1 tablespoon nuts. Serves 4.

CALORIES 173; FAT 12.6g (sat 2.9g, mono 7.3g, poly 1.9g); PROTEIN 4.6g; CARB 13g; FIBER 2.7g; CHOL 6mg; IRON 1.4mg; SODIUM 256mg; CALC 80mg

Bing Cherry Sorbet with Prosecco

Hands-on time: 30 min.
Total time: 4 hr. 30 min.

For an elegant yet easy dessert, try this sorbet. Blended with amaretto and served frozen with prosecco, the Bing cherries shine perfectly in taste and bold crimson color.

1	cup sugar
$^2/_3$	cup water
4	cups pitted fresh Bing cherries (about 1$^1/_3$ pounds)
3	tablespoons amaretto (almond-flavored liqueur)
2	tablespoons fresh lime juice
2$^2/_3$	cups prosecco or other sparkling white wine, chilled

1. Combine 1 cup sugar and $^2/_3$ cup water in a 2-cup glass measuring cup. Microwave at HIGH 2 minutes. Cool completely. Place sugar syrup, cherries, amaretto, and lime juice in a blender; process 1 minute or until smooth. Pour mixture into the freezer can of a table-top ice-cream freezer; freeze according to manufacturer's instructions. Spoon sorbet into a freezer-safe container; cover and freeze 4 hours or until firm. Pour $^1/_3$ cup prosecco into each of 8 chilled bowls; spoon about $^1/_3$ cup sorbet into each bowl. Serves 8.

CALORIES 214; FAT 0.2g (sat 0g, mono 0.1g, poly 0g); PROTEIN 0.8g; CARB 41g; FIBER 1.6g; CHOL 0mg; IRON 0.3mg; SODIUM 0mg; CALC 11mg

Fresh Cherry Galette

Hands-on time: 26 min.   Total time: 1 hr. 11 min.

A galette sounds complicated but is simply a beautiful, rustic, free-form tart. Rainier cherries have pale, creamy flesh and are larger and sweeter than Bing cherries. If you opt for another variety, add an extra tablespoon of sugar.

½   (14.1-ounce) package refrigerated pie dough

3   tablespoons granulated sugar, divided

1½   teaspoons cornstarch

3½   cups pitted fresh Rainier cherries (about 1¼ pounds)

½   teaspoon grated lemon rind

2   teaspoons fresh lemon juice

1½   tablespoons buttermilk

1   tablespoon turbinado sugar

1. Preheat oven to 400°.

2. Line a baking sheet with parchment paper. Unroll pie dough onto parchment, and roll into a 12½-inch circle. Combine 1 tablespoon granulated sugar and cornstarch, stirring with a whisk. Sprinkle cornstarch mixture over dough, leaving a 2-inch border.

3. Combine cherries, 2 tablespoons granulated sugar, rind, and juice; toss well to coat. Arrange cherry mixture over dough, leaving a 2-inch border. Fold dough border over cherries, pressing gently to seal (dough will only partially cover cherries). Brush edges of dough with buttermilk. Sprinkle turbinado sugar over cherries and edges of dough. Bake at 400° for 25 minutes or until dough is browned and juices are bubbly. Remove from oven; cool on pan at least 20 minutes before serving. Serves 6 (serving size: 1 wedge).

CALORIES 227; FAT 8.9g (sat 3.8g, mono 3.2g, poly 0.6g); PROTEIN 2.3g; CARB 38g; FIBER 1.9g; CHOL 4mg; IRON 0.3mg; SODIUM 177mg; CALC 12mg

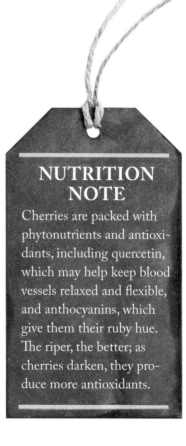

NUTRITION NOTE

Cherries are packed with phytonutrients and antioxidants, including quercetin, which may help keep blood vessels relaxed and flexible, and anthocyanins, which give them their ruby hue. The riper, the better; as cherries darken, they produce more antioxidants.

CITRUS

The tangy, sweet, vibrantly fresh flavors of lemons, limes, grapefruit, and oranges add life and lightness to any dish.

SEASON: Fall through spring, depending on the type

CHOOSING: The refreshing power of citrus comes not only from the juice and flesh, but also, critically, from the zest, which is filled with aromatic oils that carry the flavor through time and temperature. Pristine fruit is key. Select blemish-free fruit that's heavy for its size, which means it's full of juice. If areas of yellow or orange skin appear green, don't worry. The fruit is ripe.

STORING: Citrus fruit is beautiful in a bowl on the kitchen counter, but after a few days it loses moisture and softens. For best quality, place citrus in a produce bag in the vegetable bin of your refrigerator for up to a week. Some varieties will last much longer. To easily add the essence of citrus to dishes, store grated rind in the freezer (see page 31).

GROWING: Who wouldn't love a basket of homegrown lemons? Those in cold areas envy the hedges of citrus in California, but we can all enjoy beautiful plants if we protect them during winter. Whether grown in a patio pot or in the backyard, there is an option for everyone to enjoy. Typically, citrus fruit grows on trees ranging in height from 3 to 12 feet, but there are dwarf options. The trees are evergreen, fragrant in bloom, a manageable size, usually thorn-free, and wonderfully fruitful.

Those who enjoy mild winters have no excuse not to plant these fragrant evergreens. Try varieties not commonly offered in supermarkets, such as Buddha's Hand citron, Meyer or Ponderosa lemon, Key or Mexican lime, or the colorful blood orange. Where temperatures rarely drop below the mid-20s, gardeners can succeed by choosing varieties that are especially cold-hardy and by planting on a south-facing wall for extra winter warmth. Select the most cold-hardy types, such as Mandarin oranges (tangerines, clementines, and satsumas), kumquats, calamondins, Meyer lemons, and Eustis limequats. Be prepared to cover plants to protect them if temperatures dip in a severe winter since fruit can be damaged at 28°. The best coverings are nonabsorbent blankets made of spun bonded polypropylene or polyethylene, which you can purchase from horticultural suppliers. These coverings, usually listed as floating row covers or frost blankets, allow rain to pass through so they don't become heavy but they hold in heat absorbed by the soil during the day. They can stay on as long as needed. Old bed linens work, too, in an unexpected frost, but they absorb moisture and should be used for overnight protection only. For container gardeners, good choices include Ponderosa and Meyer lemons, Bearss or kaffir limes, calamondin oranges, and Nagami or Meiwa kumquats. Move them inside during extreme cold.

What's the scoop on rootstock? Plantsmen smartly figured out that dwarf fruit varieties or cold-hardy plants can be successfully adapted when grafted upon the trunk base or "rootstock" of another tree with those ideal characteristics. Your local garden center can guide you in choosing the right fruit for your climate and size needs.

No matter where or how citrus plants are grown, they need eight hours of sunshine, well-drained soil, and fertilizer that includes micronutrients. Be sure to cut your fruit from the tree, rather than letting it fall on its own, to avoid damage and a shortened storage life.

Cilantro-Jalapeño Limeade

Hands-on time: 12 min.
Total time: 3 hr. 42 min.

4½ cups water
¾ cup sugar
½ cup agave nectar
1 cup coarsely chopped cilantro
2 large jalapeño peppers, seeded and chopped (about ½ cup)
2 tablespoons sugar
¼ teaspoon salt
9 lime wedges, divided
1½ cups fresh lime juice (about 10 limes)
4 cups ice

1. Combine first 3 ingredients in a medium saucepan over medium-high heat; bring to a boil. Remove from heat; stir in cilantro and jalapeño. Let stand 30 minutes. Pour jalapeño mixture into a large bowl; cover and chill at least 3 hours.
2. Combine 2 tablespoons sugar and salt in a shallow dish. Rub rims of 8 glasses with 1 lime wedge. Dip rims of glasses in sugar mixture.
3. Strain cilantro mixture through a fine sieve over a bowl, discarding solids. Stir in lime juice. Fill each prepared glass with ½ cup ice. Add ¾ cup limeade to each glass. Garnish with 8 lime wedges. Serves 8.

CALORIES 155; FAT 0g; PROTEIN 0.2g; CARB 41.3g; FIBER 0.2g; CHOL 0mg; IRON 0.1mg; SODIUM 56mg; CALC 7mg

Lemon Squares

Hands-on time: 15 min.   Total time: 3 hr.

Lemons are such an integral part of so many recipes, but this is one that truly frames its freshness, fair and square. Pine nuts in the sweet cookie crust balance the boldness of the lemon filling.

3.4   ounces all-purpose flour
      (about ¾ cup)
¼   cup powdered sugar
3   tablespoons pine nuts, toasted
      and coarsely chopped
⅛   teaspoon salt
2   tablespoons chilled unsalted
      butter, cut into small pieces
2   tablespoons canola oil

Cooking spray
¾   cup granulated sugar
2   tablespoons all-purpose flour
1   teaspoon grated lemon rind
½   cup fresh lemon juice
2   large eggs
1   large egg white
2   tablespoons powdered sugar

1. Preheat oven to 350°.
2. Weigh or lightly spoon 3.4 ounces flour (about ¾ cup) into a dry measuring cup; level with a knife. Place 3.4 ounces flour, ¼ cup powdered sugar, pine nuts, and salt in a food processor; pulse 2 times to combine. Add butter and canola oil. Pulse 3 to 5 times or until mixture resembles coarse meal. Press in bottom of an 8-inch square glass or ceramic baking dish coated with cooking spray. Bake at 350° for 20 minutes or until lightly browned. Reduce oven temperature to 325°.
3. Combine granulated sugar and next 5 ingredients (through egg whites) in a medium bowl, stirring with a whisk until smooth. Pour mixture over crust. Bake at 325° for 20 minutes or until set. Remove from oven, and cool completely in pan on a wire rack. Cover and chill at least 2 hours. Sprinkle squares evenly with 2 tablespoons powdered sugar. Serves 16 (serving size: 1 square).

CALORIES 124; FAT 5g (sat 1.3g, mono 2g, poly 1.2g); PROTEIN 2g; CARB 18.5g; FIBER 0.3g; CHOL 30mg; IRON 0.5mg; SODIUM 31mg; CALC 6mg

Freezing the Season's Zest

Recipes often use citrus juice more frequently than rind, but don't let unused rind go to waste. If you juice several lemons or limes for a recipe, go ahead and zest them fully (a Microplane grater or vegetable peeler makes fast work of this); then place clumps in heavy-duty zip-top plastic bags for up to six months.

Orange Salad with Arugula and Oil-Cured Olives

Hands-on time: 11 min. Total time: 11 min.

The best way to use fresh market or garden produce is often in its simplest, purest form. This dish highlights the color of oranges for an elegant presentation. (If you can find blood oranges, use them; the color is stunning.) You can peel and slice the oranges ahead, if you like, arranging the slices on a plate and covering with plastic wrap. You can prep the other components ahead, too. Make the dressing several hours or even a day ahead; just bring to room temperature before tossing with the arugula. Buy washed and ready-to-use arugula to save time.

Dressing:
⅓ cup thinly sliced shallots
¼ cup fresh lemon juice
2 tablespoons finely chopped mint leaves
1 teaspoon sugar
2 teaspoons Dijon mustard
⅛ teaspoon kosher salt
⅛ teaspoon freshly ground black pepper
¼ cup extra-virgin olive oil

Salad:
1 (5-ounce) package arugula
5 oranges, peeled and thinly sliced crosswise
30 oil-cured black olives
Freshly ground black pepper (optional)

1. To prepare dressing, combine first 7 ingredients in a medium bowl, stirring with a whisk. Gradually add oil, stirring constantly with a whisk.
2. To prepare salad, combine arugula and three-fourths of dressing in a large bowl; toss gently to coat. Arrange about ½ cup arugula mixture on each of 10 plates; arrange orange slices evenly over salads. Drizzle remaining one-fourth of dressing evenly over salads; top each salad with 3 olives. Sprinkle with black pepper, if desired. Serve immediately. Serves 10.

CALORIES 132; FAT 9.5g (sat 1.6g, mono 6.6g, poly 1.3g); PROTEIN 1g; CARB 16.7g; FIBER 5.3g; CHOL 0mg; IRON 0.5mg; SODIUM 284mg; CALC 56mg

FIGS

Fresh figs have it all—stunning, sticky flesh rife with seeds and heavy with syrupy, sweet juice. This sublime fruit needs little embellishment.

SEASON: Summer and fall. Some figs will have two crops a year in warm climates.

CHOOSING: Figs don't ripen once picked, so buy them when they're soft and sweet. That also means that they don't ship well, so stick with local figs for the best flavor. The ideal fig is one that has a bend at the stem, showing that it curled downward on the tree from its own weight. It may even have a split or two, but no mold.

STORING: Figs are highly perishable, so eat them soon after you purchase or pick. To store them, place ripe figs in a produce bag in your vegetable bin. They will remain in good condition for two to five days, depending on the variety—the darker figs will last longer than the green ones.

GROWING: Figs are the ideal home-garden fruit. The plant, which grows into a large shrub or small tree that drops its leaves in winter, loves mild winters and warm summers. Black Mission figs are a California favorite but won't work as well elsewhere. Instead, try Alma, Brown Turkey, Celeste, Conadria, Green Ischia, Petite Negri, or White Marseille. In areas where temperatures dip into the single digits, Celeste, Conadria, and Chicago Hardy are good options.

When planting, choose a location on the south or west side of a building that will be sheltered from cold and not exposed to morning sun, which can be damaging when the plant is frozen. Even if the tree is killed to the ground in a hard winter, it will usually grow back from the roots. Cover it with a blanket of mulch to provide some protection.

Like most fruiting plants, figs need full sun, well-drained soil, regular water, and fertilizer. Pruning can help make tall plants more manageable and make the fruit easier to pick. Figs are also popular as espalier forms, graceful structures against a garden wall. The fruit ripens over several weeks, so make daily pickings part of your routine in season. Figs will soften as they ripen and begin to droop on the plant. Gently lift each ripe fruit, and it will separate from the stem without tearing.

Granola with Honey-Scented Yogurt and Baked Figs

Hands-on time: 18 min. Total time: 53 min.

This recipe will make you think you've awakened in a five-star B&B every morning. The granola gets rave reviews separately and will be a breakfast staple with all your fresh fruits, but the true gems are the figs baked with vanilla and honey.

1	cup old-fashioned rolled oats	1/8	teaspoon ground nutmeg
1/3	cup chopped pecans	2	tablespoons maple syrup
1	large egg white		Cooking spray
1 1/8	teaspoons vanilla extract, divided	2	tablespoons plus 2 teaspoons honey, divided
2	tablespoons brown sugar	9	firm, fresh dark-skinned figs, stemmed and quartered
3/8	teaspoon ground cinnamon, divided		
1/4	teaspoon salt, divided	3	cups plain fat-free Greek yogurt

1. Preheat oven to 300°.
2. Combine oats and pecans in a small bowl. Combine egg white and 1/8 teaspoon vanilla in a medium bowl; beat egg mixture with a mixer at medium speed until foamy. Fold oat mixture into egg white mixture. Combine brown sugar, 1/4 teaspoon cinnamon, 1/8 teaspoon salt, and nutmeg; fold sugar mixture into oat mixture. Fold in maple syrup.
3. Spread granola evenly on a foil-lined baking sheet coated with cooking spray. Bake at 300° for 25 minutes, stirring once. Remove granola from oven; stir to loosen granola from foil. Cool on a wire rack.
4. Increase oven temperature to 350°.
5. Combine 2 teaspoons honey and 1 teaspoon vanilla in a large bowl; add figs, stirring gently to coat. Arrange figs, cut sides up, in a single layer on a foil-lined baking sheet. Sprinkle figs evenly with 1/8 teaspoon cinnamon and 1/8 teaspoon salt.
6. Bake at 350° for 10 minutes or until fig juices begin to bubble. Remove from oven, and cool completely. Combine 2 tablespoons honey and yogurt in a small bowl. Spoon 1/2 cup yogurt mixture into each of 6 bowls; top each serving with about 2 1/2 tablespoons granola and 6 fig quarters. Serves 6.

CALORIES 277; FAT 5.6g (sat 0.6g, mono 2.9g, poly 1.8g); PROTEIN 13.3g; CARB 45.7g; FIBER 4.2g; CHOL 0mg; IRON 1.2mg; SODIUM 152mg; CALC 117mg

Finding the Right Fig

One of the best ways to find a tasty fig variety that's adapted to your area is to ask a neighbor for a clipping. There are shoots at the base of the plant that can be dug up and shared.

Prosciutto, Fresh Fig, and Manchego Sandwiches

Hands-on time: 20 min.   Total time: 20 min.

If the birds allow you to share in the fig harvest, this sandwich is a must-have. Don't skimp on quality ingredients like artisan bread and fine prosciutto. Layers of spicy Dijon, salty prosciutto, Manchego cheese, and peppery arugula balance the sweetness of figs and jam.

4　teaspoons Dijon mustard
8　(³/₄-ounce) slices Italian bread, toasted
1　cup baby arugula
2　ounces very thin slices prosciutto
2　ounces Manchego cheese, shaved (about ½ cup)
8　fresh figs, cut into thin slices
2　tablespoons fig jam

1. Spread 1 teaspoon mustard over 4 bread slices. Arrange ¼ cup arugula over each bread slice. Divide prosciutto evenly over bread slices; top evenly with cheese and fig slices. Spread 1½ teaspoons jam over remaining 4 bread slices. Top each serving with 1 bread slice, jam side down. Serves 4 (serving size: 1 sandwich).

CALORIES 295; FAT 5.3g (sat 2.6g, mono 2.1g, poly 0.6g); PROTEIN 11.5g; CARB 52.3g; FIBER 4.2g; CHOL 18mg; IRON 1.8mg; SODIUM 805mg; CALC 114mg

Fig and Lime Jam

Hands-on time: 10 min.   Total time: 3 hr. 43 min.

Three ingredients are a smash together for a jam best served on bread, crackers, or perhaps with a bite of pork tenderloin. We tested with Brown Turkey figs, but should you find sweeter Black Mission figs, you may need to reduce the sugar.

2　cups sugar
¼　cup fresh lime juice (about 3 limes)
2　pounds fresh Brown Turkey figs, cut into ¼-inch pieces (about 6 cups)

1. Combine all ingredients in a large heavy saucepan; mash fig mixture with a potato masher until combined. Let stand 2 hours. Bring mixture to a boil over medium heat. Reduce heat; simmer 35 minutes or until mixture begins to thicken slightly, stirring occasionally. Cool completely. Cover and chill overnight. Serves 32 (serving size: 2 tablespoons).

CALORIES 70; FAT 0.1g (sat 0g, mono 0g, poly 0.1g); PROTEIN 0.2g; CARB 18.1g; FIBER 0.8g; CHOL 0mg; IRON 0.1mg; SODIUM 0mg; CALC 10mg

Prosciutto, Fresh Fig, and Manchego Sandwiches

MELONS

Refreshing watermelon, cantaloupe, and honeydew melon sweeten any dish.

SEASON: Summer and fall, peaking in August

CHOOSING: Ripe cantaloupes and honeydew melons will smell noticeably fruity at the site where the stem was attached. The other end will give slightly when pressed if the melon is ripe. Ripe watermelons should be heavy with a waxy rind, and the spot where the melon was sitting on the soil should be pale yellow. Also, they'll sound hollow when thumped. Avoid melons with obvious cuts or bruises.

STORING: Cantaloupes and honeydew melons will continue to ripen if kept at room temperature. Once ripe, place them in the refrigerator for up to a week. Watermelons are as ripe and sweet as they'll ever be once picked, but they will continue to soften and develop lycopene (see page 42). They'll remain in good condition for up to a week in the refrigerator. Wrap any cut melon in plastic, and plan to use it within three days.

GROWING: Cantaloupes, honeydew melons, and watermelons all grow on vines that ramble around the garden, often requiring lots of room to stretch. Some varieties are bush-type, having short vines that are more manageable in small spaces and in containers. Because they can fill your refrigerator, varieties with smaller fruit are popular options. Read the growing instructions on the label to learn what to expect from the variety you choose.

Melons are summer crops that relish warm days and nights that don't dip below the 60s. Plant seeds in already-warm soil at the spacing recommended on the seed packet. Some varieties push the limit in areas with a limited growing season, needing 70 to 90 days of warmth to mature. Seedlings can be transplanted while young, so if your season is too short, start seeds indoors about two weeks before planting, and choose the warmest location you have, such as one near masonry or paving.

Choose a sunny, well-drained area. Prepare your garden soil by enriching it with compost or other organic matter. Watermelons are deep rooted and drought-resistant once they get going, though other melons may need supplemental watering. You know a cantaloupe or honeydew melon is ready by how easily it detaches from the vine and by the sweet scent. A watermelon is trickier. Look for the curly tendril closest to the melon. When it turns brown, the melon is usually ready.

Grilled Pork Chops with Two-Melon Salsa

Hands-on time: 28 min.   Total time: 28 min.

1   cup chopped seedless
     watermelon
1   cup chopped honeydew melon
3   tablespoons finely chopped
     sweet onion
1   tablespoon finely chopped
     jalapeño pepper
1   tablespoon chopped fresh
     cilantro
1   tablespoon fresh lime juice

⅛   teaspoon salt
2   teaspoons canola oil
1½   teaspoons chili powder
½   teaspoon garlic powder
½   teaspoon salt
¼   teaspoon freshly ground black
     pepper
4   (4-ounce) boneless center-cut
     loin pork chops, trimmed
Cooking spray

1. Combine first 7 ingredients in a large bowl; set aside.
2. Heat a grill pan over medium-high heat. Combine oil and next 4 ingredients (through black pepper) in a small bowl. Rub oil mixture over both sides of pork chops. Coat pan with cooking spray. Add pork to pan; cook 4 minutes on each side or until done. Serve with salsa. Serves 4 (serving size: 1 pork chop and ½ cup salsa).

CALORIES 256; FAT 13.5g (sat 4.3g, mono 6.4g, poly 1.6g); PROTEIN 25g; CARB 8.7g; FIBER 0.9g; CHOL 70mg; IRON 0.9mg; SODIUM 458mg; CALC 37mg

Melon, jalapeño, and cilantro make for a refreshing salsa that is good enough to eat on its own. Consider smaller, personal-sized watermelons such as Sugar Baby if refrigerator space is limited.

Honeydew-Kiwi Daiquiris

Hands-on time: 12 min.   Total time: 42 min.

3   cups chopped honeydew melon
4   kiwifruit, peeled and coarsely
     chopped
2   cups crushed ice

½   cup light rum
2   tablespoons sugar
1   teaspoon grated lime rind
2   tablespoons fresh lime juice

1. Arrange melon in a single layer on a baking sheet; freeze at least 30 minutes or until firm.
2. Place frozen melon and remaining ingredients in a blender; process until smooth. Serves 4 (serving size: 1¼ cups).

CALORIES 183; FAT 0.6g (sat 0.1g, mono 0g, poly 0.3g); PROTEIN 1.6g; CARB 29.7g; FIBER 3.4g; CHOL 0mg; IRON 0.5mg; SODIUM 26mg; CALC 35mg

Melon and Fig Salad with Prosciutto and Balsamic Drizzle

Hands-on time: 15 min.   Total time: 30 min.

Melon and prosciutto—it's a pairing as popular as peas and carrots. Try adding the sweet flesh of fig and the tangy bite of balsamic for a twist on a favorite appetizer.

½	cup balsamic vinegar	½	pound honeydew melon, peeled, seeded, and thinly sliced
2	teaspoons extra-virgin olive oil	½	pound cantaloupe, peeled, seeded, and thinly sliced
1	teaspoon fresh lemon juice	4	very thin slices prosciutto, torn (about 1 ounce)
¼	teaspoon freshly ground black pepper		
4	cups gourmet salad greens	4	fresh figs, quartered

1. Bring vinegar to a simmer in a small saucepan over medium-low heat; cook until syrupy and reduced to 3 tablespoons (about 10 minutes), stirring occasionally. Remove from heat.

2. Combine oil, juice, and pepper in a bowl, stirring with a whisk. Add salad greens; toss gently. Divide melon among 4 plates; top with salad greens. Arrange prosciutto and figs over salad greens; drizzle with balsamic syrup. Serves 4 (serving size: ¼ pound melon, about 1 cup salad greens, 1 slice prosciutto, 1 quartered fig, and about 2 teaspoons balsamic syrup).

CALORIES 153; FAT 3.2g (sat 0.6g, mono 1.7g, poly 0.3g); PROTEIN 4.1g; CARB 28.3g; FIBER 3.7g; CHOL 6mg; IRON 1.3mg; SODIUM 239mg; CALC 44mg

Summer Pea, Watermelon, and Farro Salad

Hands-on time: 9 min.   Total time: 32 min.

This unusual combination brings the delicious fresh flavors of sweet watermelon and peas to farro and pecorino cheese. Try it as your next grain salad standout at the neighborhood cookout. If you don't think it's unusual enough, try it with a sweet yellow watermelon to turn a few heads.

1 cup uncooked farro or wheat berries
1 cup shelled green peas (about ³⁄₄ pound unshelled)
½ teaspoon salt
¼ teaspoon freshly ground black pepper
1 cup cubed seeded watermelon
1 cup coarsely chopped fresh flat-leaf parsley
1½ ounces shaved fresh pecorino Romano cheese (about ⅓ cup)

1. Place farro in a large saucepan, and cover with water to 2 inches above farro. Bring to a boil. Cover, reduce heat, and simmer 23 minutes or until desired degree of doneness.
2. Add green peas to pan with farro, and cook 2 minutes or until crisp-tender. Drain and rinse farro mixture with cold water; drain.
3. Combine farro mixture, salt, and pepper in a large bowl. Add watermelon and parsley, and toss gently to combine. Top salad with cheese. Serves 4 (serving size: 1 cup).

CALORIES 188; FAT 4.2g (sat 1.9g, mono 0.9g, poly 0.2g); PROTEIN 10g; CARB 35.5g; FIBER 6g; CHOL 11mg; IRON 1.7mg; SODIUM 433mg; CALC 146mg

PEACHES

The intoxicating sweet fragrance of fresh peaches is your first introduction to the succulent flesh that awaits beneath the fuzzy skin.

SEASON: Depending on where you live, peaches may make an appearance as early as May and as late as October, but they peak in June, July, and August.

CHOOSING: When it comes to peaches, local is ideal. When soft and ripe, peaches are highly perishable, and impossible to ship. Luckily, they ripen well in their basket or on your counter, going from rock hard on market day to dripping with sweet juice three to five days later. Select fruit that is not bruised. If the color behind the blush of pink is yellow (or white for white-fleshed peaches), the peaches are mature, will soften, and you cannot lose.

STORING: Store unripe peaches on the counter at room temperature in a single layer. Check them daily. Transfer those that have softened to the refrigerator to stop the ripening process, and eat them within a week.

GROWING: Peach trees are a year-round project—with delicious rewards. Trees are reasonably small and self-fruitful, so you need only one. When planting peaches, consider what you want to do with them. Eating fresh or freezing? Plant a freestone peach (those in which the pit releases easily from the flesh). Canning? Plant cling (those with pits that adhere to the flesh). Early-ripening peach varieties tend to be cling. Choose the right variety for your area, one that needs about the same amount of winter chill that you get in an average season. Growers and Cooperative Extension agents can help you pick the best variety. If not well matched to your climate, your tree may bloom too soon and have the flowers killed by a late frost, or it may not bloom at all.

A backyard tree can be managed in a simple cycle of late-winter pruning, pest-preventing oil spray during the dormant season, fertilizing, thinning a heavy crop, and thorough cleanup of fallen fruit from under the tree.

Peach Lemonade

Hands-on time: 12 min.   Total time: 3 hr. 42 min.

A quick chop, blend, whir, and stir, and fresh, homemade peach lemonade will be chilling in the fridge. Keep this on hand in the hot summer months as a satisfying thirst-quencher. Add a little white bourbon or rum for garden parties.

4	cups water	4	cups ice	
2	cups coarsely chopped peaches	1	peach, pitted and cut into	
¾	cup sugar		8 wedges	
1	cup fresh lemon juice (about 6 lemons)			

1. Combine first 3 ingredients in a medium saucepan over medium-high heat. Bring to a boil; reduce heat, and simmer 3 minutes. Place peach mixture in a blender; let stand 20 minutes. Remove center piece of blender lid (to allow steam to escape); secure blender lid on blender. Place a clean towel over opening in blender lid (to avoid splatters). Blend until smooth. Pour peach mixture into a large bowl. Refrigerate at least 3 hours.

2. Press peach mixture through a sieve over a bowl, reserving liquid; discard solids. Stir in lemon juice. Place ½ cup ice in each of 8 glasses. Pour about ⅔ cup lemonade into each glass; garnish each glass with 1 peach wedge. Serves 8.

CALORIES 98; FAT 0.1g (sat 0g, mono 0g, poly 0g); PROTEIN 0.5g; CARB 25.9g; FIBER 0.8g; CHOL 0mg; IRON 0.1mg; SODIUM 0mg; CALC 4mg

Planting Peaches

Although you will find only a handful of peach varieties in your local garden center, you could potentially encounter hundreds of varieties online. The variety you choose depends on your area. Here's a very brief primer:

Yellow-fleshed peaches are best for eating fresh and preserving.

Contender (late, freestone, very cold-tolerant tree)

Desertgold (early, semi-cling, desert southwest)

Elberta (late, freestone, a classic peach)

Flordaking (early, semi-cling, warm regions from California to Florida)

Garnet Beauty (midseason; semi-cling; enjoy fresh, canned, or frozen)

Harrow Diamond (early, semi-cling, disease-resistant fruit)

La Feliciana (late, freestone, some disease resistance)

Loring (late, freestone, great taste)

Ranger (midseason, freestone, great for cold climates)

White-fleshed peaches are sweeter, less acidic than their yellow counterparts. They're best eaten fresh.

Belle of Georgia (late, freestone)

Flordaglo (early, semi-cling, for warmest regions)

Sugar Giant (late midseason, freestone, a big sweet peach)

Skillet Pork Chop Sauté with Peaches

Hands-on time: 20 min.　Total time: 20 min.

Generations before ours preserved summer's bounty by pickling peaches in a spiced, sweet syrup that paired well with Sunday suppers of pork or poultry. Take the easier route with this go-to pan sauté that complements pork in a big way. Serve over quick-cooking couscous.

2	teaspoons olive oil	2	teaspoons chopped fresh thyme
4	(4-ounce) boneless center-cut loin pork chops, trimmed	2	peaches, each cut into 8 wedges
½	teaspoon salt	½	cup dry white wine
½	teaspoon freshly ground black pepper	½	cup fat-free, lower-sodium chicken broth
2	tablespoons thinly sliced shallots	2	teaspoons honey
		2	teaspoons butter

1. Heat a large skillet over medium-high heat. Add oil to pan; swirl to coat. Sprinkle pork evenly with salt and pepper. Add pork to pan; cook 3 minutes on each side or until done. Remove pork from pan, and keep warm. Add shallots, thyme, and peaches to pan; cook 2 minutes. Stir in wine, scraping pan to loosen browned bits; bring to a boil. Cook until reduced to ⅓ cup (about 2 minutes). Stir in broth and honey; bring to a boil. Cook until reduced to ⅓ cup (about 2 minutes). Remove from heat; stir in butter. Spoon sauce over pork. Serves 4 (serving size: 1 pork chop, 4 peach wedges, and about 1½ tablespoons broth mixture).

CALORIES 235; FAT 8.6g (sat 2.8g, mono 3.7g, poly 0.8g); PROTEIN 26.2g; CARB 13.6g; FIBER 1.1g; CHOL 83mg; IRON 1.3mg; SODIUM 433mg; CALC 26mg

Fiery Grilled Peach and Habanero Salsa

Hands-on time: 18 min. Total time: 38 min.

Make this salsa a summer staple when peaches are in season. It dresses up grilled chicken, pork, or fish with caramelized sweet heat.

4   large peeled peaches, halved and pitted (about 1 pound)
2   (¼-inch-thick) slices red onion
Cooking spray
2   tablespoons chopped fresh cilantro
1   tablespoon fresh lime juice
1   teaspoon sugar
1   teaspoon grated orange rind
1   teaspoon finely chopped seeded habanero pepper
½   teaspoon salt

1. Preheat grill to medium-high heat.
2. Lightly coat peaches and onion with cooking spray. Place peaches and onion on grill rack coated with cooking spray; grill peaches 2 minutes on each side. Cool and chop peaches. Grill onion 3 minutes on each side. Cool and chop onion. Combine peaches, onion, cilantro, and remaining ingredients in a medium bowl; toss well. Let stand 15 minutes. Serves 15 (serving size: ¼ cup).

CALORIES 20; FAT 0.1g (sat 0g, mono 0g, poly 0g); PROTEIN 0.4g; CARB 5g; FIBER 0.7g; CHOL 0mg; IRON 0.1mg; SODIUM 78mg; CALC 4mg

PEARS

Ripe pears are sensuous with a dripping juice and a honey-buttery sweetness. They're an excellent pairing for many sweet and savory ingredients.

SEASON: Fall is generally peak season, but the wide variety ensures availability much of the year.

CHOOSING: European pears (Bartlett, Bosc, Comice, Anjou, and many more) will continue to ripen and soften after being picked, so buy unblemished pears free of wrinkles. Unlike European pears, Asian pears are apple-shaped and are usually crisp. The hybrid Kieffer has characteristic grit and is primarily used for preserves, although Seckel is also good to eat fresh when ripe. Pears ripen and soften from the inside out, so buy a few days before you hope to use, and let them ripen on the counter.

STORING: Place Asian pears in the refrigerator in a produce bag to maintain their crisp quality. European pears can be ripened on the counter, but transfer to the refrigerator for storage when they reach the ideal softness. Always place pears in the coldest part of your refrigerator.

GROWING: For a home garden, a semidwarf tree may be the ideal size, growing as tall as 20 feet. A smaller dwarf tree can be maintained at a height that doesn't require a ladder to reach the fruit, but a support will be needed. Asian pears may be more home-garden friendly, growing only 8 to 12 feet tall. While the European pears may wait six years to fruit, Asian pears produce in as few as three.

Select a site that receives full sun and has well-drained, deep soil. Because the spring flowers are quite ornamental, a pear tree can blend beautifully into your landscape. Because most pear trees are not self-fruitful, at least two varieties are needed to set a crop. Like apples, pears can host unwanted insects and diseases that need monitoring and occasional intervention. Consult local experts, such as your Cooperative Extension agent, for advice on growing pears in your area.

Pear and Gruyère Strata

Hands-on time: 20 min.   Total time: 9 hr. 25 min.

Finally, an excuse to buy that enticing cinnamon swirl bread in the store. Anjou, a farm favorite, is an excellent all-purpose pear whose dense flesh makes it ideal for eating fresh or cooking—it shines in this strata. Or use golden green Concorde pears or cinnamon-hued Bosc, which will hold their shape in baking. Pear and Gruyère go together like peanut butter and jelly; this rich, stuffed French toast dish is no exception.

4   cups sliced peeled Anjou or Concorde pear
2   teaspoons butter, melted
6   tablespoons granulated sugar, divided
12   (1-ounce) slices cinnamon swirl bread, cut in half diagonally
Cooking spray

4   ounces shredded Gruyère cheese (about 1 cup)
1½   cups 1% low-fat milk
1   cup egg substitute
½   teaspoon ground cinnamon
1   tablespoon turbinado sugar
½   cup maple syrup

1. Combine pear, butter, and 1 tablespoon granulated sugar in a large bowl; toss gently.

2. Arrange half of bread in an 11 x 7-inch glass or ceramic baking dish coated with cooking spray. Spoon pear mixture evenly over bread; top with cheese. Arrange remaining bread over cheese.

3. Combine 5 tablespoons granulated sugar, milk, egg substitute, and cinnamon, stirring with a whisk. Pour milk mixture over bread, pressing down to submerge. Cover and chill 8 hours or overnight.

4. Preheat oven to 350°.

5. Uncover dish. Sprinkle turbinado sugar evenly over bread. Bake at 350° for 55 minutes or until a knife inserted in center comes out clean. Let stand 10 minutes. Cut into 8 equal pieces; drizzle with syrup. Serves 8 (serving size: 1 strata piece and 1 tablespoon syrup).

CALORIES 355; FAT 10g (sat 4.3g, mono 3.7g, poly 0.6g); PROTEIN 13.1g; CARB 55.1g; FIBER 5.3g; CHOL 20mg; IRON 1.6mg; SODIUM 295mg; CALC 216mg

Cheese and Pear Pork

Hands-on time: 47 min.   Total time: 1 hr. 6 min.

This is an elegant presentation of a flawless flavor combination. Walnuts, pear, and blue cheese create the filling for pork tenderloin. Serve slices dressed with the sauce over a bed of sweet, fresh spinach and thinly sliced pear.

2   tablespoons olive oil, divided
4   shallots, thinly sliced
1   cup chopped firm Anjou pear
½   cup riesling or other white wine
1   tablespoon chopped fresh thyme
Dash of ground red pepper
½   cup chopped walnuts, toasted
2   ounces crumbled blue cheese (about ½ cup)

⅓   cup fresh breadcrumbs
2   tablespoons chopped fresh parsley
2   (12-ounce) pork tenderloins, trimmed
½   teaspoon kosher salt
1¼   cups fat-free, lower-sodium chicken broth

1. Preheat oven to 425°.

2. Heat a large skillet over medium heat. Add 1 tablespoon oil to pan; swirl to coat. Add shallots to pan; cook 6 minutes. Add pear, wine, thyme, and pepper; cook 2 minutes. Cool. Stir in nuts, cheese, breadcrumbs, and parsley.

3. Slice pork lengthwise, cutting to, but not through, other side. Open halves. Place pork between sheets of plastic wrap; pound to ¼-inch thickness. Top pork with pear mixture, leaving a ½-inch border. Roll up, starting with long side; secure pork with picks. Sprinkle with salt.

4. Heat a large ovenproof skillet over medium-high heat. Add 1 tablespoon oil to pan; swirl to coat. Add pork; sauté 5 minutes, browning on all sides. Bake at 425° for 12 minutes or until a thermometer registers 145°. Remove pork from pan, and let stand 5 minutes. Slice. Bring broth to a boil in pan over medium-high heat, scraping pan to loosen browned bits. Cook 4 minutes. Serve sauce with pork. Serves 6 (serving size: 3 ounces pork and 1 tablespoon sauce).

CALORIES 321; FAT 16.1g (sat 3.8g, mono 5.8g, poly 5.6g); PROTEIN 28.7g; CARB 13g; FIBER 1.8g; CHOL 81mg; IRON 2mg; SODIUM 478mg; CALC 72mg

PLUMS

With their puckery-sweet flesh and tart skin, plums offer magical flavor.

SEASON: May to October, with the peak in mid- to late summer

CHOOSING: Bring home smooth-skinned, wrinkle-free plums without injuries or brown spots. If not perfectly ripe, they'll continue to ripen on the kitchen counter.

STORING: When plums are as ripe as needed, place them in a plastic produce bag in the refrigerator to stop the ripening. This will keep them in good condition for up to five days.

GROWING: Plums grow on a small tree that fits nicely into a home landscape. With white—and occasionally pink—spring flowers, a plum tree could be mistaken for a purely ornamental tree.

European plums are the elongated, deep purple, or green fruit that can be eaten fresh or dried to make prunes and jams. Varieties include Damson, Green Gage, Italian Prune, and Stanley. These generally require more winter cold and tolerate less heat.

Japanese plums are round, pink to red, and juicy. For gardeners with moderate to mild winters, these are the ones to choose. Select favorites such as AU Producer, Burbank, Methley, Santa Rosa, Shiro, and many others.

The third group is made up of hybrid plums, sometimes called cherry plums, that are the result of crossing native American with Japanese species. These originated in northern states and Canada. However, gardeners far and wide can benefit from these hardy trees and shrubs, including Opata, Sapa, Sapalta, Superior, and Underwood.

When adding a plum to your landscape, plan for two. You almost always need two trees for cross-pollination, and even if your tree is self-fruitful, it will bear more fruit if there is a second plum tree. However, your pollinator usually needs to be from the same family of plums.

Open-Faced Prosciutto and Plum Sandwiches

Hands-on time: 20 min.   Total time: 20 min.

¼ cup fig preserves	4 (2-ounce) slices country wheat bread, toasted
1 tablespoon fresh lemon juice	1 cup loosely packed arugula
¼ teaspoon grated peeled fresh ginger	2 ripe plums, cut into thin wedges
3 ounces soft goat cheese (about ⅓ cup)	3 ounces very thin slices prosciutto

1. Combine first 3 ingredients in a small bowl, stirring with a whisk; set aside.
2. Spread ¾ ounce cheese evenly over each bread slice; divide arugula, plum wedges, and prosciutto evenly among sandwiches. Drizzle each sandwich with about 1 tablespoon fig preserves mixture. Serves 4 (serving size: 1 sandwich).

CALORIES 318; FAT 9.1g (sat 5.1g, mono 3.1g, poly 0.6g); PROTEIN 13.1g; CARB 45.5g; FIBER 1.9g; CHOL 26mg; IRON 4.4mg; SODIUM 589mg; CALC 161mg

Plums are the tart star of the show on this beautiful open-faced sandwich. Consider making bite-sized versions on baguette slices for a party appetizer. Choose red or purple plums with bright, unblemished skin to slice into thin wedges.

Fizzy Plum Bellini

Hands-on time: 12 min.   Total time: 2 hr. 2 min.

½ cup water	1 teaspoon eau-de-vie or brandy
3 tablespoons sugar	2 cups prosecco
2 ripe, red-skinned plums, pitted and quartered	

1. Combine first 3 ingredients in a medium saucepan over medium-high heat; bring to a boil. Cook 5 minutes, stirring occasionally. Remove from heat; cool completely. Strain syrup through a sieve over a bowl; reserve plums. Stir eau-de-vie into syrup; chill. Remove plum skins, and discard. Place plums in a blender; process until smooth. Chill puree. Spoon 2 teaspoons puree into each of 6 flutes; discard remaining puree. Divide syrup evenly among glasses. Top each serving with ⅓ cup prosecco; stir. Serves 6.

CALORIES 183; FAT 0.6g (sat 0.1g, mono 0g, poly 0.3g); PROTEIN 1.6g; CARB 29.7g; FIBER 3.4g; CHOL 0mg; IRON 0.5mg; SODIUM 26mg; CALC 35mg

Roast Pork Tenderloin with Plum Barbecue Sauce

Hands-on time: 15 min.   Total time: 1 hr. 5 min.

Plum season extends from May to October, starting with Japanese varieties and ending with more cold-tolerant European ones. That's good news, as this entrée is one that friends and family will hope appears regularly in rotation. Once it's cooked, set aside 2½ cups of sauce to serve with the pork, and use the remainder to baste as it cooks.

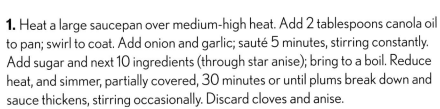

¼   cup canola oil, divided
1   cup chopped onion
2   garlic cloves, finely chopped
¼   cup packed brown sugar
¼   cup rice wine vinegar
¼   cup ketchup
2   tablespoons lower-sodium soy sauce
2   teaspoons dry mustard
1   teaspoon ground ginger
½   teaspoon freshly ground black pepper

⅛   teaspoon crushed red pepper
2   whole cloves
1½   pounds black plums, quartered and pitted
1   star anise
2   (1-pound) pork tenderloins, trimmed
½   teaspoon salt
½   teaspoon freshly ground black pepper

1. Heat a large saucepan over medium-high heat. Add 2 tablespoons canola oil to pan; swirl to coat. Add onion and garlic; sauté 5 minutes, stirring constantly. Add sugar and next 10 ingredients (through star anise); bring to a boil. Reduce heat, and simmer, partially covered, 30 minutes or until plums break down and sauce thickens, stirring occasionally. Discard cloves and anise.
2. Preheat oven to 450°.
3. Heat a large skillet over medium-high heat. Add 2 tablespoons oil to pan; swirl to coat. Sprinkle pork evenly with salt and ½ teaspoon black pepper. Add pork to pan; sauté 7 minutes, turning to brown on all sides.
4. Transfer pork to a foil-lined jelly-roll pan; coat with ½ cup plum sauce. Roast pork at 450° for 15 minutes. Remove pork from oven. Turn pork over; coat with an additional ½ cup plum sauce. Roast 7 minutes or until a thermometer inserted in thickest portion of pork registers 145°. Remove from pan; let stand 10 minutes. Slice crosswise. Serve with remaining plum sauce. Serves 8 (serving size: 3 ounces pork and about ⅓ cup sauce).

CALORIES 378; FAT 10.3g (sat 1.6g, mono 5.6g, poly 2.4g); PROTEIN 25.2g; CARB 50.7g; FIBER 4.7g; CHOL 62mg; IRON 2mg; SODIUM 417mg; CALC 22mg

RASPBERRIES

Sweet-tart raspberries are a delicate summer fruit that's worth the wait.

SEASON: Early summer through fall, depending on where the berries are grown

CHOOSING: When it comes to raspberries, it doesn't pay to plan too far ahead. Raspberries are delicate and highly perishable. Select berries that are firm without signs of juice stains or mold.

STORING: Mold can appear within hours if raspberries are not handled properly. Refrigerate unwashed berries as soon as you get them home. Use or freeze them (see page 58) within two days of purchase, rinsing them gently just before use.

GROWING: Raspberries grow on canes that are often arching and thorny. A trellis helps maintain an orderly planting and makes berry picking, mulching, fertilizing, and weed control less prickly. They need cold weather, so they'll be challenging to grow in the warmest regions of the country. Heritage is a variety that does well in borderline areas.

Ever-bearing red and yellow raspberries can produce fruit twice each season. Canes that grew the previous year will produce berries in late spring or early summer. Once berries are picked, prune the canes back to soil level. New canes will emerge and bear a second delicious crop in the fall. After harvest, don't trim them back; they'll produce again the following spring.

Black and purple raspberries grow in a clump and produce one crop of berries each year in summer. Cutting back the canes the first year to force branching means more fruit the following summer. As with red raspberries, the canes will die after they fruit; remove them at the soil level. At the same time, prune only new canes to 2 to 3 feet to encourage branching.

Pick raspberries in the morning when the berries are sweetest. A shallow basket lined with a clean paper towel is ideal. The berries are fragile and won't tolerate the weight of many berries on top of them.

Raspberry Thumbprint Cookies

Hands-on time: 36 min.   Total time: 9 hr. 18 min.

¾   cup grated almond paste
⅔   cup sugar
5   tablespoons butter, softened
¼   teaspoon vanilla extract
1   large egg white

5.6   ounces all-purpose flour (about 1¼ cups)
¼   teaspoon salt
6   tablespoons Raspberry Refrigerator Jam

1. Preheat oven to 325°. Line 2 large baking sheets with parchment paper; secure to baking sheets with masking tape.
2. Place first 3 ingredients in a large bowl; beat with a mixer at medium speed 4 minutes or until light and fluffy. Add vanilla and egg white; beat well.
3. Weigh or lightly spoon flour into dry measuring cups; level with a knife. Add flour and salt to almond paste mixture; beat at low speed until well blended. Turn dough out onto a lightly floured surface, and shape dough into 36 (1-inch) balls. Place balls 1 inch apart on prepared baking sheets, and press thumb into center of each cookie, leaving an indentation. Bake at 325° for 10 minutes or until golden. Remove cookies from pans; cool on wire racks. Spoon about ½ teaspoon Raspberry Refrigerator Jam into center of each cookie. Serves 36 (serving size: 1 cookie).

CALORIES 31; FAT 2.3g (sat 1.1g, mono 0.8g, poly 0.2g); PROTEIN 0.8g; CARB 9.5g; FIBER 0.4g; CHOL 4mg; IRON 0.3mg; SODIUM 29mg; CALC 6mg

Raspberry Refrigerator Jam

Hands-on time: 18 min.   Total time: 9 hr. 18 min.

8   cups fresh raspberries, divided
2¼   cups sugar, divided
¾   cup warm water (100° to 110°)

1   (1.75-ounce) package no-sugar-added pectin

1. Place 6 cups raspberries in a blender; process until smooth. Strain mixture through a fine sieve; discard seeds. Combine raspberry puree and 2 cups raspberries in a large bowl; partially mash raspberries with a spoon. Stir in 1½ cups sugar. Combine ¾ cup warm water and pectin in a small saucepan, stirring to dissolve. Stir in ¾ cup sugar; bring to a boil over medium heat, stirring constantly. Remove from heat; add pectin mixture to raspberry mixture, stirring until combined. Cool to room temperature. Spoon into airtight containers; cover and chill 8 hours or overnight. Serves 32 (serving size: 2 tablespoons).

CALORIES 74; FAT 0.1g (sat 0g, mono 0g, poly 0.1g); PROTEIN 0.3g; CARB 18.3g; FIBER 1.4g; CHOL 0mg; IRON 0.2mg; SODIUM 0mg; CALC 6mg

Two recipes in one: an almond-paste thumbprint cookie and a simple refrigerator jam. Both get high marks in the Test Kitchen. Almond paste makes the dough moist and pliable. The large holes of a box grater work well for grating the almond paste. A handy tip for deeper, more uniform imprints: Use a wine cork instead of your thumb. In the jam, the ratio of sugar to pectin is ideal; the jam thickens as it cools and will keep in the refrigerator for up to three weeks.

Mesclun with Berries and Sweet Spiced Almonds

Hands-on time: 10 min.   Total time: 44 min.

Any raspberries—red, purple, black, or yellow—will stand out with the crisp greens and spicy sweet almonds.

5	cups gourmet salad greens	¼	teaspoon salt
1¾	cups fresh raspberries	⅛	teaspoon freshly ground black pepper
¼	cup chopped fresh chives	1	tablespoon canola oil
3	tablespoons champagne or white wine vinegar	6	tablespoons Sweet Spiced Almonds
2	teaspoons honey		
½	teaspoon country-style Dijon mustard		

1. Combine first 3 ingredients in a large bowl. Combine vinegar and next 4 ingredients in a small bowl; gradually add oil, stirring with a whisk. Drizzle vinegar mixture over lettuce mixture; toss gently to coat. Arrange 1 cup salad on each of 6 plates; top each serving with 1 tablespoon Sweet Spiced Almonds. Serves 6.

CALORIES 84; FAT 4.2g (sat 0.3g, mono 2.4g, poly 1.3g); PROTEIN 2g; CARB 11.2g; FIBER 3.8g; CHOL 0mg; IRON 1.1mg; SODIUM 123mg; CALC 47mg

Freezing Fresh Berries

To help preserve some of the season, you can freeze berries. Simply spread unwashed berries in a single layer on a baking sheet, making sure none are touching, and place the pan in your freezer. Once frozen, transfer to a heavy-duty zip-top plastic bag. Give the berries a wash after they've thawed and just before you plan to use them.

Sweet Spiced Almonds

Hands-on time: 4 min.   Total time: 44 min.

1	cup sliced almonds	½	teaspoon ground cumin
⅓	cup packed brown sugar	1	large egg white, lightly beaten
1	teaspoon ground cinnamon		Cooking spray
½	teaspoon ground coriander		

1. Preheat oven to 325°.

2. Combine first 5 ingredients in a bowl. Stir in egg white. Spread mixture onto a foil-lined baking sheet coated with cooking spray. Bake at 325° for 10 minutes. Stir mixture; bake an additional 15 minutes or until crisp. Transfer foil to a wire rack; cool. Break mixture into small pieces. Serves 32 (serving size: 1 tablespoon).

Note: Store at room temperature in an airtight container for up to one week.

CALORIES 27; FAT 1.5g (sat 0.1g, mono 1g, poly 0.4g); PROTEIN 0.8g; CARB 2.9g; FIBER 0.4g; CHOL 0mg; IRON 0.2mg; SODIUM 3mg; CALC 11mg

STRAWBERRIES

The summer months bring the delicious juiciness and sweet fragrance and flavor of in-season strawberries.

SEASON: Berries are available from farms from spring until December. However, peak season for gardeners is May through August.

CHOOSING: Look for bright red, firm berries that have bright green caps and are free of mushy spots. If the package has a berry with mold, avoid the box entirely, as the mold will spread. Strawberries do not ripen after they are picked. Look for locally grown berries if possible.

STORING: Leave the caps attached until you're ready to eat the berries. The injury of removing them will cause the quality of the berries to decline quickly. Refrigerate unwashed berries as soon as you bring them home. Place the entire container in a produce bag to prevent drying.

GROWING: Strawberries grow on a hardy perennial plant that hugs the ground and spreads by runners that root wherever they touch the soil. A single plant this year can easily become four plants next season.

In colder regions, plant in early spring as soon as the soil can be worked. In warmer zones where the soil doesn't freeze, fall-planted strawberries can get a head start on the spring season by growing roots all winter long.

Choose a location that receives at least eight hours of sun each day. The soil should be loose and well drained. Adding a generous amount of compost will make the planting bed fluffy and deep—just what makes strawberry plants thrive. Set plants so that the crown, or the fragile base of the plant just above its roots, is just above the soil level; take care not to bury it. Space plants about 18 inches apart, allowing plenty of room for the offspring to spread out.

If you do not have enough room for a big bed of strawberries, try growing them in a large pot or strawberry jar, a big pot with pockets for plants all around the sides as well as the top. These are easy to move into a garage or close to the house during hard freezes.

Ever-bearing varieties produce a lot of berries in spring, but they also give a few all through the season. June-bearing varieties produce more berries at the same time, which is ideal for making preserves.

Strawberry-Lemon Shortcakes

Hands-on time: 35 min.   Total time: 1 hr. 30 min.

This is a quintessential dish for strawberries in season. Lightly macerating them with lemon and sugar makes the fresh berries you've just brought home even better suited for sandwiching between shortcakes. For slightly taller shortcakes with soft sides, pack the biscuits into a round cake pan; for shortcakes with crisp edges, arrange them on a baking sheet with space between.

9	ounces all-purpose flour (about 2 cups)
¼	cup granulated sugar
1	tablespoon baking powder
½	teaspoon baking soda
¼	teaspoon salt
6	tablespoons chilled butter, cut into small pieces
1¼	cups low-fat buttermilk
1	tablespoon grated lemon rind

	Cooking spray
½	cup all-purpose flour
1	tablespoon butter, melted
1	tablespoon turbinado sugar
4	cups sliced fresh strawberries
¼	cup granulated sugar
1	tablespoon fresh lemon juice
1¼	cups frozen fat-free whipped topping, thawed

1. Preheat oven to 425°.

2. Weigh or lightly spoon 9 ounces flour (about 2 cups) into dry measuring cups; level with a knife. Combine 9 ounces flour, ¼ cup granulated sugar, baking powder, baking soda, and ¼ teaspoon salt in a large bowl. Cut in butter with a pastry blender or 2 knives until mixture resembles coarse meal. Combine 1¼ cups buttermilk and grated lemon rind. Add buttermilk mixture to flour mixture, and toss gently with a fork to combine. (Dough should be wet and about the texture of cottage cheese.)

3. Coat a 9-inch round cake pan or baking sheet with cooking spray. Place ½ cup flour in a shallow dish. Scoop 10 equal dough portions into dish. Gently shape each portion into a round by tossing in flour to help shape dough. Arrange in pan. Discard excess flour. Brush dough with melted butter, and sprinkle evenly with 1 tablespoon turbinado sugar. Bake at 425° for 22 minutes or until shortcakes are lightly browned. Cool in pan 10 minutes on a wire rack. Remove shortcakes from pan. Cool on wire rack.

4. Combine berries, ¼ cup granulated sugar, and lemon juice; toss to coat. Let stand 15 minutes. Split each shortcake in half; spoon about ⅓ cup berry mixture and 2 tablespoons whipped topping into each. Serves 10 (serving size: 1 filled shortcake).

CALORIES 267; FAT 8.8g (sat 5.3g, mono 2.2g, poly 0.5g); PROTEIN 4.5g; CARB 46.2g; FIBER 2.2g; CHOL 23mg; IRON 1.6mg; SODIUM 338mg; CALC 126mg

Strawberry-Buttermilk
Sherbet

Chicken and Strawberry Salad

Hands-on time: 20 min.   Total time: 20 min.

Dressing:

1	tablespoon sugar
2	tablespoons red wine vinegar
1	tablespoon water
1/8	teaspoon salt
1/8	teaspoon freshly ground black pepper
2	tablespoons extra-virgin olive oil

Salad:

4	cups torn romaine lettuce
4	cups arugula
2	cups quartered fresh strawberries
1/3	cup vertically sliced red onion
12	ounces skinless, boneless rotisserie chicken breast, sliced
2	tablespoons unsalted cashews, halved
2	ounces crumbled blue cheese (about 1/2 cup)

Plate this no-cook recipe for a sophisticated dinner or pack it for a picnic—you'll need to pack the dressing separately and dress just before serving to keep the greens from wilting. Serve with a baguette for a great garden meal.

1. To prepare dressing, combine first 5 ingredients in a small bowl. Gradually add oil, stirring constantly with a whisk.

2. To prepare salad, combine romaine and next 4 ingredients (through chicken) in a bowl; toss gently. Place about 2 cups chicken mixture on each of 4 plates. Top each serving with 1 1/2 teaspoons cashews and 2 tablespoons cheese. Drizzle about 4 teaspoons dressing over each serving. Serves 4.

CALORIES 333; FAT 16.4g (sat 4.9g, mono 8.3g, poly 2.1g); PROTEIN 32g; CARB 14.8g; FIBER 3.5g; CHOL 83mg; IRON 2.5mg; SODIUM 347mg; CALC 156mg

Strawberry-Buttermilk Sherbet

Hands-on time: 10 min.   Total time: 1 hr. 40 min.

2	cups chopped fresh strawberries
1/3	cup agave nectar
1 1/2	cups whole buttermilk
3	tablespoons Chambord (raspberry-flavored liqueur)
1	tablespoon fresh lemon juice (optional)

Strawberries from the garden or farmers' market will make you a Pick Fresh philosophy devotee for life. Nothing like their out-of-season supermarket counterparts, these smaller berries pack intense flavor and riper flesh. Spare a couple of cups for this light and refreshing sherbet.

1. Place berries and nectar in a blender; process until smooth (about 1 minute). Add buttermilk; process until well blended. Add liqueur; pulse to mix. Add juice, if desired. Chill mixture 1 hour. Pour into the freezer can of an ice-cream freezer; freeze according to manufacturer's instructions. Serves 6 (serving size: about 3/4 cup).

CALORIES 135; FAT 2.2g (sat 1.3g, mono 0.6g, poly 0.2g); PROTEIN 2.4g; CARB 24.4g; FIBER 1.1g; CHOL 9mg; IRON 0.2mg; SODIUM 73mg; CALC 9mg

VEGETABLES

Local vegetables are one of the seasons' triumphs, offering vivid color and unmatched flavor.

ARTICHOKES

Fresh artichokes have a nutty flavor and firm, meaty texture that surpasses their jarred counterparts. The extra prep is worth it.

SEASON: Artichokes peak in spring and produce a second crop in fall.

CHOOSING: Whether you are buying artichokes or deciding when to cut them from your plants, the guidelines are the same: Select tight buds. Letting a bud remain on the plant to get bigger means it will not be as tender.

STORING: Store fresh artichokes in a produce bag in the refrigerator for one to two weeks.

GROWING: The ideal climate for perennial artichokes is coastal California, where winter is gentle and summer mornings are foggy and cool. In gardens where winters are harsh, the plants are spring-planted annuals, producing a single late-summer harvest. In all cases, the season lasts for weeks.

Artichokes are big, beautiful plants, growing about 3 to 4 feet tall and wide.

Select a place in full sun, unless you live in a hot climate, where a little afternoon shade is helpful. Good, rich garden soil will give the best results. Depending on the variety, artichokes need four to six months to produce buds. If your season is short, start seeds indoors in winter, and move them outside after the last frost.

Use mulch in summer to keep the roots cool and moist. Gardeners in areas that have hard freezes should cut the plant back, mulch heavily for the winter, and hope for the best, as it is more likely to be an annual in that climate.

When an artichoke plant blooms, the first bud is the biggest, followed by secondary buds that branch from the flower stalk. After all the buds have been cut from a stalk, remove the stalk at its base. New shoots will emerge from the roots to make next season's crown. Cut artichokes 1 to 1½ inches below the bud. For best quality, eat immediately.

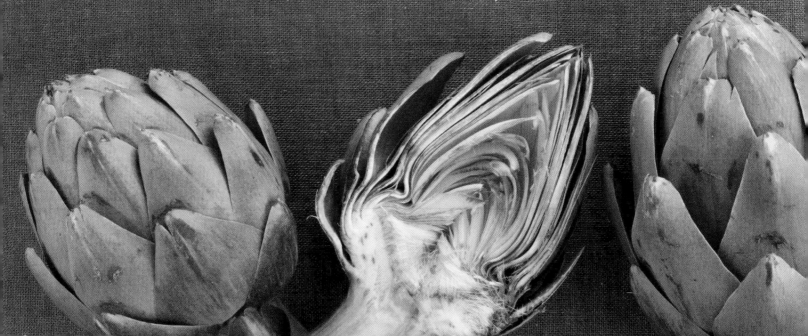

Artichokes with Roasted Garlic-Wine Dip

Hands-on time: 22 min.   Total time: 2 hr. 10 min.

Plucking leaves one by one to dip in melted butter is a classic way to enjoy fresh artichokes. If you're not convinced, this garlicky wine sauce will convert you. You'll want to dip all your steamed and roasted veggies in it! Since garlic mellows as it cooks, add the roasted garlic in two stages: Cook half with wine and broth to soften the flavor, and add the rest at the end for a more potent taste. If you plan to serve the remaining wine with this first course, choose a crisp, acidic pinot grigio or sauvignon blanc, which pairs well with artichokes. Otherwise, any dry white will work for the sauce.

2	whole garlic heads
4	medium artichokes (about 3½ pounds)
½	cup dry white wine
1	cup organic vegetable broth
1	tablespoon butter
¼	teaspoon kosher salt
	Chopped fresh parsley (optional)

1. Preheat oven to 400°.

2. Remove white papery skin from garlic heads (do not peel or separate cloves). Wrap each head separately in foil. Bake at 400° for 45 minutes; cool 10 minutes. Separate cloves; squeeze to extract garlic pulp. Discard skins.

3. Cut off stems of artichokes, and remove bottom leaves. Trim about ½ inch from tops of artichokes. Place artichokes, stem ends down, in a large Dutch oven filled two-thirds full with water; bring to a boil. Cover, reduce heat, and simmer 45 minutes or until a leaf near center of each artichoke pulls out easily. Remove artichokes from pan; keep warm.

4. Combine half of garlic pulp and wine in a small saucepan; bring to a boil. Cook 2 minutes. Add broth; cook until reduced to ½ cup (about 8 minutes). Remove from heat; stir in butter and salt. Pour mixture into a blender, and add remaining half of garlic pulp. Remove center piece of blender lid (to allow steam to escape); secure blender lid on blender. Place a clean towel over opening in blender lid (to avoid splatters). Blend until smooth. Transfer to serving bowl. Sprinkle with parsley, if desired. Serve dip with warm artichokes. Serves 4 (serving size: 1 artichoke and 3 tablespoons dip).

CALORIES 135; FAT 3.1g (sat 1.9g, mono 0.7g, poly 0.2g); PROTEIN 5.2g; CARB 19.8g; FIBER 7.2g; CHOL 8mg; IRON 1.9mg; SODIUM 403mg; CALC 84mg

Roasted Baby Artichokes and Fingerling Potatoes

Hands-on time: 21 min.   Total time: 51 min.

Baby artichokes and fingerling potatoes are big treats in small packages. Simply roasting these gems means you don't mask their flavor, while lemon juice, lemon rind, and fresh parsley are the perfect light and bright accents.

6   cups water
2   tablespoons fresh lemon juice
2   pounds baby artichokes
2   tablespoons extra-virgin olive oil
1¼   pounds small red fingerling potatoes, halved lengthwise
Cooking spray

1   tablespoon butter
2   teaspoons chopped fresh parsley
1   teaspoon grated lemon rind
1   teaspoon kosher salt
½   teaspoon freshly ground black pepper

1. Preheat oven to 425°.
2. Combine 6 cups water and lemon juice in a large bowl. Cut off stem of each artichoke to within 1 inch of base; peel stem. Remove bottom leaves and tough outer leaves, leaving tender heart and bottom. Cut each artichoke in half lengthwise. Place artichokes in lemon water.
3. Combine oil and potatoes; toss well. Arrange potatoes in a single layer on a jelly-roll pan coated with cooking spray. Bake at 425° for 15 minutes. Drain artichokes; add artichokes to potatoes, tossing to combine. Bake an additional 15 minutes or until tender. Place vegetables in a large bowl. Toss with butter and remaining ingredients. Serve immediately. Serves 8.

CALORIES 123; FAT 4.9g (sat 1.4g, mono 2.8g, poly 0.4g); PROTEIN 3.2g; CARB 17.4g; FIBER 3.4g; CHOL 4mg; IRON 1.3mg; SODIUM 292mg; CALC 22mg

Artichoke Galette

Hands-on time: 49 min. Total time: 1 hr. 19 min.

Baby artichokes are the younger, less mature buds along the stem of the plant. Their tender flesh, paired with the peppery zing of French breakfast radishes, makes a delicate, savory galette.

3	cups water, divided
2	tablespoons fresh lemon juice
8	baby artichokes
½	cup crisp white wine
1½	teaspoons black peppercorns
Cooking spray	
5	shallots, peeled and quartered
5	French breakfast radishes, halved lengthwise
½	(14.1-ounce) package refrigerated pie dough
1	garlic clove, halved
⅓	cup pine nuts, toasted and chopped
3	ounces Asiago cheese, shredded (about ¾ cup)
2	teaspoons thyme leaves
½	teaspoon freshly ground black pepper
¼	teaspoon kosher salt

1. Preheat oven to 400°.

2. Combine 1 cup water and juice in a bowl. Cut off stem of each artichoke to within 1 inch of base; peel stem. Remove bottom leaves and tough outer leaves, leaving tender heart and bottom. Cut each artichoke into quarters. Place artichokes in lemon water. Combine 2 cups water and wine in a saucepan. Place peppercorns on a double layer of cheesecloth; gather edges together, and tie securely. Add sachet to pan; bring to a simmer. Drain artichokes; add to pot. Simmer 5 minutes; drain. Discard sachet. Heat a small skillet over medium-high heat. Coat pan with cooking spray. Add shallots; sauté 5 minutes. Combine shallots, artichokes, and radishes.

3. Roll dough into a 15-inch circle; rub with garlic. Place dough on a baking sheet. Sprinkle with nuts and cheese, leaving a 2-inch border. Top with artichoke mixture, thyme, black pepper, and salt. Fold edges of dough over to partially cover. Bake at 400° for 30 minutes or until browned. Serves 6 (serving size: 1 wedge).

CALORIES 304; FAT 18.4g (sat 6g, mono 5.5g, poly 5.4g); PROTEIN 9.3g; CARB 30.8g; FIBER 5g; CHOL 13mg; IRON 1.9mg; SODIUM 503mg; CALC 177mg

All Choked Up

If you like the earthy goodness of big globe artichokes but find them fussy, buy a bunch of baby ones instead. Here's the deal: They're choke-free (the choke is that fuzzy part) and almost entirely edible, and they require less prep overall. "Baby" is also somewhat of a misnomer. They're fully grown; they just sprout low on the stalks.

ARUGULA

*This small leaf may look delicate but it packs
a peppery punch that intensifies as it grows.*

SEASON: Arugula prefers cool weather, usually the refreshing days of spring and fall.

CHOOSING: Look for unblemished green leaves with no sign of yellowing or wilting. If picking from the garden, snip off just the outer leaves; this way, the plant can produce more for your next salad or stir-fry.

STORING: If you buy arugula, keep it from wilting by placing it in a produce bag in the refrigerator. It will last about a week. When growing arugula, the best way to keep it fresh is to leave it in the garden until you need it.

GROWING: Arugula is mild-mannered when young but becomes downright spicy as the plant matures or the weather gets warm. If it becomes too piquant for your taste, mix it with a blend of mild lettuces for a flavorful salad with contrasting tastes and textures. Or wilt it in a sauté pan as you would other bitter greens.

In early spring, place young plants of arugula in a sunny, well-prepared bed. You can also sow seeds directly into your garden or into a container of good potting soil. Thin or transplant crowded seedlings so that plants grow about 12 inches apart.

Arugula grows fast, so replant again every two to three weeks to be sure you have good greens. This is particularly helpful in the spring, when the days get warmer and plants start maturing.

Each plant will grow into a rosette. When hot weather triggers flowering, arugula can grow as tall as 3 feet with white flowers. While the leaves may be too peppery for dinner, the flowers make a nice addition to a salad or as a garnish. If seeds are allowed to fall into garden beds, your arugula will return when the time is right.

Roasted Potatoes with Arugula-Pistachio Pesto

Hands-on time: 18 min. Total time: 58 min.

For those fans of peppery pesto, grow seeds with *selvatica* in the name, sometimes marketed as "wild rocket." The toothed leaves have a much more intense heat and flavor than common arugula and are favored for pesto and pizza sauces. Make extra of this pesto while the arugula is fresh; it freezes well.

2 pounds fingerling potatoes, halved lengthwise
1/4 cup extra-virgin olive oil, divided
3/4 teaspoon kosher salt, divided
3/8 teaspoon freshly ground black pepper, divided
1 1/2 cups packed arugula leaves (about 1 1/2 ounces)
3 tablespoons grated fresh Parmesan cheese
1 1/2 tablespoons pistachios
2 teaspoons water
1 1/2 teaspoons fresh lemon juice
1 garlic clove

1. Place a jelly-roll pan in oven. Preheat oven to 400°.
2. Combine potatoes and 1 tablespoon oil in a medium bowl; toss well. Arrange potatoes in a single layer on preheated pan. Sprinkle potatoes with 1/2 teaspoon salt and 1/4 teaspoon pepper. Bake at 400° for 20 minutes; toss potatoes. Bake an additional 25 minutes or until tender, stirring every 10 minutes.
3. Place 3 tablespoons oil, 1/4 teaspoon salt, 1/8 teaspoon pepper, arugula, and remaining ingredients in a food processor; process until smooth. Combine arugula mixture and hot potatoes in a medium bowl; toss well. Serves 6 (serving size: 1 cup).

CALORIES 245; FAT 10.8g (sat 1.8g, mono 7.3g, poly 1.4g); PROTEIN 5.3g; CARB 33.1g; FIBER 3.7g; CHOL 2mg; IRON 1.9mg; SODIUM 303mg; CALC 62mg

Steak House Pizza

Hands-on time: 30 min. Total time: 30 min.

Wider, less-lobed *Eruca sativa* varieties, which are more palatable in larger quantities when dressed simply, would be a great topping on this pizza. This is a new take on a "steak and salad with a side of bread" and a fun way to enjoy dinner in a bite.

1	pound fresh pizza dough	¼	cup thinly sliced red onion
8	teaspoons olive oil, divided	3	tablespoons balsamic vinaigrette
2	garlic cloves, minced	2	ounces crumbled blue cheese
2	(4-ounce) beef tenderloin steaks		(about ½ cup)
4	cups loosely packed arugula leaves	¼	teaspoon freshly ground black pepper

1. Preheat oven to 450°.

2. Place dough in a microwave-safe bowl; microwave at MEDIUM (50% power) 45 seconds. Let stand 5 minutes. Roll dough into a 14-inch circle. Place on pizza pan; pierce with a fork. Combine 2 tablespoons oil and garlic; brush over dough. Bake at 450° for 14 minutes.

3. Heat a skillet over medium-high heat. Add 2 teaspoons oil to pan; swirl to coat. Add steaks to pan; cook 3 minutes on each side. Remove from pan; let stand 5 minutes. Cut across grain into slices.

4. Combine arugula, onion, and vinaigrette. Arrange over crust; top with steak, cheese, and pepper. Serves 6.

CALORIES 360; FAT 14.6g (sat 3.7g, mono 6.8g, poly 1.2g); PROTEIN 17.3g; CARB 37.4g; FIBER 5.7g; CHOL 30mg; IRON 1.8mg; SODIUM 564mg; CALC 80mg

Quick Dough Trick

For fast pizzas, refrigerated dough from the grocer's bakery section is a time-saver. Let it stand at room temperature for at least 15 minutes—30 minutes is ideal—to make it easier to roll. But when there isn't time to spare, try this trick: Put the dough in a microwave-safe bowl, and microwave at HIGH for 30 seconds or at MEDIUM (50% power) for 45 seconds. If the dough shrinks or snaps back as you roll it out, let it rest for several minutes—the gluten will relax, letting it stretch to the desired size.

Arugula Salad with Goat Cheese, Bacon, and Balsamic-Fig Dressing

Hands-on time: 24 min. Total time: 24 min.

If you're lucky enough to harvest or happen upon the freshest of arugula greens, you'll want to eat an entire salad of them. The sweet figs in the balsamic dressing and the tangy goat cheese are a strong pairing with the peppery greens and the salty bite of bacon. Make the dressing up to three days ahead, and refrigerate. This will be your go-to green salad in season.

Dressing:
3   tablespoons balsamic vinegar
3   dried Black Mission figs, chopped
3   tablespoons water
2   tablespoons fat-free, lower-sodium chicken broth
2   tablespoons extra-virgin olive oil
1½ teaspoons honey
½   teaspoon minced shallots
¼   teaspoon chopped fresh thyme

Salad:
8   cups trimmed arugula (about 4 ounces)
¼   cup thinly sliced red onion
¼   teaspoon freshly ground black pepper
⅛   teaspoon salt
3   center-cut bacon slices, cooked and crumbled
2   tablespoons crumbled goat cheese

1. To prepare dressing, combine balsamic vinegar and figs in a small saucepan over medium-high heat; bring to a boil. Cover, remove from heat, and let stand 15 minutes. Place vinegar mixture, 3 tablespoons water, and next 5 ingredients (through thyme) in a blender; process until smooth.

2. To prepare salad, place 1⅓ cups arugula on each of 6 plates. Divide onion evenly among plates. Drizzle about 3 tablespoons dressing over each serving; sprinkle evenly with pepper and salt. Sprinkle evenly with bacon. Top each serving with 1 teaspoon goat cheese. Serve immediately. Serves 6.

CALORIES 91; FAT 4.5g (sat 1.3g, mono 2.4g, poly 0.6g); PROTEIN 3g; CARB 10.9g; FIBER 1.7g; CHOL 5mg; IRON 0.9mg; SODIUM 147mg; CALC 88mg

ASPARAGUS

The beauty of these elegant spears is their versatility.
They also shine when briefly boiled and seasoned.

SEASON: Look for asparagus in the market from February to June, with April being the peak.

CHOOSING: Fresh asparagus will be bright green with no signs of shriveling. The tender tips may have a purplish cast, but they should be firm and tight, never mushy. The cut end will be thick and fibrous—the plant's reaction to the injury of cutting. This end is cut off before cooking, but if the shoots are fresh, you may lose only an inch.

STORING: You can place asparagus in a produce bag in your vegetable bin; however, it's more likely to get bruised, broken, or left too long. To keep asparagus in prime condition, trim the cut ends, stand them in a glass of water, cover with plastic, and refrigerate (glass and all) for up to two days.

GROWING: Gardeners in all but the coldest and warmest parts of the country can grow asparagus. The perennial underground roots need a season long enough to store energy for lots of fat spears, and they need enough cold weather to go dormant for a while.

If you plant asparagus from seed, you should wait three years before the first harvest since picking early will drastically reduce yield as well as quality. To get a jump start, begin in spring with 1-year-old crowns (bare plant roots without leaves) rather than seeds as harvest can begin to a limited degree the next year. Opt for the male hybrid plants that outproduce older types. Once they mature, expect to harvest about ½ pound per crown. How much to plant depends on how much your family likes asparagus, but about five crowns per person is a good place to start.

You only get one chance to prepare a bed that will sustain these plants for years to come, so do it right. (See Third Year's the Charm on page 79.) Select a site that is sunny, well drained, and out of the way of other garden activities. Work aged manure and compost into a bed 2 feet wide, and dig a 6- to 8-inch trench the length of the bed. Sprinkle superphosphate fertilizer into the trench as you would salt popcorn. Then set the crowns 1½ feet apart. If you have two rows, space them 6 feet apart. Cover the crowns, mulch, and water well.

Ginger-Scented Corn and Asparagus Stir-Fry

Hands-on time: 30 min.   Total time: 30 min.

Stir-fries are the perfect opportunity to show off your mélange of garden goods. A colorful mix of fresh corn, sweet red pepper, green asparagus, and sizzling browned tofu makes this an inexpensive, memorable weeknight meal.

4	tablespoons canola oil, divided
10	ounces extra-firm tofu, drained and cut into $\frac{3}{4}$-inch cubes
$\frac{2}{3}$	cup fresh corn kernels
1	tablespoon grated peeled fresh ginger
4	garlic cloves, minced
1	small onion, vertically sliced (about $\frac{3}{4}$ cup)
1	julienne-cut red bell pepper (about 1 cup)
6	ounces asparagus, steamed and cut into 1-inch pieces (about 2 cups)
$\frac{1}{4}$	cup organic vegetable broth
2	tablespoons lower-sodium soy sauce
3	tablespoons rice wine vinegar
$\frac{1}{4}$	teaspoon crushed red pepper
2	cups hot cooked short-grain rice
2	thinly sliced green onions (about $\frac{1}{4}$ cup)

1. Heat a large cast-iron skillet over medium-high heat. Add 2 tablespoons oil to pan; swirl to coat. Add tofu; sauté 10 minutes or until golden brown, stirring frequently. Remove tofu from pan with a slotted spoon; wipe pan dry with a paper towel. Heat 2 tablespoons oil in pan; swirl to coat. Add corn and next 4 ingredients (through bell pepper); stir-fry 5 minutes. Add tofu, asparagus, and next 4 ingredients (through crushed red pepper). Stir-fry 1 minute or until asparagus and tofu are heated. Place $\frac{1}{2}$ cup rice on each of 4 plates. Spoon about 1 cup corn mixture over each serving, and top each with 1 tablespoon green onions. Serves 4.

CALORIES 380; FAT 18.8g (sat 1.6g, mono 12.1g, poly 4.6g); PROTEIN 12.2g; CARB 43.8g; FIBER 4g; CHOL 0mg; IRON 4.2mg; SODIUM 421mg; CALC 153mg

Grilled Asparagus with Caper Vinaigrette

Hands-on time: 11 min. Total time: 11 min.

If you are in your third year of growing your own asparagus, here comes your first harvest! If you have an established patch, it's still a great pleasure to snap them in the garden and eat them raw. Those that make it to the kitchen table are best served lightly grilled with this caper vinaigrette. Don't skip the fresh basil.

1½	pounds asparagus spears, trimmed	½	teaspoon Dijon mustard
3	tablespoons extra-virgin olive oil, divided	¼	teaspoon freshly ground black pepper
½	teaspoon kosher salt, divided	1	garlic clove, minced
Cooking spray		2	teaspoons capers, coarsely chopped
1	tablespoon red wine vinegar	¼	cup small basil leaves

1. Preheat grill to medium-high heat.

2. Place asparagus in a shallow dish. Add 1 tablespoon oil and ¼ teaspoon salt, tossing well to coat. Place asparagus on grill rack coated with cooking spray, and grill 4 minutes or until crisp-tender, turning after 2 minutes.

3. Combine ¼ teaspoon salt, vinegar, and next 3 ingredients (through garlic); stir with a whisk. Slowly pour 2 tablespoons oil into vinegar mixture, stirring constantly with a whisk. Stir in capers. Arrange asparagus on a serving platter; drizzle with vinaigrette, and sprinkle with basil. Serves 6 (serving size: about 4 asparagus spears and about 2 teaspoons vinaigrette).

CALORIES 91; FAT 7.2g (sat 1.1g, mono 5g, poly 1.1g); PROTEIN 2.6g; CARB 4.8g; FIBER 2.5g; CHOL 0mg; IRON 2.5mg; SODIUM 198mg; CALC 32mg

Third Year's the Charm

Growing asparagus from seed is a three-year process with tasty rewards. Here are some tips to help ensure success:

Year 1: Let asparagus grow unharvested. When spears emerge from the ground the first year, don't cut them. Resist the temptation—you'll be rewarded in the years to come. Those spears will develop into 4- to 6-foot-tall stalks of fine foliage. Let it stand all summer, and cut it away in winter.

Year 2: Harvest a few spears until new shoots are thin. Allow yourself a light harvest in spring of the second year, stopping when the diameter of the spears is reduced to the size of a pencil.

Year 3: Your asparagus investment pays off—eat up! You can now begin a normal harvest cycle, gathering spears over a month or more. Remember to snap the spears off at the soil level every couple of days. Using a knife to cut below ground may yield longer spears, but it risks damaging new spears still emerging.

Spring Asparagus Risotto

Hands-on time: 56 min.   Total time: 56 min.

Asparagus popping out of the soil is one of the first signs of spring in the garden. The days are warming up, but the nights are still chilly—an ideal time for warm bowls of rich asparagus risotto. Save the more tender tips for the risotto pieces, and blend the larger chopped pieces of asparagus into the broth used to cook the risotto. Garnish with shaved Parmigiano-Reggiano, if you like, for a pretty finish.

1½   pounds asparagus, cut into 1-inch slices (about 4 cups), divided
3   cups fat-free, lower-sodium chicken broth, divided
1½   cups water
1   tablespoon butter
2   cups chopped onion (about 1 large)
2   cups uncooked Arborio rice or other medium-grain rice
½   cup dry white wine
4   ounces grated fresh Parmigiano-Reggiano cheese, divided (about 1 cup)
¼   cup heavy whipping cream
1   teaspoon salt
½   teaspoon freshly ground black pepper

1. Place 1 cup asparagus and 1 cup broth in a blender; puree until smooth. Combine puree, 2 cups broth, and 1½ cups water in a medium saucepan; bring to a simmer (do not boil). Keep warm over low heat.
2. Melt butter in a large heavy saucepan over medium heat. Add onion to pan; cook 8 minutes or until tender, stirring occasionally. Stir in rice; cook 1 minute, stirring constantly. Stir in wine, and cook 2 minutes or until liquid is nearly absorbed, stirring constantly. Add ½ cup broth mixture; cook 2 minutes or until liquid is nearly absorbed, stirring constantly. Add remaining broth mixture, ½ cup at a time, stirring constantly until each portion of broth is absorbed before adding the next (about 30 minutes total). Stir in 3 cups asparagus; cook 2 minutes.
3. Stir in ¾ cup cheese, cream, salt, and pepper. Transfer risotto to a bowl. Top with ¼ cup cheese. Serves 8 (serving size: 1¼ cups risotto and 1½ teaspoons cheese).

CALORIES 283; FAT 7.7g (sat 4.4g, mono 2g, poly 0.3g); PROTEIN 10.5g; CARB 44g; FIBER 4.1g; CHOL 23mg; IRON 2.2mg; SODIUM 634mg; CALC 144mg

BEANS

Beans are magical: The many varieties keep boredom at bay, and they're amazingly good for you.

SEASON: Summer

CHOOSING: Green beans should be bright green and crisp, with only moderate bulges from the beans snuggled inside the pods. Overly mature beans will be tough, and brown bruises and drying are signs they're not fresh. For fresh, tender limas, the pods should be green.

STORING: Beans to be eaten green should be stored in a produce bag in the vegetable bin of your refrigerator for up to a week. (See page 83 for information about drying beans.)

GROWING: Snap beans, pole beans, wax beans, lima beans, yard-long beans (Chinese long beans), kidney beans, pinto beans, rattlesnake beans—the list goes on. In a nutshell, there are two plant types: pole or runner beans, which need a trellis, and bush beans, which stand on their own.

The plants produce both snap beans and shelling beans.

Green snap beans are eaten whole, pod and all, while young and tender. They become shelled beans when allowed to mature on the plant to the point that the pod is too tough to eat. Ultimately, the pods will turn brown and the dried beans can be shelled.

Plant beans in full sun in late spring or early summer. Push seeds into well-prepared beds at the spacing recommended on the seed packet, usually 4 inches apart. If you are growing bush beans, consider planting every three weeks for a continuous harvest. Pole beans will produce over a longer period.

When the days are warm and moisture is plentiful, it's surprising how fast beans grow. Pick at least every other day, refrigerating each day's harvest until you have enough to cook. Be careful not to pull beans and break the stem, which will reduce the number of beans to come. Either use two hands to separate the beans from the vine, or use small snips. In the case of the superproductive yard-long beans, clippers are almost essential.

Vegetable Chili with Harvest Beans

Hands-on time: 33 min. Total time: 3 hr. 39 min.

Beans named after painted ponies (Appaloosa), beans with sorrowful stories (Cherokee Trail of Tears black beans), and beans that sound like they have a fun beat (Calypso) are just a few of the many colorful varieties to choose from for this eclectic pot of chili. You can soak the beans overnight or use the quick-hydrate method below. Garnish with fresh cilantro, if you like.

1	cup dried black beans
1	cup dried calypso or pinto beans
1	cup dried snowcap, Appaloosa, or pinto beans
2	tablespoons olive oil
1¾	cups diced onion
¾	cup diced red bell pepper
¾	cup diced green bell pepper
¾	cup diced yellow bell pepper
½	cup minced seeded jalapeño pepper (about 4 large)
3	garlic cloves, minced
2½	tablespoons chili powder
2	tablespoons ground cumin
1	teaspoon ground red pepper
½	teaspoon salt
⅛	teaspoon freshly ground black pepper
½	cup masa harina or cornmeal
2	tablespoons unsweetened cocoa
5	(14.5-ounce) cans organic vegetable broth

1. Sort and wash beans; place in a large Dutch oven. Cover with water to 2 inches above beans, and bring to a boil; cook 2 minutes. Remove from heat; cover and let stand 1 hour. Drain beans in a colander, and set aside.

2. Heat a large skillet over medium-high heat. Add oil to pan; swirl to coat. Add onion and next 5 ingredients (through garlic); sauté 10 minutes or until tender. Add chili powder and next 4 ingredients (through black pepper); sauté 1 minute. Stir in masa harina and cocoa. Add beans and broth; stir well. Bring to a boil; reduce heat, and simmer, uncovered, 2 hours or until beans are tender, stirring occasionally. Serves 13 (serving size: 1 cup).

CALORIES 220; FAT 3.1g (sat 0.4g, mono 1.6g, poly 0.4g); PROTEIN 10.6g; CARB 37.6g; FIBER 9.3g; CHOL 0mg; IRON 3.1mg; SODIUM 523mg; CALC 55mg

Dried on the Vine

Drying beans is an excellent way to preserve a taste of the season. To dry beans, allow the pods to mature and brown in the garden. They can then be shelled, air-dried, and reserved for winter soups or for planting the following year. Put the container of dried beans in the freezer for a couple of days to kill any insects that may have gotten that far and then transfer them to a pantry or other cool, dark, dry location for longer storage.

Quick-Pickled Dilly
Green Beans

Quick-Pickled Dilly Green Beans

Hands-on time: 10 min. Total time: 2 hr. 10 min.

¼	cup chopped fresh dill	2	teaspoons sugar
½	pound green beans, trimmed	2	teaspoons salt
1	cup white wine vinegar	2	teaspoons pickling spice
1	cup water	1	garlic clove, peeled

1. Combine dill and green beans in a medium bowl.

2. Combine vinegar and remaining ingredients in a small saucepan. Bring to a boil; cook 1 minute or until sugar and salt dissolve. Pour over bean mixture. Let stand 2 hours. Drain, or serve with a slotted spoon. Serves 12 (serving size: about ⅓ cup).

CALORIES 6; FAT 0g; PROTEIN 0.4g; CARB 1.4g; FIBER 0.7g; CHOL 0mg; IRON 0.2mg; SODIUM 41mg; CALC 7mg

Dilly beans make appearances as crisp, crunchy garnishes and picnic snacks, and in the occasional Bloody Mary. They're easy to prepare and will keep for up to a week in the refrigerator. For a colorful presentation, use Golden Wax and green beans, and even throw in a baby carrot or red okra pod.

Three-Bean Salad with Almonds and Pecorino

Hands-on time: 17 min. Total time: 36 min.

1½	cups fresh lima beans	2	teaspoons olive oil
½	pound fresh yellow wax beans, trimmed and cut into 2-inch pieces	¼	teaspoon salt
		¼	teaspoon freshly ground black pepper
½	pound fresh green beans, trimmed and cut into 2-inch pieces	1	ounce shaved fresh pecorino Romano cheese (about ¼ cup)
3	tablespoons sherry or red wine vinegar	2	tablespoons slivered almonds, toasted

1. Sort and wash lima beans; place in a small saucepan. Cover with water to 2 inches above beans, and bring to a boil. Cover, reduce heat, and simmer 20 minutes or until tender. Drain.

2. Cook wax and green beans in boiling water 5 minutes or until tender. Drain and plunge beans into ice water; drain.

3. Combine lima, wax, and green beans in a large bowl. Add vinegar, olive oil, salt, and pepper; toss well. Top with cheese and slivered almonds. Serves 6 (serving size: about 1 cup bean mixture, about 2 teaspoons cheese, and 1 teaspoon almonds).

CALORIES 127; FAT 4.4g (sat 1.2g, mono 2.2g, poly 0.7g); PROTEIN 6.7g; CARB 15.6g; FIBER 5g; CHOL 3mg; IRON 2.3mg; SODIUM 185mg; CALC 102mg

Beans, beans, beans. Three-bean salads are a thing of the past, present, and future because there are so many choices. This isn't your grandmother's recipe, though, as it's light on calories and especially tasty served warm. Pair crunchy green beans with buttery limas, or substitute pink-eyed peas.

BEETS

Fresh beets offer great earthy flavor, meaty texture, and color—from golden yellow to deep purple.

SEASON: Beets prefer the cool weather of spring and fall.

CHOOSING: Select small to medium beets with firm, smooth skin and no soft spots or punctures. Those with stems and leaves still attached are best. The foliage should be green and fresh-looking.

STORING: Store beets, greens and all, in a produce bag in the coldest part of your refrigerator for up to two weeks. If you don't have room for all that foliage, snip it off about an inch above the root, but save the greens. They're tasty, too.

GROWING: Beets are grown from seeds sown as early as possible in spring, beginning about a month before the last frost date if the soil can be worked. Plant again in late summer for beets that mature in the cool days of fall. If you garden where summers are very mild, make repeated plantings from early spring until fall. In areas where winters are gentle, grow beets in fall, through winter, and into spring.

Each beet seed is actually a group of seeds. Space them about 2 inches apart. When the cluster of seedlings starts growing, snip off all but one so it can develop a proper root. As plants grow larger, thin them to about 4 inches apart. Save the leaves you remove for a fresh salad.

If you have beets growing in your fall garden, mulch them well and let them remain there, unless your soil freezes deeply. Harvest beets as you need them.

Beets seem to be sensitive to drought, so if your area experiences a period of little rain, be sure to water your beet patch. Fertilize with liquid or granular fertilizer about a month after planting at the rate recommended on the label.

Winter Salad with Roasted Beets and Citrus Reduction Dressing

Hands-on time: 15 min.   Total time: 1 hr. 47 min.

Don't say you don't like beets until you've tried them roasted. A tip for avoiding a horror scene in the kitchen: Use thin latex gloves to rub the skins off roasted beets hot from the oven so hands don't get stained. This salad combines the glorious colors of red and golden beets with a tangy citrus dressing. The earthiness of the beets is a good contrast to the bright and bitter greens, too.

4	medium beets (red and golden)	½	teaspoon freshly ground black pepper, divided
	Cooking spray		
¾	cup fresh orange juice (about 4 oranges)	¼	cup extra-virgin olive oil
		4	cups torn Boston lettuce
½	teaspoon sugar	2	cups trimmed watercress
1	tablespoon minced shallots	2	cups torn radicchio
2	tablespoons white wine vinegar	2	ounces goat cheese, crumbled (about ½ cup)
¾	teaspoon kosher salt, divided		

1. Preheat oven to 400°.

2. Leave root and 1-inch stem on beets; scrub with a brush. Place beets on a foil-lined jelly-roll pan coated with cooking spray. Lightly coat beets with cooking spray. Bake at 400° for 1 hour and 10 minutes or until tender. Cool slightly. Trim off roots and stems; rub off skins. Cut beets into ½-inch-thick wedges.

3. Bring juice and sugar to a boil in a small saucepan; cook 10 minutes or until reduced to 2 tablespoons. Pour into a medium bowl; cool slightly. Add shallots, vinegar, ½ teaspoon salt, and ¼ teaspoon pepper, stirring with a whisk. Gradually add oil, stirring constantly with a whisk.

4. Combine lettuce, watercress, and radicchio. Sprinkle lettuce mixture with ¼ teaspoon salt and ¼ teaspoon pepper; toss gently to combine. Arrange about 1 cup lettuce mixture on each of 8 plates. Divide beets evenly among salads. Drizzle about 1 tablespoon dressing over each salad; sprinkle each salad with 1 tablespoon cheese. Serves 8.

CALORIES 127; FAT 9.1g (sat 2.4g, mono 5.4g, poly 0.8g); PROTEIN 3.1g; CARB 8.2g; FIBER 1.7g; CHOL 6mg; IRON 1mg; SODIUM 253mg; CALC 53mg

NUTRITION NOTE

Unlike many other red vegetables, which get their color from lycopene, beets get their hue from betalains, pigments with antioxidant and anti-inflammatory properties. Betalains range from purple-red to yellow and are found in a limited number of grains, vegetables, and fruits; red beets are one of the richest edible sources.

Beet and Brown Rice Sliders

Hands-on time: 49 min. Total time: 49 min.

If you roast beets for another recipe, make one or two extra to save a step in this slider recipe the next night. A seemingly unusual mix of flavors comes together well in a neat presentation that will wow your burger-loving guests.

16 thin slices sourdough bread
    Cooking spray
1   cup cooked, cooled whole-grain brown rice blend
¾   cup grated cooked beets (about 1 medium)
½   cup panko (Japanese breadcrumbs)
6   tablespoons chopped walnuts, toasted
¼   cup chopped fresh flat-leaf parsley
2   tablespoons finely chopped shallots
½   teaspoon kosher salt
¼   teaspoon freshly ground black pepper
2   tablespoons Dijon mustard
1   large egg
2   tablespoons olive oil, divided
1   (3-ounce) log goat cheese, cut crosswise into 8 slices
1   cup watercress

1. Preheat broiler.
2. Cut each bread slice into a 3-inch circle using a round cutter; reserve scraps for another use (such as breadcrumbs or croutons). Lightly coat bread rounds with cooking spray. Arrange bread rounds in a single layer on a baking sheet. Broil 2 minutes on each side or until lightly toasted. Cool on a wire rack.
3. Reduce oven temperature to 400°. Place a baking sheet in oven to preheat.
4. Combine rice and next 7 ingredients (through pepper) in a medium bowl. Combine mustard and egg, stirring well. Add egg mixture to rice mixture; stir until well blended. Spoon ⅓ cup rice mixture into a (2½-inch) round cookie cutter; pack mixture down. Remove mold. Repeat procedure 7 times to form 8 patties.
5. Heat a large skillet over medium-high heat. Add 1 tablespoon oil to pan; swirl to coat. Carefully add 4 patties to pan, and cook 2 minutes. Carefully transfer patties to preheated baking sheet, turning patties over and arranging in a single layer. Repeat procedure with 1 tablespoon oil and 4 patties. Place pan in oven; bake patties at 400° for 9 minutes. Top each patty with 1 cheese slice; bake an additional 1 minute or until cheese is soft and patties are set.
6. Place 8 toasted bread rounds on a flat surface; top each round with 1 patty. Divide watercress evenly among sliders; top with remaining toasted bread rounds. Serves 4 (serving size: 2 sliders).

CALORIES 405; FAT 21g (sat 5.3g, mono 7.6g, poly 6.5g); PROTEIN 14.4g; CARB 41.4g; FIBER 3.3g; CHOL 63mg; IRON 3.1mg; SODIUM 745mg; CALC 85mg

Potato-Beet Gnocchi

Hands-on time: 23 min.   Total time: 1 hr. 45 min.

Using both the greens and the root of the beet is especially smart and nutritious. In this case, it also makes for beautiful presentation. Bull's Blood is a favorite variety, grown sometimes as an ornamental in fall containers, though it's entirely edible; Detroit Dark Red is one we've grown (to love) in the *Cooking Light* garden.

1	(8-ounce) medium-sized red beet with greens		Cooking spray
1	pound medium baking potatoes	6	quarts water
5.6	ounces all-purpose flour (about 1¼ cups), divided	4	cups vertically sliced onion
¾	teaspoon kosher salt, divided	½	teaspoon pepper
		1	ounce shaved fresh Parmesan cheese (about ¼ cup)

1. Preheat oven to 400°.

2. Remove greens and stems from beet. Chop greens to measure 2 cups. Pierce beet and potatoes with a fork. Bake potatoes 1 hour; bake beet 1 hour and 15 minutes. Peel beet and potatoes; press through a potato ricer into a bowl. Weigh or lightly spoon 4.5 ounces flour (about 1 cup) into a dry measuring cup; level with a knife. Combine potato mixture, 4.5 ounces flour, and ½ teaspoon kosher salt. Stir to form dough. Knead on a floured surface until smooth. Divide into 4 equal portions. Shape each into a 16-inch-long rope, dusting with remaining flour to prevent sticking. Cut each rope into 20 pieces. Roll each piece down the tines of a lightly floured fork; place on a baking sheet coated with cooking spray.

3. Bring 6 quarts water to a boil in a stockpot. Add half of gnocchi; cook 2½ minutes or until done. Remove gnocchi with a slotted spoon; place in a colander to drain. Repeat with remaining gnocchi. Heat a nonstick skillet over medium-high heat. Add onion to pan; sauté 4 minutes. Add gnocchi, greens, ½ teaspoon pepper, and ¼ teaspoon salt; cook 2 minutes. Sprinkle with cheese. Serves 4 (serving size: 1½ cups gnocchi mixture and 1 tablespoon cheese).

CALORIES 362; FAT 3g (sat 1.4g, mono 0.7g, poly 0.4g); PROTEIN 11.8g; CARB 73.3g; FIBER 8.1g; CHOL 6mg; IRON 3.5mg; SODIUM 568mg; CALC 162mg

Flour: A Weighty Issue

In lighter cooking, measuring flour properly is key. Adding as little as 2 tablespoons of extra flour can leave you with a product that's tough and dry. Adding too much flour is easy, since one cook's cup of flour may be another cook's 1¼ cups. The reason for the discrepancy: Some people scoop flour out of the canister and pack it into the measuring cup, or tap the cup on the counter, and then top it off with more flour. Both methods yield too much. Measuring by weight is the most accurate way and keeps you from having to worry about how you scoop. If you don't have a kitchen scale, lightly spoon the flour into dry measuring cups (i.e., don't pack it in), and then level with the flat side of a knife to ensure you get the same results we do.

BROCCOLI

This vibrant green vegetable is a nutrient star with wide appeal.

SEASON: It's available all year, but it's at its best during peak season: October through April.

CHOOSING: Look for heads that are heavy with small buds tightly packed together. Yellowing is a sign that the broccoli is headed downhill.

STORING: Place broccoli in a produce bag in the coldest part of your refrigerator. If it was fresh when you brought it into your kitchen, it should be good for another 10 days.

GROWING: Although you can grow from seeds, broccoli transplants are available at most garden centers, and they give you a healthy head start. This is especially important in spring because plants will be maturing as the weather is getting warm.

Set out transplants about a month before the last expected frost date. Choose a sunny, well-drained spot with well-prepared soil. Space plants about 18 inches apart, and give them a good start by watering them with a dilute liquid fertilizer. Water regularly, and feed again about three weeks later with liquid or granular fertilizer.

The plants are handsome with big, gray-green leaves. Watch the tip of the stem for the developing flower buds—that's the broccoli—appearing two to three months after planting. Nearly all of the plant is edible, so don't despair when your garden plants produce smaller heads than what you see in the produce aisle. Once you cut the main head, smaller side shoots will form on the stalk. These are perfect for steaming or stir-frying. You can also eat the stem (peeled and cooked) and the leaves.

Creamy Linguine with Shrimp and Veggies

Hands-on time: 30 min.   Total time: 30 min.

Broccoli florets add texture to this creamy pasta dish. If you like, add a dash of crushed red pepper with the shrimp. When shopping for shellfish, look for the Marine Stewardship Council stamp to ensure you're making a sustainable choice.

6	quarts water	2	garlic cloves, minced
1	teaspoon salt, divided	12	ounces peeled and deveined
8	ounces uncooked linguine		medium shrimp
3	cups small broccoli florets	1	julienne-cut carrot
1½	tablespoons butter	6	ounces ⅓-less-fat cream
1	cup chopped onion		cheese (¾ cup)
8	ounces sliced mushrooms	¼	teaspoon black pepper

1. Bring 6 quarts water to a boil in a saucepan. Add ½ teaspoon salt and pasta; cook 5 minutes. Add broccoli; cook 3 minutes or until pasta is al dente. Drain through a sieve over a bowl, reserving ½ cup pasta water.

2. Melt butter in a Dutch oven over medium-high heat. Add onion and mushrooms to pan; sauté 5 minutes, stirring occasionally. Add garlic, and sauté 1 minute, stirring constantly. Add ½ teaspoon salt, shrimp, and carrot; sauté 3 minutes, stirring occasionally. Add pasta mixture, reserved ½ cup pasta water, cream cheese, and pepper to pan; cook 3 minutes or until cheese melts and shrimp are done, stirring occasionally. Serves 4 (serving size: 2 cups).

CALORIES 501; FAT 16.3g (sat 9.4g, mono 3.9g, poly 1.2g); PROTEIN 32.2g; CARB 57g; FIBER 5.6g; CHOL 171mg; IRON 4.8mg; SODIUM 691mg; CALC 136mg

Beef and Broccoli Bowl

Hands-on time: 20 min.   Total time: 20 min.

Fast and easy, with great flavors, this stir-fry dinner is good for a weeknight meal.

1	(3½-ounce) bag boil-in-bag long-grain rice	2	teaspoons canola oil
¼	cup lower-sodium soy sauce	2	cups broccoli florets
1	tablespoon cornstarch	1	cup vertically sliced red onion
1	tablespoon hoisin sauce	1	cup sliced carrot
1	(12-ounce) boneless sirloin steak, cut into thin strips	½	cup water
		2	teaspoons dark sesame oil
		⅓	cup sliced green onions

1. Cook rice according to package directions.
2. Combine soy sauce, cornstarch, and hoisin in a medium bowl. Add beef; toss to coat. Heat a large wok or skillet over high heat. Add oil to pan; swirl to coat. Remove beef from bowl, reserving marinade. Add beef to pan; cook 2 minutes or until browned, stirring occasionally. Remove beef from pan. Add broccoli and next 4 ingredients (through sesame oil) to pan; cook 4 minutes or until broccoli is crisp-tender, stirring occasionally. Add reserved marinade to pan; bring to a boil. Cook 1 minute. Return beef to pan; cook 1 minute or until thoroughly heated. Sprinkle evenly with green onions. Serve over rice. Serves 4 (serving size: 1 cup stir-fry and about ½ cup rice).

CALORIES 311; FAT 9.3g (sat 2g, mono 3.9g, poly 2g); PROTEIN 23.5g; CARB 32.5g; FIBER 3g; CHOL 36mg; IRON 3.2mg; SODIUM 529mg; CALC 71mg

Broccoli with Dijon Vinaigrette

Hands-on time: 15 min.   Total time: 21 min.

2¼   pounds fresh broccoli
2   teaspoons olive oil
¼   cup finely chopped green onions
1   teaspoon fresh tarragon
½   teaspoon dry mustard
3   garlic cloves, minced
2   tablespoons red wine vinegar
2   tablespoons water
1   tablespoon Dijon mustard
¼   teaspoon freshly ground black
      pepper
⅛   teaspoon salt

1. Remove broccoli leaves, and cut off tough ends of stalks; discard. Wash broccoli; cut into spears. Arrange broccoli in a steamer basket over boiling water. Cover and steam 6 minutes or until crisp-tender. Place in a serving bowl; keep warm.

2. Heat a small saucepan over medium heat. Add oil to pan; swirl to coat. Add green onions and next 3 ingredients (through garlic); sauté 3 minutes. Remove from heat; add vinegar and remaining ingredients, stirring with a wire whisk until blended. Drizzle over broccoli, tossing gently to coat. Serves 8.

CALORIES 43; FAT 1.5g (sat 0.2g, mono 0.8g, poly 0.2g); PROTEIN 2.3g; CARB 6.3g; FIBER 2.2g; CHOL 0mg; IRON 0.7mg; SODIUM 109mg; CALC 43mg

BRUSSELS SPROUTS

This vegetable has a reputation for bitterness, but when properly cooked, sprouts offer complex flavor with a subtle crunch.

SEASON: Although readily available almost year-round, the peak season is from September to mid-February.

CHOOSING: The best-tasting, most tender sprouts are only 1 to 1½ inches in diameter—the smaller the head, the sweeter the taste. They should be compact, firm, and green, with minimal nicks and torn or yellowing leaves. Try to choose sprouts of similar size so they'll cook evenly.

STORING: Remove any damaged or loose outer leaves, and store in a produce bag in the coldest part of your refrigerator. Although they'll last a couple of weeks, try to cook them as soon as possible; their flavor will start to become unpleasantly strong after three or four days.

GROWING: A cool-weather vegetable, Brussels sprouts require three months to mature. It's best to plant in summer for harvest in the fall. They can also be planted in early spring, about a month before the last frost, for harvest in early summer. If summers are very hot where you live, Brussels sprouts can be a difficult vegetable to grow.

Because they take so long to mature, buy transplants to save time. Set them in a sunny, well-prepared bed, spacing them about 2 feet apart. Feed them at planting with a dilute solution of liquid fertilizer and again about three weeks later.

These grow unlike any of your cool-season crops, spiraling up the stalk. If you intend to harvest all at once, pinch the tip from the stalk one to two weeks in advance so the heads will mature at the same time. Otherwise, choose 1- to 2-inch sprouts individually as they mature from the bottom up, removing accompanying leaves as you go up the stem.

Maple-Glazed Chicken with Apple-Brussels Sprouts Slaw

Hands-on time: 20 min. Total time: 20 min.

Serve this fresh slaw of Brussels sprouts, crisp apples, and currants alongside chicken glazed with pure maple syrup—the lighter the syrup, the more delicate the taste. Thinly slice the sprouts to ensure the dressing coats well (this also cuts down on the bitterness), or simply separate the leaves for a pretty presentation.

8   (2-ounce) chicken cutlets
1/2 teaspoon kosher salt, divided
1/2 teaspoon freshly ground black pepper, divided
2   tablespoons olive oil, divided
3   tablespoons red wine vinegar, divided

2   tablespoons maple syrup
8   ounces Brussels sprouts
1/4 cup dried currants
1   medium Fuji or Gala apple, cut into 1/8-inch-thick slices

1. Heat a large skillet over medium-high heat. Sprinkle chicken with 1/4 teaspoon salt and 1/4 teaspoon pepper. Add 1 tablespoon oil to pan; swirl to coat. Add chicken to pan; cook 3 minutes on each side or until done. Remove from pan; keep warm. Add 2 tablespoons vinegar and syrup to pan; bring to a boil. Cook 1 minute or until reduced to 3 tablespoons. Return chicken to pan; turn to coat with glaze.
2. Cut Brussels sprouts in half lengthwise, and thinly slice crosswise. Place 1 tablespoon oil, 1 tablespoon vinegar, 1/4 teaspoon salt, and 1/4 teaspoon pepper in a large bowl; stir well with a whisk. Add Brussels sprouts, currants, and apple; toss to combine. Serve slaw with chicken. Serves 4 (serving size: 2 cutlets and about 3/4 cup slaw).

CALORIES 282; FAT 8.7g (sat 1.4g, mono 5.4g, poly 1.5g); PROTEIN 28.6g; CARB 23.4g; FIBER 3.7g; CHOL 66mg; IRON 2.1mg; SODIUM 331mg; CALC 54mg

NUTRITION NOTE

Brussels sprouts are packed with phytonutrients (natural plant compounds), which may help protect against cancer, and are also a good source of vitamins A and C (1/2 cup of cooked sprouts provides more than 50% of the recommended daily amount of vitamin C), potassium, folate, and fiber.

Brussels Sprouts Gratin

Brussels Sprouts with Pecans

Hands-on time: 18 min.   Total time: 18 min.

2   teaspoons butter
1   cup chopped onion
4   garlic cloves, thinly sliced
8   cups Brussels sprouts, halved and thinly sliced (about 1½ pounds)
½   cup fat-free, lower-sodium chicken broth
1½ tablespoons sugar
½   teaspoon salt
8   teaspoons coarsely chopped pecans, toasted

1. Melt butter in a large nonstick skillet over medium-high heat. Add onion and garlic; sauté 4 minutes or until lightly browned. Add Brussels sprouts; sauté 2 minutes. Add broth and sugar; cook 5 minutes or until liquid almost evaporates, stirring frequently. Stir in salt. Sprinkle with pecans. Serves 8 (serving size: about ⅔ cup).

CALORIES 82; FAT 3g (sat 0.8g, mono 1.3g, poly 0.7g); PROTEIN 3.6g; CARB 12.6g; FIBER 3.9g; CHOL 3mg; IRON 1.3mg; SODIUM 207mg; CALC 45mg

Slicing the sprouts into slivers by hand or on a mandoline cuts down on the cooking time. The combination of butter, garlic, onion, and sugar makes for a great foil to the cabbage-like taste of sprouts. Pecans top this off for a crowd-pleaser.

Brussels Sprouts Gratin

Hands-on time: 27 min.   Total time: 36 min.

2   hickory-smoked bacon slices
4   large shallots, thinly sliced
2   pounds Brussels sprouts, trimmed and halved
1   cup water
½   teaspoon kosher salt, divided
¼   teaspoon black pepper
Cooking spray
1   (2-ounce) slice French bread baguette
3   tablespoons butter

1. Preheat broiler.
2. Cook bacon in a skillet over medium heat until crisp. Remove bacon, reserving drippings; crumble. Increase heat to medium-high. Add shallots to pan; sauté 2 minutes or until tender. Add sprouts and 1 cup water; bring to a boil. Cover pan loosely with foil; cook 6 minutes or until almost tender. Uncover and remove from heat. Sprinkle with ¼ teaspoon salt and pepper; toss. Spoon sprouts mixture into a 2-quart broiler-safe glass or ceramic baking dish coated with cooking spray.
3. Place bread in a food processor; process until finely ground. Melt butter in a skillet over medium-high heat. Add breadcrumbs and ¼ teaspoon salt; sauté 2 minutes or until toasted. Add bacon to breadcrumb mixture; sprinkle over sprouts mixture. Broil 3 minutes or until golden. Serves 6 (serving size: about ¾ cup).

CALORIES 133; FAT 5.8g (sat 3.2g, mono 1.1g, poly 0.3g); PROTEIN 5.9g; CARB 17.9g; FIBER 4.6g; CHOL 14mg; IRON 2.1mg; SODIUM 280mg; CALC 57mg

Bacon, breadcrumbs, and broiled sprouts—we are really trying to change your opinion about Brussels sprouts! To serve for a dinner party or special occasion, you can braise the Brussels sprouts and toast the bread up to a day ahead. Then assemble and reheat before serving.

CABBAGE

This versatile veggie adds color, crunch, and a pungent flavor to dishes when raw, which softens, mellows, and sweetens when cooked.

SEASON: Late spring through summer

CHOOSING: Look for a firm head that seems heavy for its size and doesn't appear dry or cracked.

STORING: Cabbage likes to stay cool in the garden and the refrigerator. Place it in a produce bag in the coldest section, where it will keep for up to two weeks. Once cut, it remains usable for only a few days.

GROWING: The cool seasons of spring and fall are ideal for growing cabbage. Look for harvests in late spring and early summer, as well as late fall. Cabbage grown in cool climates like Alaska grows all summer.

Start with transplants for a leg up on a long growing season. A miniature head needs as little as 45 days to mature, while the jumbo heads may take as long as 100 days. Set your transplants out a month before the last frost in spring, or 8 to 12 weeks before the first frost in fall. For an extended harvest, plant several different kinds of cabbage that will mature at different times.

Set transplants in a sunny, well-prepared bed, allowing at least 12 inches between plants and up to 24 inches for large varieties. If the transplant seems to be floppy with a long stem, bury it a little deeper. Settle transplants into their new home with a dilute solution of liquid fertilizer. Mulch well to conserve soil moisture and keep out weeds. Water weekly and fertilize again after three to four weeks. Leafy vegetables like this require a lot of nitrogen and nutrients.

Cabbage is ready to harvest when the head is firm. If you wait too long, the head may split, which gives diseases and insects an open door. When you harvest, use a knife to cut the stalk just below the head. It is best not to break it off, because injuries lessen the shelf life.

Kimchi-Style Cabbage

Hands-on time: 16 min.   Total time: 7 days 16 min.

If you want to use cabbage for something more exciting than simple slaw, kimchi is worth the wait. It's a spicy Korean condiment that is often fermented and aged—sometimes for months. Our recipe is shortened to one week. It's traditionally served with steamed white rice and pairs well with stir-fries.

½   cup kosher salt, divided
2¾ pounds napa (Chinese) cabbage, quartered lengthwise
2   cups thinly sliced green onions (about 2 bunches)
2   cups finely grated peeled daikon radish (about 1 medium)
1½ cups water

½   cup rice vinegar
2   tablespoons sugar
2   tablespoons minced fresh garlic
1½ tablespoons grated peeled fresh ginger
3   tablespoons sambal oelek (ground fresh chile paste)

1. Reserve ½ teaspoon salt; set aside. Place cabbage in a large bowl; sprinkle remaining salt over cabbage, sprinkling between leaves. Weigh down cabbage with a smaller bowl filled with cans. Let stand at room temperature 2 hours; drain. Rinse cabbage thoroughly under cold water; drain. Remove cabbage leaves from core; discard core.

2. Combine reserved ½ teaspoon salt, onions, and remaining ingredients in a medium bowl. Spread radish mixture onto cabbage leaves; arrange leaves in layers in a 1-quart airtight container, pressing leaves to compress mixture. Top leaves with any remaining radish mixture. Cover and refrigerate 1 week. Store in an airtight container in refrigerator up to 2 weeks. Serves 32 (serving size: about 1½ ounces).

CALORIES 16; FAT 0g; PROTEIN 0.5g; CARB 3.4g; FIBER 0.8g; CHOL 0mg; IRON 0.1mg; SODIUM 179mg; CALC 35mg

Whole-Grain and Italian Sausage-Stuffed Cabbage

Hands-on time: 30 min.   Total time: 1 hr. 40 min.

2   cups water
½   cup dried porcini mushrooms, crushed (about ½ ounce)
1¼   cups uncooked bulgur
2   teaspoons butter
1   teaspoon olive oil
1   cup finely chopped onion
⅔   cup finely chopped celery
⅔   cup finely chopped carrot
2   garlic cloves, minced

¼   teaspoon freshly ground black pepper
1   pound hot turkey Italian sausage
12   large Savoy cabbage leaves
2   cups canned crushed tomatoes
1½   tablespoons red wine vinegar
2   teaspoons brown sugar
2   tablespoons chopped fresh parsley

1. Bring 2 cups water to a boil in a saucepan. Stir in mushrooms; cover, remove from heat, and let stand 10 minutes.

2. Uncover pan; bring mushroom mixture to a boil. Stir in bulgur; cover, remove from heat, and let stand 30 minutes or until liquid is absorbed. Spoon bulgur mixture into a large bowl.

3. Heat butter and oil in a large nonstick skillet over medium-high heat. Add onion, celery, carrot, and garlic to pan; sauté 7 minutes or until tender and lightly browned. Add vegetables to bulgur mixture; cool slightly. Stir in pepper. Remove casings from sausage. Crumble sausage into bulgur mixture; stir well to combine.

4. Add water to a large Dutch oven to a depth of 2 inches; set a large vegetable steamer in pan. Bring water to a boil over medium-high heat. Add cabbage leaves to steamer. Steam cabbage, covered, 6 minutes or until tender and pliable. Remove cabbage from steamer (do not drain water). Rinse cabbage with cold water; drain and pat dry.

5. Working with 1 cabbage leaf at a time, place ½ cup bulgur mixture in center of leaf. Fold in edges of leaf; roll up. Repeat procedure with remaining cabbage leaves and bulgur mixture to form 12 cabbage rolls. Stack rolls evenly in steamer.

6. Return Dutch oven to medium-high heat; bring water to a boil. Steam rolls, covered, 30 minutes, adding more water if necessary.

7. Combine tomatoes, red wine vinegar, and sugar in saucepan; cook over medium heat 5 minutes or until thoroughly heated, stirring occasionally. Remove from heat; stir in parsley. Serve sauce with rolls. Serves 6 (serving size: 2 cabbage rolls and about ⅓ cup sauce).

CALORIES 322; FAT 10.9g (sat 3.3g, mono 4.1g, poly 2.3g); PROTEIN 19.6g; CARB 40.2g; FIBER 10.3g; CHOL 48mg; IRON 4.1mg; SODIUM 645mg; CALC 86mg

Savoy cabbages have stunning, deeply crinkled leaves that can span a few feet in the garden. Make them more pliable for wrapping and stuffing by steaming them. They may be slightly harder to find in markets and more suitable to grow yourself, as the softer leaves don't ship well.

Chicken Soup with Cabbage and Apple

Hands-on time: 29 min.   Total time: 39 min.

This German-inspired soup is a hearty bowl of healthy goodness, complete with earthy cabbage, shredded chicken, chicken sausage, and potatoes. Tart, crunchy apple slices add a nice balance.

2	teaspoons caraway seeds
1/2	teaspoon fennel seeds
1	tablespoon olive oil
1 1/2	cups chopped onion
1/2	cup chopped carrot
1/2	cup chopped celery
3	garlic cloves, minced
4	ounces chicken apple sausage, sliced
5	cups fat-free, lower-sodium chicken broth
8	ounces chopped Yukon gold potato
3	cups thinly sliced green cabbage
2	cups shredded cooked chicken breast (about 8 ounces)
2	cups sliced Granny Smith apple
1	tablespoon cider vinegar
1/4	teaspoon kosher salt
1/4	teaspoon freshly ground black pepper

1. Heat a small skillet over medium heat. Add caraway and fennel; cook 2 minutes, stirring constantly. Place in a spice or coffee grinder; process until ground.
2. Heat a Dutch oven over medium heat. Add oil to pan; swirl to coat. Add onion, carrot, celery, and garlic; cook 6 minutes. Add sausage; cook 1 minute. Add ground spices; cook 30 seconds, stirring constantly. Add broth and potato; bring to a boil. Cover, reduce heat, and simmer 10 minutes. Increase heat to medium-high. Add cabbage and remaining ingredients; cook 3 minutes. Serves 4 (serving size: about 1 1/2 cups).

CALORIES 328; FAT 9.8g (sat 2.2g, mono 3.7g, poly 1.2g); PROTEIN 28.5g; CARB 33.2g; FIBER 6.4g; CHOL 85mg; IRON 2.5mg; SODIUM 369mg; CALC 94mg

CARROTS

Freshly harvested carrots are full of earthy sweetness. And they're easy to grow!

SEASON: Spring and fall

CHOOSING: Select carrots that are blemish-free and unbroken. If the green foliage is still attached, it shouldn't be wilted.

STORING: If the green tops are still attached, snip them off about 2 inches above the orange root. This prevents the leaves from pulling moisture out of the carrot. Place carrots in a produce bag, and store them in the coldest part of your refrigerator.

GROWING: Carrots are best grown from seeds sown directly into sunny, well-prepared beds. If the soil in your garden is heavy or rocky, carrots may be stunted, misshapen, or forked, so either amend the soil or try small, round varieties such as Paris Market. Grow carrots in a raised bed or in a container for best results.

Seeds can take up to three weeks to push through the soil, so many gardeners like to sow a row of carrots next to a row of radishes to mark the spot. The radishes pop out of the ground quickly and will be ready to harvest by the time the carrots begin growing.

Thin carrots to stand 2 to 4 inches apart, giving each room to grow. Keep the soil evenly moist by watering weekly. You can pull and eat them anytime, whether they are small or large. Leave your fall carrots in the soil until you are ready to use them. If a severe freeze is expected, mulch to prevent the soil from freezing.

Carrot Cake

Hands-on time: 35 min. Total time: 1 hr. 53 min.

Elevate an old-fashioned favorite by mixing in the pride that comes with a homegrown harvest or fresh market find.

Cake:

10.1 ounces all-purpose flour (about 2¼ cups)
2 teaspoons baking powder
1½ teaspoons ground cinnamon
¼ teaspoon salt
2 cups grated carrot
1 cup granulated sugar
½ cup packed brown sugar
6 tablespoons butter, softened
3 large eggs
1 teaspoon vanilla extract
½ cup low-fat buttermilk
Cooking spray

Frosting:

7 ounces cream cheese, softened
2 tablespoons butter, softened
½ teaspoon vanilla extract
⅛ teaspoon salt
3 cups powdered sugar
¼ cup chopped pecans, toasted

1. Preheat oven to 350°.

2. To prepare cake, weigh or lightly spoon flour into dry measuring cups, and level with a knife. Combine flour and next 3 ingredients (through ¼ teaspoon salt) in a medium bowl, stirring with a whisk. Add carrot, tossing to combine.

3. Place granulated sugar, brown sugar, and 6 tablespoons butter in a large bowl. Beat with a mixer at medium speed until combined. Add eggs, 1 at a time, beating well after each addition. Stir in 1 teaspoon vanilla. Add flour mixture and buttermilk alternately to sugar mixture, beginning and ending with flour mixture. Spread batter into a 13 x 9-inch metal baking pan coated with cooking spray. Bake at 350° for 28 minutes or until a wooden pick inserted in center comes out clean. Cool cake completely on a wire rack.

4. To prepare frosting, place softened cream cheese and next 3 ingredients (through ⅛ teaspoon salt) in a medium bowl. Beat with a mixer at medium speed until fluffy. Gradually add powdered sugar, beating at medium speed until combined (don't overbeat). Spread frosting evenly over top of cake. Sprinkle evenly with toasted pecans. Serves 20 (serving size: 1 piece).

CALORIES 285; FAT 9.9g (sat 5.2g, mono 2.9g, poly 0.8g); PROTEIN 3.5g; CARB 46g; FIBER 0.9g; CHOL 51mg; IRON 0.9mg; SODIUM 184mg; CALC 59mg

A Lighter Carrot Cake

At some point, carrot cake became the poster child for healthy-sounding food that is actually a fat and calorie disaster—we're talking 99 grams of fat and almost 1,500 calories, and that's just for one slice. In this lightened version, creamy butter and smooth low-fat buttermilk create a perfectly moist, tender texture, while brown sugar brings out the warm cinnamon spices. Full-fat cream cheese and butter maximize the flavor of the creamy frosting, while a light sprinkling of toasted pecans tops off this special, vastly lighter treat.

Carrot Soup with Yogurt

Carrot Soup with Yogurt

Hands-on time: 21 min.   Total time: 58 min.

2	teaspoons dark sesame oil	1	teaspoon grated peeled fresh ginger
1/3	cup sliced shallots (about 1 large)		
1	pound baby carrots, peeled and cut into 2-inch pieces	1/2	cup plain 2% reduced-fat Greek yogurt
2	cups fat-free, lower-sodium chicken broth	8	mint sprigs

1. Heat a medium saucepan over medium heat. Add oil to pan; swirl to coat. Add shallots to pan; cook 2 minutes or until almost tender, stirring occasionally. Add carrot; cook 4 minutes. Add broth; bring to a boil. Cover, reduce heat, and simmer 22 minutes or until tender. Add ginger; cook 8 minutes or until carrot is very tender. Cover and let stand 5 minutes at room temperature.

2. Pour half of carrot mixture into a blender. Remove center piece of blender lid (to allow steam to escape); secure blender lid on blender. Place a clean towel over opening in blender lid (to avoid splatters). Blend until smooth. Pour into a large bowl. Repeat procedure with remaining carrot mixture. Return pureed soup to pan; heat over medium heat 2 minutes or until heated.

3. Spoon soup into small bowls, and top with yogurt and mint. Serves 8 (serving size: 1/2 cup soup, 1 tablespoon yogurt, and 1 mint sprig).

CALORIES 47; FAT 1.6g (sat 0.4g, mono 0.5g, poly 0.5g); PROTEIN 2.2g; CARB 6.5g; FIBER 1.7g; CHOL 1mg; IRON 0.6mg; SODIUM 163mg; CALC 36mg

Sweet carrots and spicy ginger complement each other well in this simple soup. Make the most of the depth of flavors by using only the freshest ingredients. Use an immersion blender for ease and convenience and a simple vegetable peeler to make slender vertical slices of carrot as a garnish.

Butter-Roasted Carrots

Hands-on time: 5 min.   Total time: 20 min.

2	cups (2-inch) diagonally cut carrot	1/4	teaspoon kosher salt
1	tablespoon butter, melted	1/4	teaspoon freshly ground black pepper
1	teaspoon olive oil		Cooking spray

1. Preheat oven to 425°.

2. Combine first 5 ingredients on a baking sheet coated with cooking spray. Bake at 425° for 15 minutes. Serves 4 (serving size: about 1/2 cup).

CALORIES 61; FAT 4.2g (sat 2g, mono 1.6g, poly 0.3g); PROTEIN 0.6g; CARB 5.9g; FIBER 1.7g; CHOL 8mg; IRON 0.2mg; SODIUM 183mg; CALC 22mg

Fresh-picked carrots are sublime. Already sweet and very aromatic, they reach new heights when roasted. The heat caramelizes the carrots, and the butter and oil create a crisp crunch for every bite. To elevate the wow factor in this easy side dish, use purple-skinned varieties like Dragon or Atomic Purple, and reveal the orange and yellow centers with diagonal cuts.

CAULIFLOWER

Fresh, raw cauliflower has a lovely crisp texture and mild, neutral character. It sparkles when roasted, yielding a creamy texture and a nutty taste.

SEASON: Cauliflower is sold fresh from early summer into fall.

CHOOSING: Look for heads that are tight and firm. Avoid those with discoloration that comes with aging.

STORING: Place cauliflower in a produce bag in the coldest part of your refrigerator, where it should last for four to seven days.

GROWING: Unless your summer or winter is extremely mild, spring and fall are the best times to grow cauliflower. Set out transplants in a sunny, well-drained, prepared bed. The seedlings need about two months to mature, so begin planting about four weeks before the last spring frost, or in late summer, two months before the first fall freeze.

Space plants about 18 to 24 inches apart so the large, gray-green leaves have room to gather the sun's energy. Feed at planting with a dilute liquid fertilizer, and then fertilize again in three to four weeks. Apply mulch to help keep the soil moist and prevent problems with weeds.

You've probably seen the leaves wrapping around the head in the market. Cauliflower has been bred to do this. It prevents sunburn on the edible portion. If your plants are not shading the developing head, use twine or a clothespin to hold them in place. Cut the head of cauliflower while it is still firm and tight. Waiting will result in a loose, mealy head.

Cauliflower "Caviar" with Frizzled Prosciutto

Hands-on time: 21 min.   Total time: 61 min.

This appetizer is a party hit: Your guests will be surprised it's cauliflower.

4   cups coarsely chopped cauliflower florets (about 2 pounds)
5   teaspoons olive oil, divided
¾   teaspoon freshly ground black pepper
¼   teaspoon kosher salt

4   ounces prosciutto, chopped
1   tablespoon minced fresh garlic
1   tablespoon sherry vinegar
¼   cup chopped fresh parsley
24 Belgian endive leaves (about 2 small heads)

1. Preheat oven to 400°.

2. Arrange cauliflower florets in a single layer on a 13 x 9–inch metal baking pan. Drizzle with 1 tablespoon olive oil; sprinkle with pepper and salt, tossing to combine. Bake at 400° for 40 minutes or until cauliflower is lightly browned.

3. Heat a small skillet over medium heat. Add 2 teaspoons oil to pan; swirl to coat. Add prosciutto to pan; sauté 10 minutes or until crisp, stirring occasionally. Add garlic; sauté 1 minute. Drain on paper towels.

4. Combine cauliflower mixture, prosciutto mixture, and vinegar in a large bowl; coarsely mash with a fork. Stir in chopped parsley. Spoon 2 tablespoons cauliflower mixture into each endive leaf. Serve warm or at room temperature. Serves 12 (serving size: 2 filled leaves).

CALORIES 59; FAT 3g (sat 0.6g, mono 1.8g, poly 0.5g); PROTEIN 3.8g; CARB 4.8g; FIBER 2.2g; CHOL 6mg; IRON 0.6mg; SODIUM 205mg; CALC 21mg

Roasted Cauliflower, Chickpeas, and Olives

Hands-on time: 5 min. Total time: 27 min.

A little saltiness from Spanish olives, a little heat from crushed red pepper, a lot of nutty roasted cauliflower, and the zip of garlic cloves come together with roasted chickpeas for a tangy side. You can use cooked fresh or soaked dried chickpeas if you have them. Serve with roasted chicken or sautéed fish.

5½ cups cauliflower florets (about 1 pound)
15 green Spanish olives, pitted and halved
8 garlic cloves, coarsely chopped
1 (15-ounce) can chickpeas (garbanzo beans), rinsed and drained

3 tablespoons olive oil
½ teaspoon crushed red pepper
3 tablespoons fresh flat-leaf parsley leaves

1. Preheat oven to 450°.
2. Combine first 4 ingredients in a small roasting pan. Drizzle with oil; sprinkle with pepper. Toss well to coat. Bake at 450° for 22 minutes or until cauliflower is browned and crisp-tender, stirring after 10 minutes. Sprinkle with parsley. Serves 6 (serving size: about ⅔ cup).

CALORIES 146; FAT 9.3g (sat 1g, mono 5.8g, poly 1.6g); PROTEIN 3.8g; CARB 12.8g; FIBER 3.3g; CHOL 0mg; IRON 1mg; SODIUM 335mg; CALC 35mg

Baked Italian-Style Cauliflower

Hands-on time: 28 min.   Total time: 28 min.

Cauliflower is chameleon-like. Steamed and blended, it is reminiscent of mashed potatoes. When roasted, it tastes nutty and creamy. In this recipe, it takes the place of potatoes or pasta. If you have homemade tomato sauce canned or frozen from the summer, this is an easy garden-to-table weeknight meal.

1	tablespoon olive oil	2	ounces pitted kalamata olives, coarsely chopped
1	cup chopped onion	1½	pounds cauliflower, cut into florets
4	garlic cloves, minced		
6	ounces ground sirloin	Cooking spray	
⅛	teaspoon kosher salt	1	ounce French bread baguette, torn into 1-inch pieces
¼	teaspoon crushed red pepper		
¼	teaspoon black pepper	1	ounce grated fresh pecorino Romano cheese (about ¼ cup)
1½	cups lower-sodium marinara sauce		

1. Heat a large skillet over medium-high heat. Add oil to pan; swirl to coat. Add onion; sauté 4 minutes. Add garlic; sauté 30 seconds, stirring constantly. Stir in beef. Sprinkle with salt and peppers, and sauté 3 minutes or until browned, stirring to crumble. Stir in sauce and olives.

2. Preheat broiler.

3. Steam cauliflower 4 minutes or until crisp-tender. Place cauliflower in an 11 x 7-inch broiler-safe glass or ceramic baking dish coated with cooking spray; top with sauce mixture.

4. Place bread in a mini chopper; pulse until coarse crumbs form. Combine crumbs and cheese; sprinkle over cauliflower mixture. Broil 4 minutes or until browned. Serves 4 (serving size: about 2 cups).

CALORIES 306; FAT 14.9g (sat 4.3g, mono 7.8g, poly 1.2g); PROTEIN 16.3g; CARB 46.8g; FIBER 5.3g; CHOL 34mg; IRON 2.3mg; SODIUM 607mg; CALC 145mg

CORN

The first ear of corn heralds the arrival of summer. Enjoy its glorious sweetness and crisp, juicy texture for as long as the season lasts.

SEASON: Summer

CHOOSING: Look for green, moist husks that cling tightly to the corn. Deep brown silk tips or ends mean it's ripe, but the whole silk shouldn't be dried up. To check, peel the husk slightly, and check the top row of kernels for plumpness and density. The ultimate test is to pierce a kernel with your fingernail. If it is milky, it's just right.

STORING: As soon as it's picked, the flavor of corn changes. The sugars immediately begin turning to starch. If possible, shop for same-day harvests in local markets to get the highest sugar content and peak of perfection. If you can't eat the corn immediately, store it in the refrigerator with the husks intact, and eat within two days of purchasing for the best taste. Don't shuck until you're ready to use.

GROWING: Plant corn after the danger of frost has passed in a well-drained location that receives a minimum of six to eight hours of sun a day. Although it's tempting to plant early to get that first ear of sweet corn, resist the urge. Corn doesn't germinate well or grow very fast when the soil is cold. It is better to wait a week or two after the last frost, when the soil has warmed, planting seeds about 1 inch deep.

Sow seeds in blocks (several rows together); instead of one 20-foot row, plant four 5-foot rows for easier pollination by wind. This improves pollination so you won't find gaps in the rows of kernels on your cob. Water weekly to ensure your corn doesn't dry out on the stalk before it's time to harvest. Corn matures in 60 to 100 days, depending on the variety, and should be ready to be picked about 20 days after the first silk strands appear. Not every ear in the row will be ready at the same time. (See the box on page 117 for more information on growing corn.)

Corn Pancakes with Smoked Salmon and Lemon-Chive Cream

Hands-on time: 32 min. Total time: 32 min.

Fresh corn will make these pancakes a household favorite. They'd be fantastic in silver dollar size for appetizers or a fresh take on blini. They are equally memorable with an heirloom tomato, bacon crumbles, and grilled zucchini in place of salmon.

1/4	cup light sour cream	1/4	teaspoon kosher salt
2	tablespoons chopped fresh chives	1/8	teaspoon ground red pepper
1	teaspoon grated lemon rind	1 1/4	cups fresh corn kernels (about 3 ears), divided
2.25	ounces all-purpose flour (about 1/2 cup)	2/3	cup low-fat buttermilk
1/2	cup yellow cornmeal	3	tablespoons butter, melted
1	teaspoon sugar	1	large egg
1/4	teaspoon baking soda	12	thin slices cold-smoked salmon (about 6 ounces)

1. Combine first 3 ingredients in a small bowl; chill.

2. Weigh or lightly spoon flour into a dry measuring cup; level with a knife. Combine flour and next 5 ingredients (through pepper) in a medium bowl. Place 1 cup corn kernels, buttermilk, butter, and egg in a blender; process until coarsely pureed. Add pureed corn mixture to flour mixture, stirring until just combined. Fold in 1/4 cup corn.

3. Pour about 2 tablespoons batter per pancake onto a hot nonstick griddle or nonstick skillet; spread gently with a spatula. Cook 3 minutes or until tops are covered with bubbles and edges look cooked. Carefully turn pancakes over; cook 3 minutes or until bottoms are lightly browned. Arrange 2 pancakes on each of 6 plates; top each pancake with 1 slice salmon and 1 teaspoon lemon-chive cream. Serve immediately. Serves 6.

CALORIES 239; FAT 9.7g (sat 5g, mono 2.9g, poly 1g); PROTEIN 10.7g; CARB 27.6g; FIBER 1.8g; CHOL 56mg; IRON 1.7mg; SODIUM 409mg; CALC 59mg

Corn Varieties

Corn is a crop that's affected by its surroundings. If two varieties are planted too close to each other, cross-pollination can alter sweetness and color. Standard sweet corn (like creamy, delicious Silver Queen) and supersweet corn (a genetic variation that makes the corn taste two to three times sweeter but isn't as creamy) should be separated from each other by at least a two-week difference in planting time to ensure each maintains its color and specific level of sweetness. There's no real flavor difference between white and yellow corn—the carotene that colors the kernels is tasteless.

Another type, sugar-enhanced sweet corn, has special appeal for home gardeners. It's sweet, creamy, and doesn't need to be isolated from other types that may be growing in the neighbor's garden. Plus, the loss of sugar is much slower. Here are a few varieties of each type:

Sweet corn: Earlivee, Golden Bantam, Honey & Cream, Silver Queen

Supersweet corn: Early Xtra-Sweet, Sun & Stars Bicolor, How Sweet It Is, Honey 'N' Pearl

Sugar-enhanced corn: Early and Often, Early Choice, Luscious, Bon Jour, Sugar Pearl, Silver King

Summer Veggie Pizza

Hands-on time: 30 min. Total time: 45 min.

Using store-bought pizza dough is a lifesaver when dinners have to be quick. These vegetable toppings use the very best of the season with fresh bell pepper, corn, and basil. Simply good.

8 ounces store-bought pizza dough
Cooking spray
2 tablespoons olive oil, divided
2 garlic cloves, crushed
1 cup sliced onion
1 thinly sliced red bell pepper
8 ounces asparagus, trimmed and cut into 1-inch pieces

2 ears shucked corn
1 tablespoon cornmeal
3 ounces shredded part-skim mozzarella cheese (about ³/₄ cup)
½ teaspoon crushed red pepper
¼ teaspoon kosher salt
⅓ cup small basil leaves

1. Preheat oven to 500°.
2. Place dough in a bowl coated with cooking spray; cover and let stand 30 minutes. Heat a small skillet over medium heat. Add 4 teaspoons olive oil and garlic to pan; cook 2 minutes or until fragrant (do not brown). Remove garlic from oil; discard garlic. Remove garlic oil from pan; set aside. Increase heat to medium-high. Add 2 teaspoons olive oil to pan; swirl to coat. Add onion and bell pepper; sauté 5 minutes. Place onion mixture in a bowl, and add asparagus. Cut corn from cob; add corn to vegetable mixture.
3. Scatter cornmeal over a lightly floured surface; roll dough into a 13-inch circle on prepared surface. Transfer dough to a baking sheet; brush with garlic oil. Top with vegetable mixture, leaving a ½-inch border; sprinkle with cheese, crushed red pepper, and salt. Bake at 500° for 15 minutes or until golden. Top with basil. Cut into 8 slices. Serves 4 (serving size: 2 slices).

CALORIES 356; FAT 12.8g (sat 3.4g, mono 5.1g, poly 2g); PROTEIN 14.8g; CARB 49.3g; FIBER 4.8g; CHOL 11mg; IRON 3.7mg; SODIUM 608mg; CALC 185mg

Grilled Corn, Poblano, and Black Bean Salad

Hands-on time: 40 min.   Total time: 40 min.

If you are already firing up the grill or want to avoid heating up the kitchen in July, these ingredients pair well with grilled meats or fish. Charring corn and poblano gives them a smoky, caramelized flavor. This salad is also perfect for showcasing black beans cooked from your jars of dried garden beans, if you have them.

2	ears shucked corn	½	cup chopped fresh cilantro
2	tablespoons extra-virgin olive oil, divided	3	tablespoons fresh lime juice
		1	teaspoon ground cumin
4	green onions	¼	teaspoon salt
1	avocado, peeled, halved, and pitted	¼	teaspoon freshly ground black pepper
1	large red bell pepper	1	(15-ounce) can unsalted black beans, rinsed and drained
1	large poblano chile		
Cooking spray			

1. Preheat grill to high heat.

2. Brush corn with 2 teaspoons oil. Place green onions, avocado, bell pepper, poblano, and corn on grill rack coated with cooking spray. Grill onions 2 minutes on each side or until lightly browned. Grill avocado 2 minutes on each side or until well marked. Grill bell pepper 6 minutes on each side or until blackened; peel. Grill poblano 9 minutes on each side or until blackened; peel. Grill corn 12 minutes or until beginning to brown on all sides, turning occasionally.

3. Cut kernels from ears of corn; place in a large bowl. Chop onions, bell pepper, and poblano; add to bowl. Add 4 teaspoons oil, cilantro, and next 5 ingredients (through beans) to bowl; toss well. Cut avocado into thin slices; place on top of salad. Serves 6 (serving size: ³⁄₄ cup).

CALORIES 167; FAT 9.9g (sat 1.4g, mono 6.7g, poly 1.3g); PROTEIN 4.6g; CARB 17.8g; FIBER 6g; CHOL 0mg; IRON 1.4mg; SODIUM 209mg; CALC 38mg

CUCUMBER

Fresh cucumber imparts a refreshingly crisp coolness to any dish.

SEASON: Cucumbers are available year-round but peak in summer.

CHOOSING: When it comes to cucumbers, bigger isn't always better. The ideal size depends on the type. The long, so-called burpless cucumber grown in gardens and greenhouses has thin skin and no seeds. Its delicate flavor is good even when it is 12 to 18 inches long. Choose slicing cucumbers that are 6 to 8 inches long. Those for pickling are best when small, about 3 to 4 inches long. In general, avoid cucumbers that appear bloated and are turning from green to yellow (except lemon cucumbers, which are supposed to look that way). Yellowing is typically a sign that the seeds are maturing and the cucumber's best days are over. If in doubt, select the smallest of the type for optimum flavor and quality.

STORING: Once picked, cucumbers lose moisture, which is why supermarket cukes are waxed or individually wrapped in plastic. Keep garden-fresh cucumbers crisp by placing them in a produce bag in the vegetable bin of your refrigerator. They'll hold for about a week.

GROWING: Cucumbers are rambling vines that need a cage, tepee, or A-frame trellis to lift the developing plants off the ground. Good choices include Straight Eight, Diva, Suyo Long, and Lemon. Those who have small gardens or grow in containers will enjoy the more compact-growing Salad Bush hybrid, Bush Slicer, or the aptly named Spacemaster.

Plant cucumber seeds or transplants in spring no sooner than two weeks after the last frost. The air should be warm, but it is also a good idea to give the soil time to lose that winter chill.

Prepare the soil by adding organic materials such as bagged garden soil or compost. Create small mounds of loose, rich soil that measure 12 to 18 inches across. Plant four to five seeds or two to three transplants along the outer edge of each little hill. Allow about 4 feet between hills.

When seeds germinate, remove all but the strongest three plants. Guide the young vines onto their support, and then they'll grab on as they grow. If you're growing bush-type varieties, be sure to mulch the soil with pine needles or wheat straw to keep the developing cucumbers clean. Use clippers to harvest rather than pulling so as to avoid damaging vines.

Cucumber Gazpacho with Shrimp Relish

Hands-on time: 20 min. Total time: 20 min.

Chilled cucumber gazpacho is so refreshing in the heat of summer. We recommend English cucumbers because they have fewer seeds and thin skin that doesn't require peeling. Look for other types marketed as Japanese or Persian, too. Blending them into a creamy summer soup is a breeze.

2	teaspoons extra-virgin olive oil
3/4	pound peeled and deveined medium shrimp, chopped
1/2	teaspoon salt, divided
1/2	teaspoon freshly ground black pepper, divided
1/4	teaspoon ground cumin
1/4	teaspoon paprika
2	cups quartered grape tomatoes
1/3	cup cilantro leaves
2 1/2	cups chopped English cucumber
1	cup fat-free, lower-sodium chicken broth
1	cup plain whole-milk Greek yogurt
1/4	cup chopped onion
2	tablespoons fresh lime juice
	Dash of ground red pepper
1	large garlic clove, peeled

1. Heat a large skillet over medium-high heat. Add oil to pan; swirl to coat. Sprinkle shrimp with 1/4 teaspoon salt, 1/4 teaspoon black pepper, cumin, and paprika. Add shrimp to pan; sauté 2 minutes or until done. Stir in tomatoes; remove from heat. Add cilantro.

2. Place 1/4 teaspoon salt, 1/4 teaspoon black pepper, cucumber, and remaining ingredients in a blender; process until smooth. Ladle 1 cup soup into each of 4 bowls; top each with 3/4 cup relish. Serves 4.

CALORIES 225; FAT 9.6g (sat 5.1g, mono 1.9g, poly 0.9g); PROTEIN 22.7g; CARB 11.5g; FIBER 2.2g; CHOL 139mg; IRON 2.4mg; SODIUM 557mg; CALC 130mg

Avoid the Bitter End

If the weather has been hot and dry, some cucumber varieties can become bitter. However, the bitterness is usually concentrated in the skin or the end of the cucumber that was attached to the vine. When in doubt, taste a cucumber before using it in a recipe. If it is bitter, peel it, removing a bit of the white flesh at the same time (a vegetable peeler makes easy work of this), and taste again to ensure that the bitterness is gone.

Herby Cucumber Salad

Hands-on time: 12 min.
Total time: 12 min.

Update the classic cucumber-dill salad with creative slicing and a medley of fresh herbs.

¼	cup plain low-fat yogurt
2	tablespoons coarsely chopped fresh dill
1	tablespoon coarsely chopped fresh parsley
2	tablespoons fresh lemon juice
1	tablespoon extra-virgin olive oil
1½	teaspoons coarsely chopped fresh mint
2	teaspoons Dijon mustard
¼	teaspoon sugar
¼	teaspoon salt
¼	teaspoon freshly ground black pepper
1	garlic clove
5½	cups thinly sliced cucumber (about 2 large)
2½	cups thinly sliced red onion

1. Place first 11 ingredients in a food processor or a blender; process until well blended. Combine cucumber and onion in a large bowl. Drizzle with yogurt mixture, and toss to coat. Serves 6 (serving size: 1 cup).

CALORIES 65; FAT 2.6g (sat 0.5g, mono 1.7g, poly 0.3g); PROTEIN 1.8g; CARB 9.9g; FIBER 1.4g; CHOL 1mg; IRON 0.5mg; SODIUM 150mg; CALC 48mg

Cucumber-Lime Granita

Hands-on time: 30 min.   Total time: 3 hr. 30 min.

We know cucumbers are cool, and sweet shaved ice is the quintessential summer refreshment. Together, the two make an ideal treat from the garden. While the recipe calls for English cucumber to save time peeling and seeding, this granita would be perfect for a garden party served in hollowed out "cups" made from the round, yellow True Lemon cucumber, and garnished with fresh mint leaves.

1	cup water	1/4	teaspoon salt
3/4	cup sugar	3	mint sprigs
1	tablespoon grated lime rind	1	pound chopped English
1/2	cup fresh lime juice		cucumber

1. Combine first 5 ingredients in a small saucepan over medium heat; bring to a boil. Cook 1 minute; remove from heat. Add mint; let stand 10 minutes. Discard mint. Place juice mixture and cucumber in a blender; process until smooth. Cool completely. Pour mixture into an 11 x 7-inch glass or ceramic baking dish. Cover and freeze 45 minutes; scrape with a fork. Freeze. Scrape mixture every 45 minutes until completely frozen (about 3 hours). Remove from freezer; scrape entire mixture with a fork until fluffy. Serves 6 (serving size: about 1/2 cup).

CALORIES 112; FAT 0g; PROTEIN 1g; CARB 28.9g; FIBER 1.1g; CHOL 0mg; IRON 0mg; SODIUM 99mg; CALC 5mg

Cool as a Cucumber

Cucumbers, by nature, are refreshing. It's not a myth or legend: On any given summer day, the inner core of a cucumber is 20° cooler than the surrounding garden.

EGGPLANT

This glossy, plump vegetable with its firm, meaty flesh is the perfect base for a host of dishes—pastas, burgers, seafood dishes, and meatless favorites.

SEASON: Although available year-round, eggplant is at its peak from July to October.

CHOOSING: When selecting, look for eggplants with firm, glossy skin. Size and color vary widely among types, but the eggplant should feel heavy. Avoid those with wrinkled skin, soft spots, or brown patches.

STORING: Store whole, unwashed eggplants in a produce bag to retain moisture and prevent shriveling. Because it can't withstand temperatures below 45° without damage, keep eggplant in your vegetable bin or the warmest section of your refrigerator.

GROWING: Like its cousin the tomato, eggplant is a summer favorite in most of the country. However, it can be grown and harvested in warmer regions like Florida from fall to spring.

The standard favorite, Black Beauty, is a good choice, but so are the long, lavender Oriental eggplants, the white ones that actually look like eggs, and even orange and green ones. The more unusual the eggplant, the more likely it will be that you need to start from seeds.

No matter which variety you choose, plant in the spring after the soil and air have warmed. Make up for the lost time by starting with transplants, even if you grow them yourself indoors.

Choose a sunny location with well-prepared soil and good drainage. Large-fruited types need to be spaced 2 to 3 feet apart, while the long, slender types can be set 1½ to 2 feet apart. It's a good idea to use a stake at planting time to support the plant later when it's heavy with fruit. Small cages often used for tomatoes are a wonderful tool for eggplant.

Feed with a dilute solution of liquid fertilizer at planting. Fertilize again every month throughout the season. Keep the soil evenly moist by watering at least an inch each week. Mulch to prevent drying. When it's time to harvest, use clippers to cut the eggplants from the plant.

What's in a Name?

The eggplant got its name from the first varieties to reach the West, which were white, round, and egg-sized. While colors range from creamy white to green, the shiny, vivid purple eggplant is now the most recognizable.

Falafel-Stuffed Eggplant with Tahini Sauce and Tomato Relish

Hands-on time: 40 min.   Total time: 1 hr. 25 min.

3	tablespoons warm water	½	teaspoon ground coriander
2	tablespoons tahini (roasted sesame seed paste)	¼	teaspoon freshly ground black pepper
4	teaspoons fresh lemon juice	¼	teaspoon ground red pepper
1	teaspoon honey	2	large eggs
½	teaspoon ground cumin	2	garlic cloves, minced
1	garlic clove, minced	1	(15-ounce) can unsalted chickpeas (garbanzo beans), rinsed and drained
2	eggplants (about 12 ounces each)		
Cooking spray		1	cup chopped seeded tomato
¾	teaspoon kosher salt, divided	½	cup chopped seeded peeled cucumber
¼	cup chopped onion		
¼	cup fresh breadcrumbs	½	cup vertically sliced red onion
¼	cup chopped fresh flat-leaf parsley	½	cup coarsely chopped fresh flat-leaf parsley
1	tablespoon tahini	1	tablespoon fresh lemon juice
2	teaspoons olive oil	1	tablespoon extra-virgin olive oil
1½	teaspoons ground cumin		

1. Combine first 6 ingredients in a small bowl, stirring with a whisk. Set aside.

2. Preheat oven to 475°.

3. Slice eggplants in half lengthwise; score cut sides in a crosshatch pattern. Place eggplant halves, cut sides down, on a baking sheet coated with cooking spray. Bake at 475° for 7 minutes or until slightly tender and browned. Remove from oven; carefully scoop out pulp, leaving a ¾-inch shell. Reserve pulp for another use. Season cut sides with ¼ teaspoon salt.

4. Place ½ teaspoon salt, onion, and next 11 ingredients (through chickpeas) in a food processor; process until smooth. Spoon ½ cup chickpea mixture into each eggplant shell. Bake at 475° for 25 minutes or until eggplant halves are tender and chickpea mixture is lightly browned.

5. Combine tomato and remaining ingredients in a bowl; stir to combine.

6. Place 1 eggplant half on each of 4 plates. Top each half with ¼ cup relish and 1½ tablespoons sauce. Serves 4 (serving size: 1 stuffed eggplant half).

CALORIES 308; FAT 15.6g (sat 2.5g, mono 7.4g, poly 3.8g); PROTEIN 12.1g; CARB 34.3g; FIBER 10.8g; CHOL 106mg; IRON 3.5mg; SODIUM 450mg; CALC 116mg

Large, oblong eggplants such as Black Beauty are best for stuffing. This is a picture-perfect way of presenting a new take on falafel without the frying. The nutty flavor of sesame seeds in tahini plays well with the fresh relish of tomato, cucumber, red onion, and parsley. Save the unused eggplant pulp for baba ghanoush or another dish.

Eggplant Parmesan

Hands-on time: 25 min. Total time: 1 hr. 45 min.

Eggplant:

2 large eggs, lightly beaten
1 tablespoon water
2 cups whole-wheat panko (Japanese breadcrumbs)
1 ounce grated fresh Parmigiano-Reggiano cheese (about ¼ cup)
2 (1-pound) eggplants, peeled and cut crosswise into ½-inch-thick slices
Cooking spray

Filling:

½ cup torn fresh basil
1 ounce grated fresh Parmigiano-Reggiano cheese (about ¼ cup)
½ teaspoon crushed red pepper
1½ teaspoons minced fresh garlic
⅛ teaspoon salt
1 (16-ounce) container part-skim ricotta cheese
1 large egg, lightly beaten

Remaining ingredients:

1 (24-ounce) jar premium pasta sauce
⅛ teaspoon salt, divided
8 ounces thinly sliced part-skim mozzarella cheese
3 ounces finely grated fontina cheese (about ¾ cup)

1. Preheat oven to 375°.

2. To prepare eggplant, combine 2 eggs and 1 tablespoon water in a shallow dish. Combine panko and 1 ounce Parmigiano-Reggiano in a second shallow dish. Dip eggplant in egg mixture; dredge in panko mixture, pressing gently to adhere and shaking off excess. Place slices 1 inch apart on baking sheets coated with cooking spray. Bake at 375° for 30 minutes or until golden, turning once and rotating baking sheets after 15 minutes.

3. To prepare filling, combine basil and next 6 ingredients (through egg) in a bowl.

4. To assemble, spoon ½ cup pasta sauce in bottom of a 13 x 9–inch glass or ceramic baking dish coated with cooking spray. Layer half of eggplant slices over pasta sauce. Sprinkle eggplant with a dash of salt. Top with about ¾ cup pasta sauce; spread half of filling over sauce, and top with a third of mozzarella and ¼ cup fontina. Repeat layers once, ending with about 1 cup pasta sauce. Cover tightly with aluminum foil coated with cooking spray. Bake at 375° for 35 minutes. Remove foil; top with remaining third of mozzarella and ¼ cup fontina. Bake at 375° for 10 minutes or until sauce is bubbly and cheese melts; cool 10 minutes. Serves 10 (serving size: 1 slice).

CALORIES 328; FAT 15g (sat 7.7g, mono 4g, poly 0.8g); PROTEIN 22.3g; CARB 27.3g; FIBER 5.8g; CHOL 87mg; IRON 2mg; SODIUM 720mg; CALC 469mg

Panko Breading Technique

A too-heavy or too-thin coating of these Japanese breadcrumbs will prevent you from getting the coveted crisp, "oven-fried" effect that is the crux of this dish. Here's how to get the crumb count just right:

1. Give the eggplant slices a quick dip in egg wash; let the excess drip off.

2. Gently press the panko onto each slice to help it adhere.

3. The whole-wheat panko barely browns, but it will create a perfectly crisp coating.

Miso Grilled Vegetables

Hands-on time: 25 min.   Total time: 25 min.

Capitalize on summer's bounty with the simplest recipe and 10 minutes on the grill. A little miso and mint bring out the fresh flavors. Japanese eggplants produce abundantly and are the perfect serving size for roasting or grilling. Try Ichiban or Malaysian Red in your garden.

2   tablespoons red or white/yellow miso (soybean paste)
1   tablespoon lukewarm water
3   tablespoons olive oil
1   pound zucchini, cut lengthwise into ⅓-inch-thick slices
8   ounces Japanese eggplant, cut lengthwise into ⅓-inch-thick slices
1   red bell pepper, cut into 6 pieces
1   orange bell pepper, cut into 6 pieces
1   small red onion, cut into 6 wedges
Cooking spray
2   tablespoons mint leaves
1   lime, cut into slices

1. Preheat grill to high heat.
2. Combine miso and 1 tablespoon lukewarm water. Gradually add oil, stirring with a whisk. Place zucchini, eggplant, and bell peppers on a jelly-roll pan. Add 5 tablespoons miso mixture; toss to coat. Brush onion with remaining miso mixture.
3. Place vegetables on grill rack coated with cooking spray. Grill zucchini, eggplant, and bell pepper 4 minutes on each side or until tender. Grill onion 6 minutes on each side or until tender. Sprinkle with mint. Serve with lime wedges. Serves 6 (serving size: about 3 zucchini slices, 2 eggplant slices, 2 bell pepper pieces, 1 onion wedge, and 1 lime slice).

CALORIES 112; FAT 7.1g (sat 1g, mono 4.9g, poly 0.8g); PROTEIN 1.8g; CARB 11.4g; FIBER 4.5g; CHOL 0mg; IRON 0.6mg; SODIUM 221mg; CALC 22mg

FENNEL

With the flavor of sweet anise, fennel is divine raw or cooked.

SEASON: Peak season is fall and winter. However, home gardeners can also slip in a quick planting in spring for an early summer harvest.

CHOOSING: Look for compact bulbs that are relatively heavy and firm. Avoid those that are splitting or browning, or have other injuries.

STORING: Remove the foliage by snipping an inch or two above the bulb. Place fennel in a produce bag to prevent moisture loss, and store it in the vegetable bin of your refrigerator for three or four days.

GROWING: Often mistaken for celery or dill, fennel is a true original. All parts of the plant (the bulb, stalk, and feathery fronds) are edible. Fennel enjoys cool weather—not hot, but not freezing. Although it's easy to germinate from seeds sown directly into the garden after the soil has warmed, transplants are helpful to get a head start in spring or in raising a fall crop that must be started in the heat of summer. It takes about three months for fennel to produce the bulb, so do the math to determine when you need to start and if you have enough time before the weather turns hot or starts freezing.

Improved varieties have been introduced in recent years. Try Zefa Fino or Trieste. They resist the urge to flower, channeling their energy into the bulb instead.

Plant fennel seeds or transplants in a sunny, well-drained bed that has been amended with compost. Thin seedlings to stand about 12 inches apart. Keep the bed moist, and be sure to feed your fennel every two to three weeks with a liquid fertilizer.

After the bulb grows to about 2 inches in length, cover it with soil or mulch, which will make it tender. Snip off any flower stalks that may form to prevent the bulb from splitting. When it's time to harvest, use clippers to snip under the bulb and cut the taproot.

Warm White Beans with Roasted Fennel

Hands-on time: 14 min. Total time: 34 min.

If you're anise-averse, roasting it may be what it takes to convert you. The caramelized flavors mixed with hearty beans and spinach create a filling and nutritious cool-weather dish. Try it with your own dried beans rehydrated and cooked for a richer flavor. Substitute kale if you don't have fresh spinach on hand.

4   cups thinly sliced fennel bulb
3   tablespoons olive oil, divided
¾   teaspoon freshly ground black pepper, divided
½   teaspoon salt, divided
¼   teaspoon ground red pepper
2   garlic cloves, minced
Cooking spray
3   tablespoons grated fresh Parmigiano-Reggiano cheese
2   (15.8-ounce) cans Great Northern beans, rinsed and drained
4   cups fresh baby spinach

1. Preheat oven to 450°.
2. Combine fennel, 1 tablespoon oil, ½ teaspoon black pepper, ¼ teaspoon salt, red pepper, and garlic in a large bowl; toss to coat fennel. Arrange fennel mixture in a single layer on a baking sheet coated with cooking spray. Bake at 450° for 15 minutes or until fennel begins to brown. Stir; sprinkle cheese evenly over fennel mixture. Bake an additional 5 minutes or until golden brown.
3. Heat a large nonstick skillet over medium heat; add 2 tablespoons oil. Add beans; cook 2 minutes or until heated. Add fennel mixture, spinach, ¼ teaspoon black pepper, and ¼ teaspoon salt. Cook 2 minutes; serve immediately. Serves 8 (serving size: about ⅔ cup).

CALORIES 140; FAT 6.1g (sat 1.1g, mono 3.9g, poly 0.7g); PROTEIN 5.8g; CARB 17.4g; FIBER 5.2g; CHOL 2mg; IRON 1.8mg; SODIUM 231mg; CALC 90mg

Slow-Cooked BBQ Fennel, Onion, and Pork Sandwiches

Hands-on time: 35 min.   Total time: 45 min.

Fennel and onion are incredible additions to this veggie-lover's version of a BBQ sandwich. Colorful shredded cabbage in red and green tops the pork with a crunch.

8	ounces boneless pork shoulder, trimmed and chopped	¼	cup cider vinegar
2	cups vertically sliced onion	2	teaspoons extra-virgin olive oil
1	large fennel bulb, thinly sliced	2	teaspoons cider vinegar
½	teaspoon kosher salt	¾	cup thinly sliced green cabbage
½	teaspoon chili powder	¾	cup thinly sliced red cabbage
½	teaspoon paprika	⅓	cup plain 2% reduced-fat Greek yogurt
¼	teaspoon ground cumin	2	tablespoons canola mayonnaise
¼	teaspoon freshly ground black pepper	1	teaspoon minced fresh garlic
¼	cup crushed tomatoes	6	(1½-ounce) whole-wheat hamburger buns, toasted

1. Heat a Dutch oven over medium-high heat. Add pork to pan; cook 2 minutes. Add onion and fennel to pan; cover and cook 15 minutes, stirring frequently. Add salt and next 4 ingredients (through pepper); cook 1 minute, stirring constantly. Add tomatoes and ¼ cup vinegar to pan. Reduce heat to medium. Uncover and cook 15 minutes or until pork is tender, stirring frequently.
2. Combine olive oil and 2 teaspoons vinegar in a medium bowl. Add green and red cabbage; toss gently to coat.
3. Combine yogurt, mayonnaise, and garlic in a small bowl. Spread about 1½ teaspoons yogurt mixture onto each bun half. Top bottom half of each bun with ¼ cup fennel mixture, ¼ cup cabbage mixture, and top half of bun. Serves 6 (serving size: 1 sandwich).

CALORIES 253; FAT 9.9g (sat 1.9g, mono 4.6g, poly 2.4g); PROTEIN 13.3g; CARB 29.5g; FIBER 5.6g; CHOL 25mg; IRON 2.2mg; SODIUM 470mg; CALC 102mg

Preparing Fennel

Use crunchy fennel bulb either raw or cooked, and save some of the feathery fronds (which look like dill but taste like anise) for a delicate garnish.

1. Remove fronds, and chop.

2. Trim and discard stalks.

3. Cut away the fibrous core.

4. Cut the trimmed fennel bulb into slices.

Shaved Fennel Salad with Orange, Green Olives, and Pistachios

Hands-on time: 20 min. Total time: 20 min.

This fennel salad has a zippy crunchiness with a potentially addictive anise flavor. It marries citrus, briny olives, and the crunch of green pistachios. Harvest or buy whole stalks of fennel for this recipe, as you use the fernlike fronds as well as the bulb. A mandoline is ideal for shaving the fibrous bulbs into delicate, thin slices.

1	tablespoon grated orange rind	¼	teaspoon freshly ground black pepper
¾	cup orange sections (about 2 large oranges)	⅛	teaspoon kosher salt
¾	cup coarsely chopped pitted green olives (about 3 ounces)	2	medium fennel bulbs with stalks (about 2 pounds)
2	tablespoons extra-virgin olive oil	1	cup shelled unsalted dry-roasted pistachios
1	tablespoon fresh lemon juice		

1. Combine first 7 ingredients in a large bowl; toss gently to combine.
2. Trim tough outer leaves from fennel, and mince feathery fronds to measure 2 tablespoons. Remove and discard stalks. Cut fennel bulbs in half lengthwise, and discard core. Thinly slice fennel bulbs. Add fennel slices to juice mixture, and toss gently to combine. Sprinkle with fennel fronds and nuts. Serves 8 (serving size: ¾ cup).

CALORIES 173; FAT 13.2g (sat 1.6g, mono 8.3g, poly 2.8g); PROTEIN 4.3g; CARB 11.7g; FIBER 3.8g; CHOL 0mg; IRON 1.1mg; SODIUM 233mg; CALC 55mg

Confusing Cousins

Some fennel varieties are grown for their bulbs, and others in the family, such as Bronze Fennel, are grown more for their foliage. Be certain of what seeds you buy.

GARLIC

Garlic rewards beginner gardeners with an abundant crop.
Flavor varies widely by variety.

SEASON: Garlic is harvested in spring and summer, but it also stores well. Fresh garlic should be available year-round.

CHOOSING: Fresh, sweet garlic is plump, firm, and heavy. If the papery covering pushes in, the cloves have shrunken. Avoid garlic heads that have green shoots.

STORING: Garlic will remain plump and usable on your countertop for a couple of months, but if you put it in your refrigerator, it will wait patiently for up to seven months for you to grab it and make a good recipe great.

GROWING: Garlic is easy to grow, and late summer into fall is the best time to plant. There are three types: softneck garlic (stores well, best for Southern gardens, easy to braid), hardneck garlic (does not store as well as softneck, best for Northern gardens, diversity of flavors), and elephant garlic (actually a leek, milder tasting, huge cloves). There are many varieties of softneck and hardneck garlic.

You can buy heads of specific varieties from seed companies or purchase garlic for planting from a local farmers' market and at the grocery store. Be aware that garlic in supermarkets is sometimes chemically treated to reduce sprouting, which isn't ideal for planting, and it might not be best suited for your climate. It's also worth exploring the differences in spiciness and color among the varieties available for the home garden.

Prepare a sunny, well-drained garden bed that has been enriched with compost or other organic matter. Remove the papery covering, and break apart the head of garlic just before planting, setting the cloves 1½ inches deep with the pointed end up. They should be spaced 6 inches apart. (Elephant garlic needs more space, so plant about 4 to 5 inches deep and 12 inches apart.)

In late spring or early summer, if you see your plant send up a flower stalk, snip it off but also enjoy its garlicky flavor in stir-fry. When the leaves start yellowing and there are about four green leaves remaining, carefully dig up the head. If the papery covering is intact and the head is well filled out, it's time to harvest.

Shrimp and White Bean Cakes with Roasted Garlic Sauce

Hands-on time: 35 min.   Total time: 1 hr. 25 min.

Growing your own garlic gives you a variety of flavor and color you won't find in the supermarket—from fiery hot to mild and streaked pink or purple. Roasting mellows it to a sweeter, caramelized paste that is great on a toasted baguette or in sauces like this one, perfect for shrimp and cannellini bean cakes.

1	whole garlic head
7	teaspoons olive oil, divided
½	cup plain fat-free Greek yogurt
1	teaspoon fresh lime juice
½	teaspoon freshly ground black pepper, divided
¼	teaspoon kosher salt, divided
½	pound peeled and deveined medium shrimp, divided
1	(15-ounce) can cannellini beans or other white beans, rinsed and drained, divided
½	cup cooked bulgur
¼	cup coarsely chopped cilantro leaves

1. Preheat oven to 375°.

2. Remove white papery skin from garlic head (do not peel or separate cloves). Drizzle 1 teaspoon oil over garlic; wrap in foil. Bake at 375° for 1 hour; cool 10 minutes. Separate cloves; squeeze into a small bowl to extract pulp. Discard skins. Mash garlic using the back of a spoon. Stir in yogurt, juice, ¼ teaspoon pepper, and ⅛ teaspoon salt.

3. Place 3 shrimp and ⅔ cup beans in a food processor; pulse until blended but not quite pureed. Add remaining shrimp, remaining beans, bulgur, cilantro, ¼ teaspoon pepper, and ⅛ teaspoon salt to food processor; pulse until coarsely chopped. Fill a ¼-cup dry measuring cup with shrimp mixture. Invert onto a platter lined with parchment paper; gently pat into a 2½-inch-wide patty. Repeat procedure with remaining shrimp mixture, forming 8 cakes. Refrigerate 20 minutes.

4. Preheat broiler.

5. Brush a jelly-roll pan with 1 tablespoon oil. Arrange chilled cakes on pan; brush tops of cakes with 1 tablespoon oil. Broil 5 minutes or until browned. Carefully turn cakes over. Brush tops of cakes with oil from pan. Broil an additional 5 minutes or until browned. Serve cakes with sauce. Serves 4 (serving size: 2 cakes and about 2 tablespoons sauce).

CALORIES 223; FAT 9g (sat 1.3g, mono 5.9g, poly 1.3g); PROTEIN 18.7g; CARB 17.2g; FIBER 3.8g; CHOL 86mg; IRON 2.6mg; SODIUM 364mg; CALC 91mg

Chicken with 40 Cloves of Garlic

Hands-on time: 30 min. Total time: 65 min.

There's no better dish for garlic than this. Count on about five or six heads of garlic to equal 40 cloves. And don't do without a single one; it's worth it! In a pinch, you can substitute six pounds of chicken pieces. Serve with steamed asparagus.

NUTRITION NOTE

Garlic has long been recognized for its medicinal properties in addition to its culinary uses. The bulbs contain a wide assortment of health-promoting antioxidants, minerals, and vitamins. When cut, crushed, or chewed, garlic produces allicin—the compound responsible for its strong odor—which has been shown to lower blood pressure and reduce risk of heart attack.

2   (3-pound) whole chickens
1   tablespoon butter
1   tablespoon extra-virgin olive oil
½   teaspoon salt
¼   teaspoon freshly ground black pepper
40 garlic cloves, peeled
1¼ cups fat-free, lower-sodium chicken broth
1   cup dry white wine
24 (¼-inch-thick) slices diagonally cut French bread baguette
Chopped fresh flat-leaf parsley (optional)

1. Remove and discard giblets and necks from chickens. Trim excess fat; remove skin. Cut each chicken into 8 pieces. Heat a 12-inch nonstick skillet over medium-high heat. Add butter and oil to pan; swirl until butter melts. Sprinkle salt and pepper evenly over chicken. Add half of chicken pieces to pan; cook 2 minutes on each side or until golden. Remove chicken from pan; keep warm. Repeat procedure with remaining chicken.

2. Reduce heat to medium. Add garlic; cook 1 minute or until garlic begins to brown, stirring frequently. Arrange chicken on top of garlic. Add broth and wine; cover and cook 25 minutes or until chicken is done.

3. Remove chicken from pan; keep warm. Increase heat to medium-high, and cook 10 minutes or until liquid is reduced to about 1 cup. Serve sauce and garlic with chicken and bread. Garnish with chopped parsley, if desired. Serves 8 (serving size: about 4 ounces chicken, 2 tablespoons sauce, 5 garlic cloves, and 3 bread slices).

CALORIES 343; FAT 13.7g (sat 3.6g, mono 4.9g, poly 3.4g); PROTEIN 29.6g; CARB 24.2g; FIBER 2g; CHOL 111mg; IRON 2.3mg; SODIUM 468mg; CALC 58mg

Green Beans with Toasted Garlic

Hands-on time: 12 min. Total time: 20 min.

Simple, garlicky beans make a great side for summer and fall. Be careful not to burn the garlic, as it toasts quickly in the olive oil.

1   pound green beans, trimmed
2   teaspoons butter
1   teaspoon olive oil
4   garlic cloves, thinly sliced
¼   teaspoon salt
¼   teaspoon freshly ground black pepper

1. Bring a large saucepan of water to a boil. Add beans; cook 5 minutes. Plunge beans into ice water; drain.

2. Heat a large skillet over medium-high heat. Add butter and oil to pan; swirl until butter melts. Add garlic; sauté 30 seconds. Remove garlic; set aside. Add beans to pan; sprinkle with salt and pepper. Cook 2 minutes, tossing frequently. Top with garlic. Serves 4 (serving size: about 1 cup).

CALORIES 67; FAT 3.2g (sat 1.4g, mono 1.3g, poly 0.3g); PROTEIN 2.3g; CARB 9.2g; FIBER 4g; CHOL 5mg; IRON 1.3mg; SODIUM 169mg; CALC 49mg

GREENS

Leafy, nutrient-rich mustard greens, collards, and Swiss chard offer wonderfully unique texture and flavor that spice up any meal.

SEASON: Although available in markets year-round, they are at their prime in spring and fall.

CHOOSING: Look for greens that are not wilted, have no physical damage, and have no areas that are turning yellow or brown.

STORING: Place greens in a produce storage bag in the coldest part of the refrigerator. Most will stay fresh for about a week.

GROWING: Most gardeners will have success growing mustard greens, collards, and Swiss chard in the spring and again in the fall. In warm, temperate gardens, greens will live through the winter. If your area has cool summers, you can grow them then, too.

Greens need full sun and rich soil to produce a lot of leafy growth very quickly. Space mustard greens 4 to 8 inches apart, collards 12 to 18 inches apart, and Swiss chard 8 to 12 inches apart. Apply a liquid fertilizer at planting time and again every three to four weeks.

In a well-prepared bed, sow seeds or set transplants two to four weeks before the last spring frost. Plants will mature in spring, making quite a display of light yellow flowers when the weather gets hot. Pull them out to make way for summer veggies.

For a fall and winter harvest, sow seeds or set out transplants in late summer or early fall. The plants will mature as the days get cooler. This is ideal for greens because light frosts actually sweeten them. Collards are the most cold-hardy of the bunch, and they frequently provide fresh greens all winter long. Harvest the outer leaves from the bottom, moving up, as soon as the leaves are large and the plant is established.

Swiss Chard with Crème Fraîche

Hands-on time: 5 min. Total time: 16 min.

The smart, tart cousin of sour cream makes a sharp partner for Swiss chard. If you need to compare it to a traditional dish, rethink creamed spinach with every colorful bite.

1½	pounds Swiss chard, trimmed	¼	teaspoon salt
1	tablespoon olive oil	¼	teaspoon freshly ground black
⅓	cup crème fraîche		pepper

1. Remove stems and center ribs from chard. Cut stems and ribs into ½-inch pieces; set aside. Coarsely chop leaves; set aside.

2. Bring a large pot of water to a boil. Add stems and ribs; cook 5 minutes. Stir in leaves; cook 2 minutes or until leaves wilt. Drain well, pressing chard with the back of a spoon to remove as much water as possible.

3. Return pan to medium heat. Add oil to pan; swirl to coat. Add chard, crème fraîche, salt, and pepper. Cook 4 minutes or until chard is tender. Serves 8 (serving size: ½ cup).

CALORIES 64; FAT 5.3g (sat 2.4g, mono 2.3g, poly 0.3g); PROTEIN 1.7g; CARB 3g; FIBER 1.3g; CHOL 9mg; IRON 1.4mg; SODIUM 244mg; CALC 40mg

Chard Prep

This earthy, nutrient-packed plant is easy to handle and ideal for wilting down to a silky texture. For easy prep, follow a few simple steps:

1. Wash leaves in a sink or large bowl of water until they're free of grit. Drain and pat dry.

2. Fold each leaf in half lengthwise; cut out the hard vein.

3. To make neat strips of chard, stack a few trimmed leaves; roll up tightly like a cigar.

4. Slice across the rolled stack to form ribbons.

Braised Pork with Slow-Cooked Collards, Grits, and Tomato Gravy

Hands-on time: 40 min. Total time: 2 hr. 40 min.

1½ tablespoons canola oil, divided
1 (20-ounce) boneless pork shoulder (Boston butt), trimmed
1 teaspoon kosher salt, divided
¾ teaspoon black pepper, divided
2 cups water, divided
2 cups unsalted chicken stock, divided
1½ teaspoons lower-sodium soy sauce
2 cups vertically sliced onion

8 cups chopped collard greens
2 teaspoons sugar
1 (28.5-ounce) can unsalted whole tomatoes, undrained
1 tablespoon all-purpose flour
⅓ cup finely chopped onion
1 ounce chopped cremini mushrooms
2 garlic cloves, minced
½ cup uncooked quick-cooking grits

1. Preheat oven to 325°.
2. Heat an ovenproof saucepan over medium-high heat. Add 1½ teaspoons oil; swirl to coat. Sprinkle pork with ½ teaspoon salt and ½ teaspoon pepper. Add pork to pan; cook 8 minutes, browning on all sides. Discard oil. Add ½ cup water, ½ cup stock, and soy sauce. Cover and bake at 325° for 2 hours or until very tender. Remove pork; reserve liquid. Place pork on a cutting board; cover with foil. Let stand 10 minutes; cut into 4 slices.
3. While pork cooks, heat a Dutch oven over medium heat. Add 1½ teaspoons oil; swirl to coat. Add sliced onion and ¼ teaspoon salt; cook 2 minutes or until golden, stirring occasionally. Add ½ cup water, ½ cup stock, greens, and sugar. Bring to a boil. Cover; reduce heat, and simmer 25 minutes or until tender, stirring occasionally.
4. Remove 1 cup tomato liquid from can; reserve remaining liquid and tomatoes for another use. Combine 1 cup tomato liquid and flour in a bowl, stirring with a whisk. Place a zip-top plastic bag inside a 2-cup glass measure. Pour pork cooking liquid into bag; let stand 5 minutes (fat will rise to the top). Seal bag; snip off 1 bottom corner of bag. Drain liquid into tomato mixture, stopping before fat layer reaches opening; discard fat. Return pan to medium-high heat. Add 1½ teaspoons oil to pan; swirl to coat. Add chopped onion and mushrooms; sauté 2 minutes. Add tomato mixture to saucepan; bring to a boil. Cook until reduced to 1 cup (about 10 minutes).
5. While gravy cooks, bring 1 cup water, 1 cup stock, ¼ teaspoon salt, ¼ teaspoon pepper, and garlic to a boil in a saucepan. Gradually add grits, stirring constantly with a whisk. Reduce heat; simmer 5 minutes or until liquid is absorbed, stirring frequently. Serve grits with gravy, pork, and greens. Serves 4 (serving size: about 3 ounces pork, ½ cup greens, ½ cup grits, and ¼ cup gravy).

CALORIES 454; FAT 24.8g (sat 7.4g, mono 11.5g, poly 3.5g); PROTEIN 27.3g; CARB 30.9g; FIBER 4.7g; CHOL 89mg; IRON 3.1mg; SODIUM 771mg; CALC 151mg

Collards are often regarded as a Southern crop—after all, the favorite variety is named Georgia—but they are appearing in fine restaurants nationwide. Collards are especially good if harvested after one or two frosts. If not, add a touch of sugar to offset any bitterness. The greens can simmer while the pork cooks (or they can be done ahead and reheated). Start the grits and gravy around the same time; you don't want the grits to sit, or they'll get too firm.

Honey-Wine Braised Chicken Thighs with Mustard Greens

Hands-on time: 33 min.   Total time: 1 hr. 14 min.

Mustard greens loom large in the pan, sound bitter and tart, and look too healthy for their own good. Yet this ginger-honey sauce wilts the greens into a mellower flavor for rave reviews. Serve over rice or lo mein noodles.

2½ teaspoons dark sesame oil
6 skinless, boneless chicken thighs (about 2 pounds)
2 cups chopped red onion (about 1 large)
¾ cup fat-free, lower-sodium chicken broth
⅓ cup Shaoxing (Chinese rice wine) or dry sherry
2½ tablespoons minced peeled fresh ginger
3 tablespoons oyster sauce
2 tablespoons honey
4 garlic cloves, minced
1½ pounds mustard greens, stems removed, coarsely chopped
1 tablespoon sesame seeds, toasted

1. Preheat oven to 350°.
2. Heat a large Dutch oven over high heat. Add oil to pan; swirl to coat. Add chicken; cook 4 minutes on each side or until browned. Add onion; stir-fry 4 minutes. Reduce heat; add broth and Shaoxing, scraping pan to loosen browned bits. Stir in ginger, oyster sauce, honey, and garlic. Cover and bake at 350° for 30 minutes.
3. Remove from oven. Remove chicken from pan; shred with 2 forks, and return to pan. Place pan over medium-low heat. Add half of greens to pan; cover. Cook 5 minutes or until greens wilt; stir well. Repeat procedure with remaining greens. Cook mixture, covered, 15 minutes. Spoon 1 cup chicken mixture into each of 6 bowls; sprinkle each serving with ½ teaspoon sesame seeds. Serves 6.

CALORIES 327; FAT 14.4g (sat 3.4g, mono 5.3g, poly 3.7g); PROTEIN 33.4g; CARB 13.5g; FIBER 0.7g; CHOL 101mg; IRON 3.8mg; SODIUM 281mg; CALC 214mg

The Shaoxing Redemption

Yes, you can use dry sherry in place of Shaoxing (shaow-SHEEN) wine, but we recommend adding this fragrant, deeply nutty wine to your pantry—you can experiment with it in stews or other recipes calling for winy flavor.

KALE

Kale's somewhat bitter flavor shines when raw, baked, sautéed, or stewed.

SEASON: Fall through spring

CHOOSING: Look for bunches that are dark green and free of yellow or brown blemishes.

STORING: Place cut kale in a plastic produce bag in your refrigerator for up to a week.

GROWING: In warm areas, kale is best grown in the cool months of spring and fall. It's also remarkably cold-hardy and will survive all but the most severe winters, remaining usable even after nights dipping to 10°. Kale is even better after one or two frosts—the leaves will develop a touch of sweetness that is worth the wait.

There are a number of delicious options for planting: the frilly Winterbor and Dwarf Blue Curled; the hardy, purple-veined Red Russian; and the blue-green Lacinato, also known as dinosaur or Tuscan kale.

Set out transplants about a month before the last frost in spring. Plant again in late summer, about two months before the first anticipated frost. In warm regions, planting can continue all winter into spring.

Kale is a leafy green requiring sun, moisture, and rich soil. Amend your soil with organic materials such as bagged garden soil, mushroom compost, or your own compost. Add timed-release fertilizer granules to the soil before planting to ensure nonstop nutrition and the best growth.

Space transplants about a foot apart. To get the most from limited garden space, plant wide rows: three rows of kale in a bed 4 square feet wide, which allows you to reach the center of the bed from each side while giving you the maximum room for planting. Water well, and mulch the bed with pine needles, wheat straw, or bark nuggets to keep the soil moist. Water at least an inch weekly.

Harvest kale sustainably by picking the outer leaves, leaving the top ones to nourish the plant.

Garlic-Roasted Kale

Hands-on time: 7 min.
Total time: 19 min.

A quick side and soon-to-be staple, this recipe is one of the ways fresh kale has raised its profile. Roasting turns the leaves from a dusty dark green to dark emerald with brown-tinged, curly edges that crunch. Be very careful to avoid burning; keep an eye on the tips of the leaves, and remove immediately when they begin to crisp.

10	ounces kale, stems removed, chopped
3½	teaspoons extra-virgin olive oil
¼	teaspoon kosher salt
1	garlic clove, thinly sliced
1	teaspoon sherry vinegar

1. Arrange oven racks in center and lower third of oven. Preheat oven to 425°. Place a large jelly-roll pan in oven 5 minutes.
2. Combine first 4 ingredients in a bowl; toss to coat. Place kale mixture on preheated pan, spreading with a silicone spatula to separate leaves. Bake at 425° for 7 minutes. Stir kale. Bake an additional 5 minutes or until edges of leaves are crisp and kale is tender.
3. Place kale in a bowl. Drizzle with vinegar; toss. Serve immediately.
Serves 4 (serving size: about ⅔ cup).

CALORIES 72; FAT 4.7g (sat 0.7g, mono 3g, poly 0.8g); PROTEIN 2.3g; CARB 7.1g; FIBER 1.4g; CHOL 0mg; IRON 1.2mg; SODIUM 125mg; CALC 93mg

Lemony Kale Salad

Hands-on time: 14 min. Total time: 19 min.

A simple lemon and oil dressing with quality pecorino cheese is a must-try. If you doubt the raw kale craze, harvest leaves after one or two winter frosts, when the starches convert to natural sugars. Lacinato kale is a good option for this salad, paired with the colorful chard variety Bright Lights.

1	tablespoon fresh lemon juice
1	tablespoon olive oil
½	teaspoon sugar
½	teaspoon freshly ground black pepper
¼	teaspoon kosher salt
4	cups torn kale leaves
2	cups torn Swiss chard leaves
4	teaspoons unsalted pumpkinseed kernels
¼	cup sliced green onions (about 2)
1	ounce shaved fresh pecorino Romano cheese (about ¼ cup)

1. Combine first 5 ingredients, stirring until sugar dissolves. Add kale and chard; toss. Let stand 10 minutes.

2. While greens stand, heat a skillet over medium heat. Add kernels to pan, and cook 5 minutes or until browned, stirring frequently. Add kernels, onions, and cheese to greens; toss. Serves 6 (serving size: 1 cup).

CALORIES 65; FAT 4g (sat 0.8g, mono 2g, poly 0.8g); PROTEIN 2.6g; CARB 6.3g; FIBER 1.4g; CHOL 2mg; IRON 1.4mg; SODIUM 234mg; CALC 87mg

Bacon, Kale, and Butternut Pasta

Hands-on time: 38 min.   Total time: 1 hr. 15 min.

Bacon, pasta, cheese, and sweet winter squash are not what you'd expect to see on the light menu, but indulge. The Test Kitchen tried multiple variations of greens: Kale, with its earthy heartiness, helps to balance the sweetness from the squash. Also, try Swiss chard or, for a more peppery bite, mustard greens.

5	cups (½-inch) cubed peeled butternut squash	1	teaspoon salt, divided
1	tablespoon olive oil	5	garlic cloves, minced
Cooking spray		2	cups fat-free, lower-sodium chicken broth, divided
12	ounces uncooked ziti (short tube-shaped pasta), campanile, or other short pasta	2	tablespoons all-purpose flour
		½	teaspoon crushed red pepper
		1	cup crème fraîche
4	cups chopped kale	1½	ounces shredded Gruyère cheese (about ⅓ cup)
2	bacon slices		
2	cups vertically sliced onion		

1. Preheat oven to 400°.
2. Combine squash and oil in a large bowl; toss well. Arrange squash mixture in a single layer on a baking sheet coated with cooking spray. Bake at 400° for 30 minutes or until squash is tender.
3. Cook pasta 7 minutes or until almost al dente, omitting salt and fat. Add kale to pan during last 2 minutes of cooking. Drain pasta mixture.
4. Cook bacon in a large nonstick skillet over medium heat until crisp. Remove bacon from pan; crumble. Add onion to drippings in pan; cook 6 minutes, stirring occasionally. Add ½ teaspoon salt and garlic; cook 1 minute, stirring occasionally.
5. Bring 1¾ cups broth to a boil in a small saucepan. Combine ¼ cup broth and flour in a small bowl, stirring with a whisk. Add flour mixture, ½ teaspoon salt, and pepper to broth. Cook 2 minutes or until slightly thick. Remove from heat; stir in crème fraîche.
6. Combine squash, pasta mixture, bacon, onion mixture, and sauce in a large bowl; toss gently. Place pasta mixture in a 13 x 9-inch glass or ceramic baking dish coated with cooking spray; sprinkle evenly with cheese. Bake at 400° for 25 minutes or until bubbly and lightly browned. Serves 8 (serving size: about 1½ cups).

CALORIES 348; FAT 19.8g (sat 5.6g, mono 11.1g, poly 2g); PROTEIN 14.5g; CARB 29.4g; FIBER 2.9g; CHOL 73mg; IRON 3.3mg; SODIUM 589mg; CALC 220mg

Oven-Bound Pasta

The casserole idea is simple: Disparate elements are combined, sauced, topped, and baked until the elements marry, absorbing flavor and melding deliciously while the cheese bubbles and browns. Apply these principles for lighter expressions of casserole perfection.

1. Start with a big pot of water to give the pasta room to move. As a general rule, use about five quarts of water for every pound of pasta. Stir the pasta occasionally during the first few minutes to prevent sticking.

2. With baked pastas—except lasagnas that use no-boil noodles—the pasta cooks twice: once when boiled, and then again in the oven. To prevent mushiness, boil noodles until they're almost al dente. After baking, the pasta will be just past al dente, soft and perfect for the dish.

3. The sauce in baked pasta is one of the main flavorings. Season it boldly with fresh herbs, garlic, and spices. Since it's also the medium that cooks the pasta for the second time, you need to have enough liquid—like broth or tomato sauce—for the noodles to absorb as they bake.

LETTUCES, ENDIVE & RADICCHIO

These greens are an excellent opportunity to add color and crunch to your meals.

SEASON: Although available all year, spring and fall are peak season for endive, radicchio, and lettuces of all types.

CHOOSING: Look for unblemished foliage that is not wilted, avoiding bunches with brown or wilted leaves.

STORING: Store salad greens in a produce bag, and place in the vegetable bin of your refrigerator. Refrain from tearing or washing them until you are ready to use them. If they're wilted, place them in an ice-cold water bath for 10 minutes, and spin dry. Most salad greens will last only a few days in your refrigerator, so buy or harvest only what you will use immediately. Radicchio will last three to four weeks.

GROWING: Nothing compares to the delicacy and fragrance of lettuce picked fresh from the garden. In areas where summers are mild, choose heat-tolerant varieties for all-summer salads.

Red and green leaf lettuces are easy-to-grow options that never curl inward or make a head; the center is open. There are dozens of varieties to choose from.

Romaine, or cos lettuce, stands taller than other lettuces and has a prominent center rib. Butterhead lettuce, which includes the popular Bibb and Boston lettuces, is a semi-heading type with smooth, mild-tasting red or green leaves.

Curly chicory, or frisée, has frilly leaves that have a little crunch and a welcome bitterness. It makes frequent appearances in mesclun blends.

Endive is a salad green grown from seeds sown in the cool days of early spring. The narrow-leaved form is called chicory, and the tall, broad-leaved one is escarole, or Batavian endive.

Radicchio is a bright red and white Italian chicory that adds color and spice to salads. A related form called witloof chicory is grown to produce healthy roots that are dug at summer's end and replanted in a warm dark place to produce Belgian endive during winter.

All of these can be grown in a rich, sun-drenched garden bed or in containers. Salad greens need compost and fertilizer for fuel. Invest in the soil so growing will be easy.

Start with either seeds or transplants. It's a good idea to use transplants in spring gardens because seeds won't germinate well when it's cold, and plants will bolt, or set bloom stalks, when days are longer and warmer. However, the fall salad garden can easily be grown from seeds in late summer, and the plants will grow strong in the bright sun and cool days of autumn. With the exception of radicchio, which needs to have the entire head cut and brought indoors, most of these lettuces can be picked by cutting off outer leaves one at a time.

Endive and Watercress Salad with Bacon-Cider Dressing

Hands-on time: 24 min. Total time: 24 min.

Smoky bacon, tangy Dijon, and maple syrup cut the bitterness of these sharp greens. As it's a very simple salad, each ingredient plays a key role. Splurge on extra-virgin olive oil, real maple syrup, and high-quality bacon.

4   center-cut bacon slices
3   tablespoons extra-virgin olive oil
2½   tablespoons cider vinegar
2   tablespoons maple syrup
1   teaspoon Dijon mustard
¼   teaspoon kosher salt
¼   teaspoon freshly ground black pepper
1   garlic clove, minced
4   cups (½-inch) diagonally cut Belgian endive
3   cups chopped radicchio
1   cup trimmed watercress

1. Heat a medium nonstick skillet over medium heat. Add bacon to pan; cook until crisp. Remove bacon from pan, reserving 2 teaspoons drippings in pan; coarsely chop bacon. Combine 2 teaspoons drippings, oil, and next 6 ingredients (through garlic) in a large bowl, stirring with a whisk. Add remaining ingredients; toss well. Sprinkle with chopped bacon. Serves 6 (serving size: about 1¼ cups).

CALORIES 108; FAT 8.2g (sat 1.6g, mono 4.9g, poly 0.8g); PROTEIN 2.1g; CARB 7.5g; FIBER 1.9g; CHOL 5mg; IRON 0.3mg; SODIUM 195mg; CALC 25mg

Charred BLT Salad

Hands-on time: 27 min.   Total time: 27 min.

This salad tops charred greens with prosciutto, crunchy bread cubes, and grape tomatoes—finishing with blue cheese that begins to melt when it hits the warm lettuce. Romaine, with its stronger rib, can withstand a little time on the grill. The sugars in the leaves concentrate, and the char on the exterior adds another dimension of flavor.

3   tablespoons extra-virgin olive
    oil, divided
2   ounces thinly sliced prosciutto,
    cut crosswise into ribbons
1½ cups (½-inch) cubed whole-grain
    bread (about 2 ounces)
1   pint grape tomatoes
¼   teaspoon freshly ground black
    pepper
⅛   teaspoon kosher salt
2   romaine lettuce hearts, halved
    lengthwise
Cooking spray
¼   cup chopped green onions
2   ounces crumbled blue cheese
    (about ½ cup)

1. Heat a large skillet over medium heat. Add 2 tablespoons oil to pan; swirl to coat. Add prosciutto; cook 4 minutes or until crisp, stirring occasionally. Remove prosciutto with a slotted spoon. Drain on paper towels. Add bread to pan; cook 3 minutes or until browned, stirring frequently. Combine prosciutto and bread. Add 1 tablespoon oil to pan; swirl to coat. Add tomatoes; cook 5 minutes or until skins begin to split, stirring frequently. Pour tomatoes and olive oil into a small bowl. Sprinkle with pepper and salt.
2. Preheat grill to medium-high heat.
3. Coat cut sides of lettuce with cooking spray. Place lettuce, cut sides down, on grill rack coated with cooking spray. Cook 2 minutes or until well marked. Place 1 lettuce half on each of 4 plates. Divide prosciutto mixture and tomato mixture evenly among servings. Top each serving with 1 tablespoon onions and ½ ounce cheese. Serves 4.

CALORIES 226; FAT 16g (sat 4.5g, mono 9.1g, poly 1.4g); PROTEIN 9g; CARB 12.9g; FIBER 2.9g; CHOL 19mg; IRON 1.5mg; SODIUM 559mg; CALC 120mg

Crisp Lamb Lettuce Wraps

Hands-on time: 20 min. Total time: 20 min.

Loose-leaf and romaine lettuces are essential in your cut-and-come-again lettuce patch, but make sure you also grow a butterhead (sometimes referred to as Boston or Bibb) variety, such as Buttercrunch or Yugoslavian Red, for wrap recipes.

2	teaspoons canola oil	½	cup chopped fresh parsley
1	cup finely chopped onion	½	cup chopped tomato
2	teaspoons minced fresh garlic	½	cup chopped cucumber
1	teaspoon ground cinnamon	¼	cup plain fat-free Greek yogurt
¾	teaspoon kosher salt	¼	cup red pepper hummus
¼	teaspoon freshly ground black pepper	8	Boston lettuce leaves
6	ounces lean ground lamb	2	tablespoons torn mint leaves
		1	tablespoon pine nuts, toasted

1. Heat a large skillet over high heat. Add oil to pan; swirl to coat. Add onion and next 5 ingredients (through lamb) to pan; sauté 5 minutes or until lamb is done. Combine parsley, tomato, and cucumber in a bowl. Stir in lamb mixture. Combine yogurt and hummus in a small bowl. Place about ¼ cup lamb mixture in each lettuce leaf. Top each wrap with 1 tablespoon hummus mixture. Divide mint and pine nuts evenly among wraps. Serves 4 (serving size: 2 wraps).

CALORIES 158; FAT 8g (sat 1.2g, mono 3g, poly 1.6g); PROTEIN 11.4g; CARB 11.3g; FIBER 3g; CHOL 24mg; IRON 2mg; SODIUM 488mg; CALC 68mg

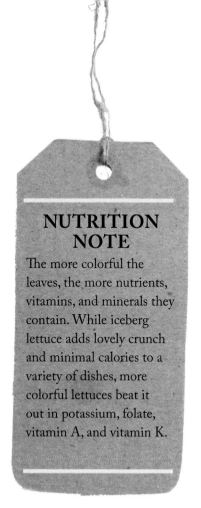

NUTRITION NOTE

The more colorful the leaves, the more nutrients, vitamins, and minerals they contain. While iceberg lettuce adds lovely crunch and minimal calories to a variety of dishes, more colorful lettuces beat it out in potassium, folate, vitamin A, and vitamin K.

OKRA

*Many folks shy away from okra because they expect a viscous texture.
But when handled right, okra is crunchy, crisp, and far from slimy.*

SEASON: May through October

CHOOSING: Look for small green or red pods, 1 to 3 inches long, that do not have much black bruising on them.

STORING: Place okra in a produce bag in the vegetable bin of your refrigerator. Use it within a week.

GROWING: Okra likes to be in full sun and good soil. Prepare the bed by loosening the soil and working in compost. Start with seeds or transplants, but wait until the soil has warmed, about two to three weeks after the last spring frost. You can warm the soil quicker by covering it with black plastic until ready to plant. Soak seeds overnight before planting. Sow seeds 6 inches apart, and thin them later to 12 to 18 inches apart. If you are using transplants, disturb the roots as little as possible. Space transplants 12 to 18 inches apart.

Okra plants take about two months to start flowering. Once they do, fertilize again with a liquid or granular product at the rate specified on the label. Pods form immediately after the flowers fade. At the peak of the season, you'll need to cut pods almost daily to prevent them from getting too big and tough. Use clippers or scissors to minimize damage to the plant. Remember to wear long sleeves when you harvest okra; it can irritate your skin. Store the pods in the refrigerator, collecting for several days until you have enough to prepare for dinner.

Standard-sized varieties such as Clemson Spineless will eventually get too tall to reach. To keep the plant under control, cut it back to 4 to 5 feet. Side branches will sprout and produce even more. For growing in containers, look for dwarf varieties that produce full-sized pods on a short stem, such as Green Fingers and Lee.

Spicy Pickled Okra

Hands-on time: 10 min. Total time: 40 min.

Pickling is a great way to make use of an abundant garden harvest, and no vegetable is more abundant than okra. In the height—and heat—of summer, it needs to be picked daily or every other day. Choose pods 5 inches or smaller for the most tender bites. For a pretty color variation, grow green and red varieties. Serve as a side dish or as part of a relish tray. Pickled okra is also a great garnish for a martini or bloody Mary. This recipe would also work for green beans.

2½ cups white vinegar
2 cups water
3 tablespoons sugar
2 tablespoons kosher salt
1 teaspoon white peppercorns
1 teaspoon coriander seeds
1 teaspoon fennel seeds
1 teaspoon cumin seeds
4 dill sprigs
2 green or red jalapeño peppers, halved lengthwise
1½ pounds small okra pods

1. Combine first 8 ingredients in a large saucepan; bring to a boil. Cook 1 minute or until sugar and salt dissolve, stirring frequently. Remove from heat; stir in dill, jalapeño, and okra. Cool completely; pour mixture into an airtight container. Cover and chill. Serves 20 (serving size: ¼ cup).

Note: Refrigerate okra in an airtight container for up to two weeks.

CALORIES 28; FAT 0g; PROTEIN 0.7g; CARB 6.8g; FIBER 1.1g; CHOL 0mg; IRON 0.3mg; SODIUM 10mg; CALC 29mg

Chicken and Sausage Gumbo

Hands-on time: 32 min.   Total time: 32 min.

To some, gumbo isn't gumbo without okra. If you have a lot of fresh okra from your summer harvest and want to freeze some for steaming bowls of spicy gumbo this winter, choose 3- to 4-inch pods to destem—without cutting into the seed pod—and quickly blanch, drain, and freeze whole. Slice into bite-sized pieces after defrosting slightly, and it's ready to use in this recipe when you're sporting sweaters.

6	ounces andouille sausage, finely chopped	1	tablespoon salt-free Cajun/ Creole seasoning
2	tablespoons butter	½	teaspoon salt
2	tablespoons canola oil	5	garlic cloves, minced
1.5	ounces all-purpose flour (about ⅓ cup)	3	cups unsalted chicken stock
		1	(14.5-ounce) can unsalted whole tomatoes, drained and crushed
8	ounces skinless, boneless chicken thighs, cut into bite-sized pieces		
1	cup chopped onion	1	cup sliced fresh okra
¾	cup chopped green bell pepper (about 1 medium)	3	cups bagged precooked brown rice
½	cup thinly sliced celery		Fresh parsley leaves (optional)

1. Heat a Dutch oven over medium-high heat. Add sausage to pan; sauté 5 minutes, turning to brown on all sides. Remove sausage from pan using a slotted spoon, reserving drippings in pan; drain on paper towels. Melt butter in drippings in pan. Add oil to pan; swirl to coat. Weigh or lightly spoon flour into a dry measuring cup; level with a knife. Stir flour into butter mixture; cook 3 minutes or until flour mixture starts to brown, stirring constantly with a whisk. Add chicken; sauté 4 minutes, stirring frequently. Add onion and next 5 ingredients (through garlic) to pan; sauté 6 minutes or until vegetables are tender, stirring occasionally. Add stock and tomatoes to pan; bring to a boil. Return sausage to pan; stir in okra. Reduce heat, and simmer 6 minutes, stirring occasionally. Serve over rice. Garnish with parsley, if desired. Serves 6 (serving size: 1 cup gumbo and ½ cup rice).

CALORIES 367; FAT 16.1g (sat 5.6g, mono 7.3g, poly 2.7g); PROTEIN 19g; CARB 36.8g; FIBER 4.2g; CHOL 57mg; IRON 2.6mg; SODIUM 559mg; CALC 70mg

Another Option: Spiced Okra

If the viscous texture of okra turns you off, try this recipe. (Even folks who usually don't like okra enjoy the taste and texture of this highly seasoned dish.)

Cook ¾ teaspoon brown mustard seeds in a large heavy skillet over medium-high heat for 30 seconds or until toasted and fragrant. Add 1 tablespoon canola oil, 1 teaspoon ground coriander, 1 teaspoon finely chopped serrano chile, ½ teaspoon kosher salt, ¼ teaspoon curry powder, and 1 pound small to medium trimmed okra pods; cook 1 minute, stirring occasionally. Cover, reduce heat to low, and cook 8 minutes, stirring occasionally. Uncover and increase heat to high; cook 2 minutes or until okra is lightly browned.

CALORIES 47; FAT 2.6g (sat 0.2g); SODIUM 163mg

Stewed Okra
with Tomatoes and Bacon

Hands-on time: 23 min. Total time: 47 min.

Let's start with bacon fat and stew a few tomatoes and lots of okra in it. How could you go wrong? Stewing okra like this makes the most of its sticky ways and brews a flavorful sauce best served over rice. A bonus? Vidalia onions. There is no substitute for their sweet, gentle flavor, compliments of the soil.

2	bacon slices	1/2	cup water
1	cup chopped Vidalia or other sweet onion	1	to 2 teaspoons hot sauce
1	cup chopped green bell pepper	1	teaspoon cider vinegar
1	garlic clove, minced	1/2	teaspoon salt
4	cups sliced fresh okra (about 1 pound)	1/2	teaspoon dried thyme
2	cups chopped tomato	1/2	teaspoon freshly ground black pepper

1. Cook bacon in a Dutch oven over medium-high heat until crisp. Remove bacon from pan, reserving 2 teaspoons drippings in pan. Crumble bacon.

2. Add onion, bell pepper, and garlic to drippings in pan, and sauté 5 minutes or until tender. Add okra and remaining ingredients; bring to a boil. Cover, reduce heat, and simmer 20 minutes or until okra is tender. Sprinkle with bacon. Serves 8 (serving size: 1/2 cup).

CALORIES 59; FAT 2.1g (sat 0.7g, mono 0.9g, poly 0.3g); PROTEIN 2.7g; CARB 8.8g; FIBER 3.1g; CHOL 3mg; IRON 0.8mg; SODIUM 212mg; CALC 59mg

ONIONS

Onions are the workhorses of the kitchen, each with its own flavor profile— from sweet to pungent—to suit your culinary needs.

SEASON: Available all year, but seasons vary around the country. You'll usually find fresh onions in spring and summer, identified by their thin layer of papery skin. Their high moisture content gives them a milder flavor. Onions harvested in cool weather are known as storage onions; they have a pungent flavor, several layers of thick skin, and a moisture content slightly lower than that of fresh onions.

CHOOSING: Look for onions that are heavy and firm with tight, dry skins and no bruises, signs of sprouting, or smell (they release their fragrance when bruised or cut).

STORING: Store in a cool, dry, dark place with lots of air circulating. Never suffocate them in plastic bags—they'll rot. Storage onions can last months; fresh ones, 30 to 90 days.

GROWING: Onions are pretty inexpensive to purchase in stores, but the beauty of growing your own is always having them at your fingertips. Dash out the door to harvest as green onions in the younger stages, or let them develop into larger bulbs for fresh eating or storage.

You'll find storage onions in shades of white, yellow, and red. They'll keep the longest if properly dried (see page 163) and stored. Sweet onions, such as Bermuda, Vidalia, Texas sweets, and Walla Walla, are best for eating fresh. Perennial multiplier onions, such as Evergreen Long White, are a wonderful garden option—they're planted whole in the fall or late winter and divide in the spring. Just pull what you need, and replant what you don't. You may never run out.

The amount of daylight your garden receives will determine the type of onion you should plant: long-day, short-day, or intermediate-day. Short-day onions develop bulbs in no more than 12 hours of daily light for a certain period of time. So, if planted in the north where summer days are longer, these plants form extremely small bulbs prematurely. Long-day onions need 14 to 16 hours, so they'll fail to form bulbs in areas with shorter summer days. Intermediate-day onions require 13 to 15 hours. Getting great bulbs in your garden isn't hard; just start with the right variety for your region, and plant at the right time in spring. Consult your local garden centers or Cooperative Extension office for help selecting the right types.

Onion Tart

Hands-on time: 20 min. Total time: 1 hr. 10 min.

Don't turn up your nose at pounds of onions in a single dish until you've had this caramelized onion and feta pie. It'll make you teary for a different reason: joy. Use Vidalia onions for sweetness, or a bushel of fresh ones from your garden. If you are growing your own, this is an ode to your harvest.

1	tablespoon olive oil		1	ounce crumbled reduced-fat feta cheese (about ¼ cup)
2½	pounds onion, sliced			
2	tablespoons chopped fresh thyme		1	ounce shredded reduced-fat Swiss cheese (about ¼ cup)
½	teaspoon kosher salt			
¼	teaspoon freshly ground black pepper		1	large egg, lightly beaten
½	(14.1-ounce) package refrigerated pie dough		2	tablespoons water

1. Preheat oven to 425°.

2. Heat a large nonstick skillet over medium-high heat. Add oil to pan; swirl to coat. Add onion, thyme, salt, and pepper; cook 20 minutes, stirring occasionally.

3. Roll dough out on a parchment paper–lined baking sheet. Sprinkle feta cheese in center, leaving a 1½-inch border; top with onion mixture. Sprinkle with Swiss cheese. Fold piecrust border up and over onion mixture, pleating as you go, leaving a 6-inch-wide opening. Combine egg and 2 tablespoons water; brush over dough. Bake at 425° for 25 minutes or until golden. Cool 10 minutes. Serves 4 (serving size: 1 wedge).

CALORIES 402; FAT 18.9g (sat 6.7g, mono 6.8g, poly 3.7g); PROTEIN 7.6g; CARB 51.4g; FIBER 5g; CHOL 13mg; IRON 0.8mg; SODIUM 606mg; CALC 146mg

Ward Off Weepiness

One way to minimize the tears brought on by onion prep is to use a sharp knife. Dull knives crush the onion's cells, releasing more of the tear-inducing sulfuric compounds. Using a sharp knife minimizes the breakage and the need for safety goggles. You can also chill the onion in the fridge for 10 to 15 minutes to help reduce the noxious output.

Sweet Onion Casserole

Hands-on time: 20 min.
Total time: 65 min.

1	tablespoon canola oil
4	cups chopped sweet onion (about 1¾ pounds)
½	cup uncooked long-grain rice
⅔	cup 2% reduced-fat milk
2	ounces shredded Gruyère cheese (about ½ cup)
¼	teaspoon salt
¼	teaspoon freshly ground black pepper
⅛	teaspoon ground allspice

Cooking spray

1⅓	ounces grated fresh Parmesan cheese (about ⅓ cup)

1. Preheat oven to 325°.
2. Heat a large skillet over medium-high heat. Add oil to pan; swirl to coat. Add onion; sauté 5 minutes or until tender. Place onion in a large bowl.
3. Cook rice in a large pot of boiling water 5 minutes. Drain.
4. Stir rice and next 5 ingredients (through allspice) into onions. Spoon onion mixture into an 8-inch square glass or ceramic baking dish coated with cooking spray. Sprinkle evenly with Parmesan cheese. Cover and bake at 325° for 40 minutes. Uncover and bake an additional 5 minutes. Serves 8 (serving size: about ½ cup).

CALORIES 144; FAT 5.6g (sat 2.3g, mono 2.3g, poly 0.7g); PROTEIN 5.7g; CARB 17.9g; FIBER 1.6g; CHOL 12mg; IRON 0.8mg; SODIUM 160mg; CALC 152mg

Diner-Style Onion Rings

Hands-on time: 25 min. Total time: 25 min.

Not only are they light, but they're also gluten-free and irresistibly crunchy. And yes, these are fried, but using proper frying techniques yields foods with healthy fat levels. The two gluten-free flours reduce oil absorption while the rings cook, which means fewer calories and less fat. The addition of baking soda and carbonated club soda to the batter also discourages oil absorption by producing gas bubbles. Save this treat for your largest bulbing onion varieties, such as Texas Supersweet, Walla Walla, or Candy.

4	cups canola oil	1	medium onion, cut into ½-inch-thick slices and separated into rings (8 ounces)
4.4	ounces gluten-free all-purpose flour (about 1 cup)		
5	ounces white rice flour (about 1 cup)	¼	teaspoon salt
1	tablespoon chili powder	¼	teaspoon garlic powder
1	teaspoon baking soda	¼	teaspoon freshly ground black pepper
1¼	cups club soda, chilled	½	cup ketchup (optional)

1. Preheat oven to 200°.

2. Clip a candy thermometer onto the side of a 4-quart Dutch oven; add oil to pan. Heat oil to 385°.

3. While oil heats, weigh or lightly spoon flours into dry measuring cups; level with a knife. Combine flours, chili powder, and baking soda in a medium bowl. Gradually add club soda, stirring with a whisk until smooth.

4. Dip onion rings, 1 at a time, in batter, coating completely. Add to hot oil. (Do not crowd pan.) Fry 1 minute on each side or until golden, maintaining oil temperature at 375°. Drain onion rings on a paper towel–lined jelly-roll pan. Place pan in oven, and keep warm at 200° until ready to serve. Combine salt, garlic powder, and black pepper. Sprinkle onion rings evenly with salt mixture just before serving. Serve with ketchup, if desired. Serves 6 (serving size: about 5 onion rings).

Note: You'll have some of the batter left over, but don't decrease the amount you use. You need the full amount so the onion rings can be immersed in the batter and get fully coated.

CALORIES 234; FAT 19g (sat 1.4g, mono 11.9g, poly 5.3g); PROTEIN 1.7g; CARB 15.4g; FIBER 1.7g; CHOL 0mg; IRON 0.4mg; SODIUM 177mg; CALC 17mg

Drying Onions

If you grow a lot of onions, they need to be dried so they can be stored for later use. When the tops begin to yellow and fall over, lift them out of the soil by digging under them with a fork, being careful not to puncture the bulb. Shake off the soil and spread the bulbs out to dry. While drying, they are healing, letting go of their leaves and roots. After 7 to 10 days, trim off the dried roots and tops. Place them in a cool, dry place that doesn't reach freezing temperatures. If you have room, store them in the vegetable bin of your refrigerator.

PEAS

Whether snow, snap, or shelling types, sweet little peas are a treat. Peas, please!

SEASON: Spring through fall

CHOOSING: Green peas for shelling should have green, glossy pods that feel firm and full. Snow pea pods should be flat with almost no visible lumps of peas inside. And edible-podded sugar snap peas should be crisp and plump. All types should be refrigerated after you buy them because their sweetness declines quickly after picking.

STORING: If you can't cook and eat them immediately, store peas in a produce bag in the vegetable bin of your refrigerator. Wait to shell peas just before you cook them.

GROWING: Plant in the cool season of spring and fall in most of the country. In northern or high-altitude areas with cool summers, they can be picked all summer. Where winters are mild with only light frosts, gardeners enjoy peas all winter.

Peas grow on vines that need a trellis, even if it's a tepee made of bamboo and twine or a section of metal fencing. Even those labeled as "bush" peas will do better with a little support. Select a sunny site, and push seeds into well-prepared soil about 1 inch deep and 2 to 3 inches apart.

All types require about two months of growth from the time seeds are sown until the first peas are ready to be picked. That means planting about a month before the last spring frost so there will be time to enjoy a long harvest before the days start to get hot. For a fall planting, sow seeds in late summer.

The tall, vining varieties have the longest harvest, about six weeks. You can make a second planting a few weeks after the first to have a continuous supply.

Fresh Pea and Garlic Gazpacho

Hands-on time: 23 min.   Total time: 27 min.

Nothing denotes spring better than freshly shelled green peas. Sweet, crisp, and light years different from anything in the frozen food aisle, shelled English peas are a garden treasure to behold. If you can avoid eating them all on the spot in your garden, try this extremely fresh, bright, light gazpacho.

2½ cups shelled fresh English peas
2¼ cups ice water
1½ cups chopped peeled English cucumber
1 cup (½-inch) cubed French bread
2 tablespoons extra-virgin olive oil
1½ tablespoons sherry vinegar
2 garlic cloves
½ teaspoon kosher salt
½ teaspoon freshly ground black pepper
Fresh pea shoots
1 tablespoon small mint leaves
1½ teaspoons extra-virgin olive oil

1. Cook peas in boiling water 4 minutes. Drain and rinse with cold water until cool. Set aside ½ cup peas. Place remaining peas, 2¼ cups ice water, and next 5 ingredients (through garlic) in a blender; process until smooth. Stir in salt and pepper. Ladle 1 cup soup into each of 6 bowls. Garnish with reserved ½ cup peas, fresh pea shoots, mint leaves, and 1½ teaspoons oil. Serves 6.

CALORIES 124; FAT 6.3g (sat 0.9g, mono 4.5g, poly 0.6g); PROTEIN 4g; CARB 12.7g; FIBER 3.5g; CHOL 0mg; IRON 1.2mg; SODIUM 200mg; CALC 25mg

Lemony Snap Peas

Hands-on time: 17 min.   Total time: 17 min.

Sugar snap peas are a spring favorite and can be eaten whole, pod and all. Harvest when the pods are tender and the peas are still tiny. This recipe makes the most of the peas' natural sugars. Cook for just a blink in boiling water, and serve with this citrusy Dijon dressing.

8   cups water
12   ounces fresh sugar snap peas, trimmed
½   teaspoon grated lemon rind
2   tablespoons fresh lemon juice
1   tablespoon extra-virgin olive oil
1   teaspoon Dijon mustard
½   teaspoon sugar
¼   teaspoon kosher salt
¼   teaspoon freshly ground black pepper
1   shallot, minced

1. Bring 8 cups water to a boil in a large Dutch oven. Add peas; cook 30 seconds or until crisp-tender. Drain and plunge into ice water; drain. Slice half of peas diagonally.
2. Combine lemon rind and remaining ingredients in a medium bowl; stir with a whisk. Add peas; toss to coat. Serves 4 (serving size: about 1 cup).

CALORIES 73; FAT 3.6g (sat 0.5g, mono 2.5g, poly 0.4g); PROTEIN 2.5g; CARB 8.4g; FIBER 2.3g; CHOL 0mg; IRON 1.8mg; SODIUM 154mg; CALC 39mg

Sautéed Snow Peas and Peppers

Hands-on time: 12 min.   Total time: 12 min.

Only three ingredients enhance the fresh flavors of snow peas and red bell pepper.

2   teaspoons dark sesame oil, divided
2½   cups fresh snow peas, trimmed
1   cup thinly sliced red bell pepper
¼   teaspoon salt
⅛   teaspoon freshly ground black pepper

1. Heat a large skillet over medium-high heat. Add 1 teaspoon oil to pan; swirl to coat. Add snow peas and bell pepper to pan; sauté 4 minutes or until vegetables are crisp-tender, stirring occasionally. Remove pan from heat. Drizzle vegetable mixture with 1 teaspoon oil. Sprinkle with salt and black pepper, and toss well to combine. Serves 4 (serving size: about ¾ cup).

CALORIES 46; FAT 2.4g (sat 0.4g, mono 0.9g, poly 1g); PROTEIN 1.4g; CARB 4.8g; FIBER 1.6g; CHOL 0mg; IRON 1mg; SODIUM 150mg; CALC 19mg

Lemony Snap Peas

PEPPERS

Peppers offer a range of flavor—from delightfully sweet to fiery heat.

SEASON: Summer and fall are peak times for peppers.

CHOOSING: Peppers come in many sizes, shapes, and Scoville units—the measurement of how hot they are, from sweat to tears. Look for peppers that are wrinkle-free, glossy, and free of injuries.

STORING: Place peppers in a produce bag, and store in the vegetable bin of your refrigerator. They'll last about a week.

GROWING: Peppers are tender plants. Frost is deadly, and cold soil is crippling for them, so don't rush to plant early. Depending on the variety, they need 70 to 90 days from the time transplants are set into warm soil until peppers are harvested. If you start from seeds, you'll need to start them early indoors to get a jump on a long season.

The plants usually grow to about 18 to 24 inches during the summer. Those with small peppers can stand unassisted, but any of the large pepper plants need to be staked or grown in a tomato cage to prevent them from falling over. It's best to put those supports in place when you first plant.

Choose a sunny bed with well-prepared soil. Plants vary in size, so read the label and space them accordingly. Buy sturdy transplants with dark green leaves. After planting, water them with a dilute solution of liquid fertilizer. Feed again lightly when peppers begin to grow.

When harvesting, use clippers to avoid breaking a branch. You can pick peppers at any time; they're never too young. However, many peppers will change colors and improve in both nutrition and flavor as they mature, so if you're growing sweet bell peppers, harvest a few green ones, but leave some on the plant to turn yellow, orange, or red.

Grilled Stuffed Jalapeños

Hands-on time: 30 min. Total time: 40 min.

Now this is a hot way to eat a pepper. Not in terms of intense heat, mind you, but in terms of popularity. A lightened version of a very addictive appetizer, this recipe gets rave reviews. For the best heat, pick jalapeños when they begin to show vertical "woody" lines and begin to age. You can let a few fully ripen to red for a sweeter heat and fun presentation.

2   center-cut bacon slices
4   ounces cream cheese (about ½ cup), softened
4   ounces fat-free cream cheese (about ½ cup), softened
1   ounce shredded extra-sharp cheddar cheese (about ¼ cup)
¼   cup minced green onions
1   teaspoon fresh lime juice
¼   teaspoon kosher salt
1   small garlic clove, minced
14 jalapeño peppers, halved lengthwise and seeded
Cooking spray
2   tablespoons chopped fresh cilantro
2   tablespoons chopped seeded tomato

1. Preheat grill to medium-high heat.

2. Cook bacon in a skillet over medium heat until crisp. Remove bacon from pan; drain on paper towels. Crumble bacon. Combine crumbled bacon, cheeses, and next 4 ingredients (through garlic) in a bowl, stirring to combine. Divide cheese mixture evenly among pepper halves. Place filled peppers, cheese sides up, on grill rack coated with cooking spray. Cover and grill peppers 8 minutes or until bottoms of peppers are charred and cheese mixture is lightly browned. Place peppers on a serving platter. Sprinkle with cilantro and tomato. Serves 14 (serving size: 2 stuffed pepper halves).

Note: If making these for a party, you can stuff the peppers, cover, and chill. Then grill just before your guests arrive.

CALORIES 56; FAT 4.1g (sat 2.2g, mono 1.1g, poly 0.2g); PROTEIN 2.9g; CARB 2.1g; FIBER 0.5g; CHOL 13mg; IRON 0.2mg; SODIUM 157mg; CALC 55mg

Jerk Chicken and Stuffed Mini Bell Peppers

Hands-on time: 30 min. Total time: 40 min.

This recipe uses both hot and sweet garden peppers. Try those sweet little Yummy peppers (yes, that's the real name) for the tongue-taming creamy stuffing. After eating the serrano-spiked jerk chicken, you'll be glad you did.

Hot Pepper Overload

The *bad* thing about growing hot peppers is that one plant is so incredibly productive. The *good* thing about growing hot peppers is that one plant is so incredibly productive. You need just one or two to spice up a recipe. One solution for a plethora of peppers is to dry them in a dehydrator, string them, crush them with mortar and pestle, or powder them with a spice grinder—you'll have a year's supply of heat at your fingertips as crushed red pepper flakes or chili powder with your personal heat preference. Two tips: Use gloves and put the dehydrator in the garage, or else you'll mace yourself!

⅓ cup sliced green onions, divided
⅓ cup chopped shallots, divided
1 tablespoon brown sugar
3 tablespoons fresh lime juice, divided
2 tablespoons olive oil
½ teaspoon ground allspice
4 garlic cloves
1 large serrano chile, stemmed
8 bone-in chicken thighs, skinned
¼ teaspoon salt
Cooking spray
3 ounces ⅓-less-fat cream cheese (about ⅓ cup)
2 tablespoons chopped fresh cilantro
2 tablespoons light sour cream
8 mini bell peppers

1. Preheat grill to medium-high heat. After preheating, reduce heat on one side to low.

2. Place ¼ cup green onions, ¼ cup shallots, sugar, 2 tablespoons juice, oil, allspice, garlic, and serrano in a mini food processor; process until smooth. Combine half of onion mixture and chicken in a medium bowl; toss well. Sprinkle with salt.

3. Place chicken on grill rack coated with cooking spray over medium-high heat. Cover and grill 5 minutes on each side. Move chicken over low heat. Cover and grill 5 minutes on each side or until done. Brush chicken with remaining onion mixture.

4. While chicken cooks, combine remaining green onions, remaining shallots, 1 tablespoon juice, cheese, cilantro, and sour cream in a bowl. Halve bell peppers lengthwise; discard seeds. Divide cheese mixture evenly among pepper halves. Place peppers on grill rack coated with cooking spray over medium-high heat. Grill 7 minutes or until peppers are lightly charred. Serves 4 (serving size: 2 thighs and 4 pepper halves).

CALORIES 338; FAT 21.2g (sat 4.3g, mono 5.1g, poly 10.1g); PROTEIN 17.5g; CARB 22.6g; FIBER 4.9g; CHOL 72mg; IRON 2.6mg; SODIUM 535mg; CALC 197mg

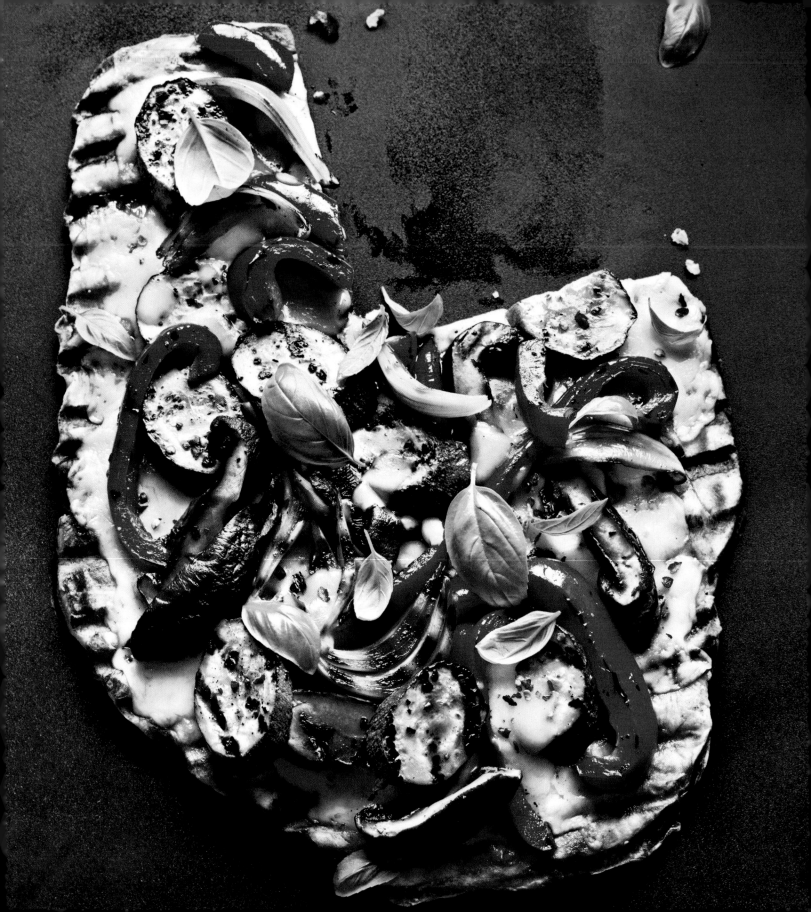

Grilled Vegetable and Fontina Pizza

Hands-on time: 32 min.   Total time: 40 min.

This grilled veggie pizza is a gorgeous medley of red pepper, zucchini, mushrooms, red onion, and sweet basil. Also consider orange, yellow, or purple sweet peppers such as Merlot, Golden Treasures, or Canary Bell. With refrigerated fresh pizza dough and a few minutes on the grill, dinner is on the table in minutes.

2   portobello mushroom caps
1   tablespoon chopped garlic
1   large red bell pepper, cut into ½-inch strips
1   medium zucchini, cut diagonally into ½-inch-thick slices
1   red onion, cut into ½-inch wedges (root end intact)
5   teaspoons extra-virgin olive oil
¼   teaspoon kosher salt
¼   teaspoon freshly ground black pepper
Cooking spray
8   ounces refrigerated fresh pizza dough
4   ounces shredded fontina cheese (about 1 cup)
¼   cup basil leaves
½   teaspoon crushed red pepper

1. Preheat grill to high heat.

2. Remove brown gills from undersides of mushrooms with a spoon; discard. Combine mushrooms, garlic, bell pepper, zucchini, onion, and oil in a bowl; toss to coat. Sprinkle with salt and pepper. Arrange vegetables on grill rack coated with cooking spray; grill 8 minutes or just until tender. Slice mushrooms.

3. Roll dough into a 12-inch oval on a lightly floured surface. Place dough on grill rack; grill 2 minutes on each side or until lightly browned.

4. Sprinkle cheese over dough, leaving a ½-inch border around edges. Arrange vegetable mixture over cheese. Grill pizza 3 minutes or until cheese melts. Sprinkle pizza with basil leaves and crushed red pepper; cut into 8 slices. Serves 4 (serving size: 2 slices).

CALORIES 344; FAT 16.1g (sat 6g, mono 6.5g, poly 2.2g); PROTEIN 14.2g; CARB 38g; FIBER 3.1g; CHOL 31mg; IRON 2.6mg; SODIUM 693mg; CALC 173mg

POTATOES

From dense, waxy varieties to fluffy, starchy versions—potatoes in all their forms are a crowd-pleaser that can be adapted to almost any cooking method.

SEASON: New potatoes are available in late spring and early summer. Mature potatoes make their appearance in late summer and fall.

CHOOSING: Look for firm potatoes that are not green or sprouting.

STORING: Place potatoes in paper or burlap bags to increase the humidity while allowing air to circulate. Store them in the coolest, darkest place in your home, such as a pantry or cabinet or in an unheated garage or basement. They'll last three to five weeks.

GROWING: To plant potatoes, you need potatoes—but not ones from the grocery store. Instead, purchase seed potatoes that are raised carefully to be disease-free. If the seed potato is large, cut it into 1¼-inch pieces that each contain an eye (the bud that causes an indentation in the surface). Let the cut pieces air-dry for a day or two before planting.

Potatoes can tolerate cold soil and frosts, so plant in a sunny spot about two weeks before the last expected frost or as soon as the soil can be worked. Prepare the soil with plenty of compost to make it loose and fertile. There are a few planting options: The trench method involves setting the seed pieces 12 inches apart in a 6-inch-deep furrow, and then covering with about 3 inches of soil. Continue to bring the soil over the developing potatoes as the plant grows, always leaving the top leaves visible.

The labor-saving surface method involves pressing the seed pieces about a foot apart into a level bed until they're almost buried, and then piling about 18 inches of leaves, straw, or other mulch on top on the bed. The mulch will settle and the potato foliage will find its way to the light. Harvesting the potatoes involves little more than pulling back the mulch and lifting the plant, potatoes attached.

You can also grow potatoes in a large container—think whiskey-barrel size. Set the seed potatoes on top of 6 inches of potting mix, and cover with a couple of inches of soil. As the potatoes grow, continue to add more potting mix and mulch until the pot is filled.

Harvesting potatoes is like digging for buried treasure. New potatoes are ready about two months after planting. For the final harvest, wait until the foliage is beginning to yellow. If you injure any potatoes with your digging fork, eat those first.

Chicken and White BBQ Potatoes

Hands-on time: 20 min.   Total time: 60 min.

Potatoes are known to be versatile, but did you know they could house your entire dinner? This comfort classic has all the trimmings of a warm and filling meal. Scale down by using Yukon gold potatoes, which tend to be smaller than larger russet (baking) potatoes.

4   (6-ounce) Yukon gold or baking
    potatoes
Cooking spray
2/3   cup canola mayonnaise
3   tablespoons white vinegar
1   tablespoon Dijon mustard
2   teaspoons freshly ground black
    pepper

1/2   teaspoon sugar
1/8   teaspoon salt
2   garlic cloves, minced
1 1/2   cups shredded skinless, boneless
    rotisserie chicken breast
3   tablespoons sweet pickle relish
1/4   cup sliced green onions

1. Preheat oven to 450°.
2. Pierce potatoes with a fork, and coat lightly with cooking spray. Bake at 450° for 50 minutes or until tender. Remove potatoes from oven, and cool slightly. Cut a lengthwise slit in each potato, cutting to but not through other side, and squeeze ends to loosen potato flesh.
3. Combine mayonnaise and next 6 ingredients (through garlic) in a medium bowl. Stir in chicken and relish. Divide chicken mixture evenly among potatoes. Top each potato with 1 tablespoon onions. Serves 4 (serving size: 1 stuffed potato).

CALORIES 489; FAT 30.8g (sat 3g, mono 16.6g, poly 8.2g); PROTEIN 14.6g; CARB 36.9g; FIBER 2.7g; CHOL 45mg; IRON 1.9mg; SODIUM 657mg; CALC 17mg

Potato and Vegetable Salad with Mustard Ranch

Hands-on time: 10 min.   Total time: 20 min.

You could use any waxy, thin-skinned potato for this salad, such as La Ratte or Russian Banana fingerlings, freshly dug red new potatoes, or even Yukon gold if you are buying from the produce aisle. The key is to highlight the colorful varieties available and the smaller, more special treats you can grow yourself or find in farmers' markets.

2	pounds multicolored fingerling potatoes, unpeeled and cut into bite-sized pieces
1½	teaspoons kosher salt, divided
¼	cup plain 2% reduced-fat Greek yogurt
¼	cup buttermilk
1	tablespoon Dijon mustard
1	tablespoon fresh lemon juice
¾	teaspoon freshly ground black pepper
½	teaspoon honey
1	garlic clove, minced
1	cup chopped red bell pepper (about 1 medium)
¾	cup chopped celery
½	cup finely chopped onion
½	cup chopped fresh flat-leaf parsley leaves
¼	cup chopped fresh chives
2	tablespoons chopped fresh dill

1. Place potato pieces and 1 teaspoon salt in a medium saucepan, and cover with water. Bring to a boil. Reduce heat, and simmer 20 minutes or until potatoes are tender but still hold their shape. Drain and rinse with cold water. Drain.
2. Combine ½ teaspoon salt, yogurt, and next 6 ingredients (through garlic) in a large bowl, stirring well with a whisk. Add potatoes, bell pepper, and remaining ingredients to yogurt mixture; toss gently to coat. Serves 8 (serving size: 1 cup).

CALORIES 107; FAT 0.7g (sat 0.3g, mono 0g, poly 0.2g); PROTEIN 3.7g; CARB 22.4g; FIBER 2.8g; CHOL 2mg; IRON 1.2mg; SODIUM 318mg; CALC 35mg

Garlic and Herb Oven Fries

Hands-on time: 18 min.   Total time: 43 min.

Some think the potato exists purely for French fries. If you're a fan of all things fried, try this oven-baked version that sizzles in garlicky butter. Russet or other starchy, larger potatoes are best for cutting into matchsticks and keeping good form. Also try the blue varieties Purple Majesty or All Blue, or the all-purpose Kennebec.

2   pounds baking potatoes, peeled
2   tablespoons canola oil
1½ tablespoons butter
1   garlic clove, minced
2   tablespoons chopped fresh parsley
½   teaspoon kosher salt
¼   teaspoon black pepper

1. Place a roasting pan in oven. Preheat oven to 450°.
2. Cut potatoes into ¼-inch matchsticks; toss with oil. Arrange in preheated pan; bake at 450° for 5 minutes. Turn oven to broil (do not remove pan from oven). Broil 20 minutes or until browned, turning once. Melt butter in a skillet. Add garlic; sauté 30 seconds. Add fries; cook 1 minute. Toss with parsley, salt, and pepper. Serves 6 (serving size: about 1½ cups).

CALORIES 209; FAT 7.7g (sat 2.2g, mono 3.7g, poly 1.5g); PROTEIN 3.1g; CARB 32.9g; FIBER 2.4g; CHOL 8mg; IRON 0.6mg; SODIUM 194mg; CALC 11mg

RADISHES

Rediscover this crisp, colorful root. In the garden,
the search for the first fat jewels is a treasure hunt.

SEASON: Available year-round in supermarkets, they're at their peak in spring.

CHOOSING: When purchasing, look for plump, firm roots, preferably with the leaves still attached. Wilted leaves are a sure sign of mealy radishes below.

STORING: When you bring radishes into the kitchen from the market or garden, chop off the greens—if they remain attached, they'll pull moisture from the crisp root. The greens have a mild, aromatic flavor and can be used raw or cooked. Store the radish roots in a produce bag in your crisper drawer for up to a week. If the radishes become spongy, crisp them by placing them in a bowl of ice water for up to an hour.

GROWING: Radishes are the ideal introduction-to-gardening crop. They have a short growing time, ideal for children whose attention spans may not last long enough for some vegetables to mature. The cool months of spring and fall are the ideal times to plant. In the warmest regions of the country, where frost is rare, radishes can be grown all winter, while in the coldest regions they can grow all summer. Young radishes and those that mature in cool weather have a mild flavor. Those harvested in the summer heat have a much sharper, almost biting taste.

Start radish prep as early as your soil can be worked, as much as a month before the last expected freeze. Because many radish varieties require only a month from seed to harvest, you can sow a few seeds every week for a continuous supply. In the fall, begin planting about a month before the first expected frost.

Because plants stay small, growing only 6 to 12 inches tall, they're a good option to plant between larger, slow-maturing vegetables. For example, spring broccoli transplants need about two months to mature. During the first month, you can raise a crop of radishes. By the time the broccoli grows tall enough to cast shade, the radishes are ready to be pulled and eaten.

Varieties of round, usually red radishes include Early Scarlet Globe, Plum Purple, Pink Beauty, German Giant, and the multicolored Easter Egg II. Long radishes include French Breakfast, White Icicle, and China Rose.

Like all root vegetables, radishes prefer loose, well-drained soil. Drag your trowel lightly to create a ½-inch-deep line for planting. Sow seeds about an inch apart, and then smooth the soil over the seeds. Allow 6 inches between rows. Water well and wait, but not for long. Seedlings will emerge in a few days. A helpful tip: Label your radish rows with the date you planted them to help you know when they're ready to harvest.

Hummus-Stuffed Pitas

Hands-on time: 15 min.   Total time: 15 min.

Radishes are easy to grow and fast to sow. Add a dotting of seeds to the garden or containers each week for a constant supply that you can slice for salads or stuff into sandwiches like this vegetarian pita. Serve it with another early sign of spring: steamed sugar snap peas.

1 teaspoon grated lemon rind
1 (8-ounce) container plain hummus
4 (6-inch) whole-wheat pitas, halved
4 green leaf lettuce leaves, halved

1¼ cups thinly sliced English cucumber
¾ cup thinly sliced radishes
½ cup crumbled feta cheese
⅓ cup thinly sliced red onion
Freshly ground black pepper

1. Combine rind and hummus. Divide hummus mixture evenly among pita halves (about 1½ tablespoons each). Divide lettuce, cucumber, radishes, cheese, and onion evenly among pita halves. Sprinkle with pepper. Serves 4 (serving size: 2 pita halves).

CALORIES 344; FAT 14.9g (sat 2.4g, mono 7.4g, poly 3.6g); PROTEIN 13.1g; CARB 47.1g; FIBER 7.7g; CHOL 13mg; IRON 3.9mg; SODIUM 758mg; CALC 141mg

Nectarine and Radish Salsa

Hands-on time: 12 min. Total time: 42 min.

Spicy-sweet and cooling with a citrus tang, this salsa is a refreshing no-cook condiment. Serve with grilled chicken, pork, or fish, or as a dip for toasted tortilla wedges.

2¼ cups (¼-inch) diced nectarines
1½ cups radishes, halved lengthwise
and thinly sliced
½ cup chopped cucumber
¼ cup finely chopped red onion
1 tablespoon fresh lime juice
2 teaspoons chopped fresh
cilantro
1½ teaspoons sugar
¼ teaspoon salt

1. Combine all ingredients in a medium bowl; toss well. Let salsa stand 30 minutes. Serves 12 (serving size: ⅓ cup).

CALORIES 18; FAT 0.1g (sat 0g, mono 0g, poly 0.1g); PROTEIN 0.5g; CARB 4.3g; FIBER 0.8g; CHOL 0mg; IRON 0.1mg; SODIUM 55mg; CALC 7mg

Granny Smith, Radish, and Radicchio Salad with Orange-Walnut Vinaigrette

Hands-on time: 17 min. Total time: 17 min.

Each of these has a bite—whether tart, peppery, or sharp—and blend together well. For consistent texture and great presentation, cut the radish, apple, and radicchio into julienne or matchstick pieces.

Don't Toss the Top!

The beauty of growing or finding Pink Beauty, Purple Plum, or Watermelon radishes goes beyond the bright Easter egg colors. Young greens pack in vitamin C and are great wilted, sautéed, fresh in salads, or stirred into creamy soups. Try replacing half of the raddicchio in this salad with sliced radish greens.

3 tablespoons fresh orange juice
3 tablespoons walnut oil
1 tablespoon red wine vinegar
2 teaspoons Dijon mustard
1/4 teaspoon freshly ground black pepper
1/8 teaspoon salt
4 cups thinly sliced radicchio (1 [12-ounce] head)
1 cup thinly sliced radishes (about 6)
2 Granny Smith apples, quartered and cut into julienne strips (about 1 pound)
1/4 cup coarsely chopped walnuts, toasted

1. Combine first 6 ingredients in a large bowl, stirring with a whisk. Add radicchio, radishes, and apples to bowl; toss gently to coat. Place about 3/4 cup salad on each of 8 plates; sprinkle each serving with 1 1/2 teaspoons nuts. Serves 8.

CALORIES 101; FAT 7.7g (sat 0.7g, mono 5g, poly 1.5g); PROTEIN 1.3g; CARB 8.2g; FIBER 1.6g; CHOL 0mg; IRON 0.5mg; SODIUM 82mg; CALC 16mg

SPINACH

The mild flavor of spinach makes it wonderfully adaptable to a range of uses in the kitchen (whether raw or cooked).

SEASON: Although available year-round, spring and fall are the peak seasons.

CHOOSING: Select leaves that are green and smell fresh, with no water-soaked, wilted, or yellowed patches.

STORING: Store spinach in a produce bag in the refrigerator for three to seven days.

GROWING: Spinach is a relatively quick crop, needing only five to six weeks from the time seeds are sown until harvest. Select a sunny bed and prepare the soil by working in plenty of compost.

The low-growing spinach lends itself to planting in a bed. (A 2- to 3-foot-wide row that can be worked from one side or the other is ideal.) Level the dirt with a rake, and scatter seeds thinly across the bed. Then rake again to cover the seeds. Water to settle seeds and soil into place. Seedlings will begin to appear in about a week. Thin as needed, and be sure to toss the leaves into your next salad.

Plant spinach seeds in the spring about a month before the last frost. For a fall garden, sow seeds one to two months before the first expected frost. The fall spinach will stop growing once the weather gets cold, but with a little protection from mulch, it will live and provide fresh greens in mild winters and the next spring.

Harvest spinach by pinching off the outer leaves, allowing the plant to remain in the garden to grow. Keeping a layer of mulch around plants will help keep soil from splashing onto the leaves when it rains.

Spinach and Parmesan Soufflés

Hands-on time: 24 min. Total time: 57 min.

Spinach, eggs, and cheese make a perfect brunch soufflé. As it's a key ingredient, Italian Parmigiano-Reggiano cheese is worth seeking out. It has a superior nutty flavor you won't find in the domestic alternatives.

Cooking spray
1½ tablespoons dry breadcrumbs
1½ cups fresh baby spinach
⅔ cup fat-free milk
2 tablespoons all-purpose flour
⅛ teaspoon salt
⅛ teaspoon ground nutmeg

⅛ teaspoon freshly ground black pepper
2 ounces grated fresh Parmigiano-Reggiano cheese (about ½ cup)
2 large egg yolks
4 large egg whites
¼ teaspoon cream of tartar

1. Place a baking sheet in oven. Preheat oven to 425°.

2. Coat 4 (6-ounce) ramekins with cooking spray, and sprinkle evenly with breadcrumbs, tilting and turning dishes to coat sides completely.

3. Heat a large skillet over medium-high heat. Coat pan with cooking spray. Add spinach; cook 2 minutes or until spinach wilts, tossing constantly. Place spinach in a colander; let stand 5 minutes. Squeeze excess liquid from spinach. Coarsely chop.

4. Combine milk and next 4 ingredients (through black pepper) in a small saucepan over medium-high heat, stirring with a whisk until smooth. Cook 2 minutes or until mixture is thick and bubbly, stirring constantly. Spoon mixture into a large bowl, and let stand 10 minutes. Stir in spinach, cheese, and egg yolks.

5. Combine egg whites and cream of tartar in a large bowl, and let stand at room temperature 15 minutes. Beat with a mixer at high speed until medium peaks form (do not overbeat). Gently stir one-fourth of egg whites into spinach mixture, and gently fold in remaining egg whites. Gently spoon mixture into prepared dishes. Sharply tap dishes 2 or 3 times on counter to level. Place dishes on preheated baking sheet; return baking sheet to 425° oven. Immediately reduce oven temperature to 350°; bake soufflés at 350° for 21 minutes or until puffy and golden brown. Serve immediately. Serves 4 (serving size: 1 soufflé).

CALORIES 163; FAT 6g (sat 2.8g, mono 1.9g, poly 0.6g); PROTEIN 13.2g; CARB 14.6g; FIBER 1.4g; CHOL 115mg; IRON 1.7mg; SODIUM 405mg; CALC 218mg

Fennel-Spinach Salad
with Shrimp

Creamed Spinach and Mushrooms

Hands-on time: 19 min.   Total time: 19 min.

4	teaspoons canola oil, divided	1	tablespoon all-purpose flour
8	ounces sliced cremini mushrooms	³/₈	teaspoon salt
2¹/₂	cups fresh baby spinach	¹/₄	teaspoon black pepper
¹/₃	cup finely chopped shallots		Dash of nutmeg
2	teaspoons minced fresh garlic	2¹/₂	ounces ¹/₃-less-fat cream
³/₄	cup fat-free milk		cheese (about ¹/₃ cup)

1. Heat a skillet over medium-high heat. Add 1¹/₂ teaspoons oil; swirl to coat. Add mushrooms; cook 6 minutes or until liquid evaporates. Remove from pan. Add 1¹/₂ teaspoons oil; swirl to coat. Add spinach; cook 1 minute or until wilted. Remove from heat.
2. Heat a Dutch oven over medium heat. Add 1 teaspoon oil to pan; swirl to coat. Add shallots and garlic; cook 1 minute, stirring constantly. Combine milk and flour in a bowl, stirring with a whisk. Add milk mixture, salt, pepper, and nutmeg to pan; bring to a boil, stirring constantly. Cook 3 minutes or until thick, stirring constantly. Add cheese; stir until cheese melts and mixture is smooth. Add mushrooms and spinach to milk mixture; toss gently to coat. Serves 6 (serving size: ¹/₂ cup).

CALORIES 102; FAT 6.1g (sat 1.8g, mono 2.7g, poly 1.1g); PROTEIN 4.8g; CARB 8.1g; FIBER 1.4g; CHOL 9mg; IRON 1.7mg; SODIUM 241mg; CALC 111mg

Creamed spinach is a quintessential, but fat-packed steak house side. Try this lightened classic with cremini mushrooms and nutmeg. Since the spinach is lightly wilted and tossed with the sauce, this recipe would showcase colorful varieties such as Bordeaux or Cardinal with deep red stems.

Fennel-Spinach Salad with Shrimp

Hands-on time: 18 min.   Total time: 18 min.

3	center-cut bacon slices	3	tablespoons extra-virgin olive oil
1	pound jumbo shrimp, peeled and deveined	2	tablespoons finely chopped shallots
2¹/₄	cups fresh baby spinach	1	tablespoon balsamic vinegar
2	cups thinly sliced fennel bulb	1	teaspoon Dijon mustard
1	cup grape tomatoes, halved	¹/₄	teaspoon salt
¹/₂	cup thinly sliced red onion	¹/₄	teaspoon black pepper

1. Cook bacon in a skillet over medium heat until crisp. Remove bacon from pan, reserving drippings; crumble. Add shrimp to pan; cook 2 minutes, turning once.
2. Combine bacon, spinach, fennel, tomatoes, and onion in a bowl. Combine oil and remaining ingredients in a small bowl, stirring with a whisk. Add shrimp and balsamic mixture to spinach mixture; toss well. Serves 4 (serving size: about 3¹/₂ cups).

CALORIES 274; FAT 13.5g (sat 2.2g, mono 7.7g, poly 19g); PROTEIN 27.5g; CARB 11.2g; FIBER 3.5g; CHOL 176mg; IRON 5mg; SODIUM 487mg; CALC 156mg

Quick, fresh, light—the perfect trifecta for a weeknight meal. Thin slices of fennel with fresh spinach leaves are nice bites that contrast with bacon and bacon-sautéed shrimp. It's fast and looks fancy.

SUMMER SQUASH

These colorful squash are easy to grow, with the promise of a bumper crop.

SEASON: Summer

CHOOSING: Look for smooth, blemish-free squashes. A small, tender squash is preferable to an oversized, seedy one.

STORING: Place squash in a produce bag in the vegetable bin of the refrigerator for up to a week.

GROWING: The basic summer squashes are yellow (crookneck or straightneck), zucchini (green or yellow, long or round), and pattypan (scallop). The plants are similar, growing like a large shrub with fuzzy leaves that make your arms itch.

Squash needs a sunny spot and is grown from seeds sown in hills—a small mound made by digging a hole and filling it full of good compost mixed with the existing soil. Plant about five seeds in the resulting 1-foot-wide, slightly raised bed. Space the hills about 3 to 5 feet apart, depending on the size of the plants you're growing.

Immediately after the danger of frost has passed, push seeds about an inch deep into each hill, water, and wait about a week. If needed, thin each hill to contain only two plants, one on each side of the hill.

If your plant is covered in blooms but you see no squash, never fear. The first blooms are male; the female flowers (those with tiny fruits at the base of the bloom) will begin appearing shortly thereafter. Harvest these edible male squash blossoms early in the morning, when they are fully open, for a homegrown delicacy stuffed and sautéed—just leave enough male and female blooms to create future fruits.

If summer squashes are left on the plant, they grow quite large, developing a hard rind and big seeds. However, these big guys lack the culinary appeal of smaller, tender squashes; remove them from the plant, and place them on the compost pile. Plant again about a month after the first sowing if you have room for a second crop.

Summer Squash, Bacon, and Mozzarella Quiche

Hands-on time: 25 min. Total time: 2 hr. 40 min.

When you are looking for ways to use up all those squash that seem to appear overnight, this will set you back at least 4 cups. Great for dinner or brunch, this quiche also introduces a crust that you can use for other homemade pies.

6.75 ounces all-purpose flour (about 1½ cups)
½ teaspoon salt
3 tablespoons chilled unsalted butter, cut into small pieces
2 tablespoons vegetable shortening, cut into small pieces
¼ cup ice water
Cooking spray
1 tablespoon extra-virgin olive oil
2 cups (⅛-inch-thick) slices yellow squash
2 cups (⅛-inch-thick) slices zucchini
¼ cup chopped shallots
1 tablespoon chopped fresh thyme
1 cup 2% reduced-fat milk
¾ teaspoon salt
¼ teaspoon black pepper
4 center-cut bacon slices, cooked and crumbled
3 large egg whites
3 large eggs
3 ounces shredded part-skim mozzarella cheese (about ¾ cup)

1. Weigh or lightly spoon flour into dry measuring cups; level with a knife. Place flour and ½ teaspoon salt in a food processor; pulse 2 times or until combined. Add butter and shortening; pulse 4 times or until mixture resembles coarse meal. With food processor on, add ¼ cup ice water through food chute, processing just until mixture is combined (do not form a ball). Press mixture into a 4-inch circle on plastic wrap, and cover. Refrigerate 1 hour.

2. Preheat oven to 400°.

3. Slightly overlap 2 sheets of plastic wrap on a slightly damp, flat surface. Unwrap and place dough on plastic wrap. Cover dough with 2 additional sheets of overlapping plastic wrap. Roll dough, still covered, into a 12-inch circle. Freeze dough 5 minutes or until plastic wrap can be easily removed. Remove top sheets of plastic wrap, and fit dough, plastic wrap side up, into a 9½-inch deep-dish pie plate coated with cooking spray. Remove remaining plastic wrap. Fold edges under; flute. Pierce bottom and sides of dough with fork. Bake at 400° for 15 minutes. Cool on a wire rack.

4. Reduce oven temperature to 350°.

5. Heat a nonstick skillet over medium-high heat. Add oil to pan; swirl to coat. Add squash, zucchini, shallots, and thyme; sauté 5 minutes or until tender. Cool slightly.

6. Combine milk and next 5 ingredients in a bowl. Arrange squash mixture evenly over crust; sprinkle with cheese. Pour egg mixture over cheese. Bake at 350° for 45 minutes or until filling is set. Cool 15 minutes on a wire rack. Serves 8.

CALORIES 265; FAT 14.1g (sat 6.3g, mono 4.3g, poly 1.5g); PROTEIN 11.2g; CARB 22.4g; FIBER 1.2g; CHOL 90mg; IRON 1.7mg; SODIUM 556mg; CALC 134mg

Summer Squash Croquettes

Hands-on time: 32 min.   Total time: 3 hr. 47 min.

A healthier version of a family dinner classic, these pan-fried croquettes will get the kids to eat squash. Make sure to drain the steamed squash well for cohesive patties.

4²/₃	cups coarsely chopped yellow squash (about 1¼ pounds)
½	cup chopped green onions
1	cup crushed saltine crackers (about 30 crackers)
½	teaspoon sugar
⅛	teaspoon salt
2	large eggs
¼	cup yellow cornmeal

Cooking spray
1   tablespoon canola oil, divided
Sliced green onions (optional)

1. Steam squash and ½ cup onions, covered, 15 minutes or until tender. Drain well. Mash mixture with a fork. Stir in crackers and next 3 ingredients (through eggs). Cover and chill 3 hours; drain well in a fine sieve.

2. Place cornmeal in a shallow dish. Divide squash mixture into 12 equal portions, shaping each portion into a ½-inch-thick patty. Dredge patties in cornmeal. Lightly coat each patty with cooking spray.

3. Heat a large nonstick skillet over medium-high heat. Add 1 teaspoon canola oil to pan; swirl to coat. Place 4 patties in pan; cook 1½ minutes on each side or until golden. Remove patties from pan. Repeat procedure 2 times with 2 teaspoons oil and 8 patties. Garnish with sliced green onions, if desired. Serve immediately. Serves 6 (serving size: 2 patties).

CALORIES 151; FAT 6.3g (sat 1g, mono 3.1g, poly 1.4g); PROTEIN 6.6g; CARB 18.6g; FIBER 2.1g; CHOL 71mg; IRON 2.2mg; SODIUM 245mg; CALC 45mg

Chocolate Chip Zucchini Bread

Hands-on time: 16 min.   Total time: 1 hr. 46 min.

If you celebrate national "Sneak Some Zucchini Onto Your Neighbors' Porch Day," at least leave them some in loaves of chocolate! This is a moist, decadent version that is also great for the freezer.

¾	cup sugar
3	tablespoons canola oil
2	large eggs
1	cup applesauce
9	ounces all-purpose flour (about 2 cups)
2	tablespoons unsweetened cocoa
1¼	teaspoons baking soda
1	teaspoon ground cinnamon
¼	teaspoon salt
1½	cups finely shredded zucchini (about 1 medium)
½	cup semisweet chocolate chips
	Cooking spray

1. Preheat oven to 350°.

2. Place first 3 ingredients in a large bowl; beat with a mixer at low speed until well blended. Stir in applesauce.

3. Weigh or lightly spoon flour into dry measuring cups; level with a knife. Combine flour and next 4 ingredients (through salt), stirring well with a whisk. Add flour mixture to sugar mixture, beating just until moist. Stir in zucchini and chocolate chips. Spoon batter into a 9 x 5-inch loaf pan coated with cooking spray. Bake at 350° for 1 hour or until a wooden pick inserted in center comes out almost clean. Cool in pan 10 minutes on a wire rack, and remove from pan. Cool completely on wire rack. Serves 16 (serving size: 1 slice).

CALORIES 161; FAT 5.1g (sat 1.6g, mono 1.4g, poly 1.7g); PROTEIN 2.9g; CARB 27.3g; FIBER 1.4g; CHOL 27mg; IRON 1.2mg; SODIUM 145mg; CALC 12mg

Get Pickled

When you're weary of sautéing it, stuffing it, baking it into bread, and unloading it on neighbors, make zucchini pickles. They're every bit as delicious as their cucumber counterparts. Follow your favorite recipe, or give this sweet-spicy version a go: Combine 4 cups (⅛-inch-thick) slices zucchini, 1 cup slivered sweet onion, and 3 thinly sliced garlic cloves in a glass bowl. Bring 1 cup white vinegar, ½ cup sugar, ¾ teaspoon crushed red pepper, 1 teaspoon mustard seeds, and ¾ teaspoon kosher salt to a boil; pour over zucchini mixture. Cover and chill 24 hours. Serves 16.

CALORIES 9; FAT 0.1 (sat 0g); SODIUM 32mg

SWEET POTATOES

This tuber combines sweet, earthy undertones with a wealth of nutrients.

SEASON: Although sweet potatoes store well and are available most of the year, fall is when the fresh crop comes in.

CHOOSING: Select sweet potatoes that are firm and free of injuries.

STORING: The ideal temperature for storing sweet potatoes is in the 50s—warmer than the refrigerator and cooler than room temperature. An unheated garage or basement or a cool, dark cabinet or pantry is ideal. If stored properly, they'll last three to six months. Otherwise, only buy as many as you can eat in a week or two.

GROWING: Sweet potatoes love hot weather and despise the cold, so wait to plant them until after the soil has warmed in spring, about three weeks after the last frost. They need 100 to 120 days to grow, depending on the variety, so get them started as early as possible.

Opt for varieties from disease-free sources. This may require you to order plants, known as slips, by mail. Create a raised, compost-enriched bed that is about a foot tall, 2 to 3 feet wide, and as long as you like in a sunny spot. Space plants about a foot apart, staggering them in the bed. Keep the soil moist until the new plants begin growing. Then water anytime the plants may be under stress from too little rain. Be sure to note the date you planted and how many days your plants need to mature.

Once the recommended number of days has passed, dig up a potato. If it's about the size you want, go ahead and harvest the rest. Leaving them in the ground longer will result in larger sweet potatoes, but they can grow so large that they are unusable. If temperatures below 40° are forecast before your sweet potatoes are scheduled to be harvested, go ahead and dig them up; cold weather can ruin the roots.

Because sweet potatoes aren't very sweet or moist when first harvested, you'll need to cure them for about eight weeks. This period of warmth and humidity helps heal any cuts and triggers the development of the sugar-creating enzymes that give these veggies their distinct flavor. Store them at 70° to 85°—the ideal location in your home may be near the water heater or on top of the refrigerator or clothes dryer—for 5 to 10 days. Then store them in the 50° range for six to eight weeks, which helps the sugars develop further.

Sweet Potato Chile Mac

Hands-on time: 22 min.   Total time: 1 hr. 32 min.

Sweet with heat! The natural sweetness of the potatoes pairs well with a bit of spice from chipotle peppers and Mexican chorizo. There's a fair amount of heat in the recipe, so if you prefer milder food, use less chipotle. A dash of green onions and cilantro tops off this fresh take on mac and cheese. Serve with a green salad to offset what seems deliciously gluttonous.

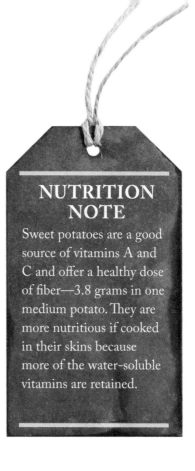

NUTRITION NOTE

Sweet potatoes are a good source of vitamins A and C and offer a healthy dose of fiber—3.8 grams in one medium potato. They are more nutritious if cooked in their skins because more of the water-soluble vitamins are retained.

3   medium-sized sweet potatoes (about 2 pounds)
1   cup fat-free milk
1½ to 2 tablespoons chopped chipotle chile, canned in adobo sauce
⅜   teaspoon kosher salt
¼   teaspoon freshly ground black pepper
3   ounces Monterey Jack cheese, shredded (about ¾ cup)
8   ounces uncooked whole-wheat penne or macaroni pasta
1   tablespoon olive oil
6   ounces fresh Mexican chorizo, casings removed
¼   cup chopped green onions
2   tablespoons chopped fresh cilantro

1. Preheat oven to 425°.
2. Pierce potatoes several times with a fork; place on a foil-lined baking sheet. Bake at 425° for 1 hour or until tender. Cool slightly; peel and mash in a large bowl. Stir in milk and next 4 ingredients (through cheese).
3. Cook pasta according to package directions, omitting salt and fat; drain. Add pasta to sweet potato mixture; set aside.
4. Preheat broiler.
5. Heat a large ovenproof skillet over medium heat. Add oil to pan; swirl to coat. Add chorizo to pan; cook 4 minutes or until browned, stirring to crumble. Place chorizo in a small bowl. Wipe pan clean. Spoon sweet potato mixture into pan; sprinkle evenly with chorizo. Broil 2 minutes or until lightly browned and crisp. Sprinkle with onions and cilantro. Serves 6 (serving size: about 1 cup).

CALORIES 456; FAT 15.5g (sat 6.2g, mono 6.9g, poly 1.4g); PROTEIN 18.6g; CARB 63.2g; FIBER 8.8g; CHOL 32mg; IRON 3.1mg; SODIUM 589mg; CALC 235mg

Roasted Sweet Potato Salad with Cranberry-Chipotle Dressing

Hands-on time: 25 min. Total time: 60 min.

A clear favorite in taste-testing, this salad is a spicy-sweet-savory mix of bold flavors. Be sure to let the cranberries cook until they start to pop; the juice helps to thicken the dressing. Don't skip the pepitas! Use your own roasted, salted pumpkinseeds when in season for a crunchy bite.

2½	pounds sweet potatoes, peeled and cut into 2-inch pieces	¼	cup water
3	tablespoons olive oil, divided	2	teaspoons honey
¾	teaspoon kosher salt	1	(7-ounce) can chipotle chiles in adobo sauce
½	teaspoon freshly ground black pepper	½	cup pepitas (pumpkinseeds)
¾	cup fresh or frozen cranberries	¾	cup chopped green onions
		¼	cup fresh cilantro leaves

1. Preheat oven to 450°.

2. Place sweet potatoes on a large jelly-roll pan. Drizzle with 2 tablespoons oil, and sprinkle with salt and pepper; toss to coat. Bake at 450° for 30 minutes or until tender, turning after 15 minutes.

3. Place 1 tablespoon oil, cranberries, ¼ cup water, and honey in a saucepan. Remove 1 or 2 chiles from can; finely chop to equal 1 tablespoon. Add chopped chiles and 1 teaspoon adobo sauce to pan (reserve remaining chiles and sauce for another use). Place pan over medium-low heat; bring to a boil. Cover, reduce heat, and cook 10 minutes or until cranberries pop, stirring occasionally. Remove from heat. Mash with a potato masher or fork until chunky.

4. Place pepitas in a medium skillet; cook over medium heat 4 minutes or until lightly browned, shaking pan frequently.

5. Combine potatoes, pepitas, onions, and cilantro in a bowl. Add cranberry mixture to bowl; toss gently to coat. Serves 8 (serving size: ¾ cup).

CALORIES 189; FAT 8.4g (sat 1.3g, mono 5.5g, poly 0.9g); PROTEIN 3.7g; CARB 25.5g; FIBER 4.5g; CHOL 0mg; IRON 1.3mg; SODIUM 335mg; CALC 40mg

Butter-Pecan Mashed Sweet Potatoes

Hands-on time: 10 min. Total time: 20 min.

Growing your own sweet potatoes is easy. And the reward is tenfold—in pounds and fun—as uncovering these in early fall is better than hunting Easter eggs. Mashing them with browned butter and topping with crunchy pecans makes a simple holiday staple. For a kid-friendly showstopper, try one of the purple varieties (you may need a little more liquid, as they tend to be starchier).

4   sweet potatoes (about 2 pounds)
1½ tablespoons butter
2   tablespoons fat-free milk
¼   teaspoon salt
¼   cup chopped pecans, toasted

1. Pierce each potato with a fork 3 to 4 times on each side. Wrap each potato in a damp paper towel. Microwave at HIGH 8 minutes, turning after 4 minutes. Cool slightly. Cut potatoes in half; scoop pulp into a bowl. Mash pulp.

2. Heat butter in a small saucepan over medium heat; cook 3 minutes or until browned. Stir butter, milk, and salt into potato pulp. Top with pecans. Serves 4 (serving size: ½ cup).

CALORIES 262; FAT 9.2g (sat 3.2g, mono 3.9g, poly 1.6g); PROTEIN 4.4g; CARB 41.5g; FIBER 7.6g; CHOL 12mg; IRON 1.4mg; SODIUM 304mg; CALC 51mg

TOMATOES

Tomatoes are the poster child for the pick-fresh movement and are the epitome of summer. Growing your own opens the door to hundreds of varieties and unrivaled flavor.

SEASON: May through September in the most temperate regions; June through August is peak season nationwide.

CHOOSING: Look for tomatoes with a bright, shiny skin and firm flesh that yields slightly to gentle pressure. The best flavor comes from vine-ripened fruits that were recently picked, so opt for those marked "locally grown."

STORING: Store them at room temperature but not in direct sunlight—the kitchen windowsill may not be the best spot. Never store tomatoes in the refrigerator. The cold destroys flavor and leaves tomatoes with a mealy texture. It's best to use tomatoes within four or five days of picking or purchasing.

GROWING: There are hundreds of varieties, with one to suit every gardener's space and taste. For containers, consider a variety that keeps a compact shape, such as Husky Cherry Red or Better Boy Bush. Cherry tomatoes are usually indeterminate, meaning they continually vine and grow on a trellis or balcony railing. Consider growing one of each of these three types: a "slicer," such as Cherokee Purple, for big, meaty fruits; a "paste" tomato, such as Roma, San Marzano, or Black Plum, for making sauces; and a cherry, such as Sun Gold, for eat-as-you-pick bites of sunshine.

Tomatoes need full sun and flourish with several gallons of water a week. When growing in containers, ensure the pots are at least 24 inches in diameter. Deep roots are the secret to keeping plants well watered and healthy. Contrary to how you normally plant, bury a tomato transplant up to its "neck," with only three or four leaves above the soil—roots will form along the stem beneath the ground to produce a stronger, sturdier plant.

Tomato Stack Salad with Corn and Avocado

Hands-on time: 30 min. Total time: 30 min.

Keep it simple with "summer on a plate." Prized tomatoes barely make it to the stovetop in the peak of summer, so stun guests with a rainbow stack of sliced tomatoes. This one is certainly a conversation starter and the best way to brag on your garden or farmers' market finds. For the prettiest presentation and a unique mix of flavors, choose purple, orange, green, red, or yellow tomatoes. Green Zebra, Black Krim, and Dr. Wyche's Yellow are favorites.

2	bacon slices, halved
¼	cup low-fat buttermilk
1	tablespoon finely chopped fresh chives
1	tablespoon finely chopped fresh basil
2	tablespoons canola mayonnaise
2	teaspoons cider vinegar
1	garlic clove, minced
½	teaspoon freshly ground black pepper, divided
2	ears shucked corn
	Cooking spray
2	large beefsteak tomatoes, cut into 8 (½-inch-thick) slices total
2	globe tomatoes, cut into 8 (½-inch-thick) slices total
⅛	teaspoon kosher salt
½	ripe peeled avocado, thinly sliced
4	teaspoons extra-virgin olive oil

1. Preheat grill to high heat.
2. Heat a large nonstick skillet over medium heat. Add bacon to pan; cook 8 minutes or until crisp, tossing occasionally to curl. Drain bacon on paper towels.
3. Combine buttermilk and next 5 ingredients (through garlic), stirring with a whisk. Stir in ¼ teaspoon pepper.
4. Coat corn with cooking spray. Place corn on grill rack; grill 8 minutes or until well marked, turning occasionally. Remove from grill; cool slightly. Cut corn kernels from cobs.
5. Sprinkle tomato slices evenly with salt. Alternate layers of tomato and avocado on each of 4 plates. Scatter corn evenly onto plates. Drizzle each tomato stack with about 1½ tablespoons dressing and 1 teaspoon oil. Sprinkle ¼ teaspoon pepper evenly over salads; top each salad with 1 bacon piece. Serves 4.

CALORIES 191; FAT 13g (sat 1.9g, mono 8g, poly 2.2g); PROTEIN 5.1g; CARB 16.1g; FIBER 4.5g; CHOL 5mg; IRON 0.9mg; SODIUM 228mg; CALC 40mg

NUTRITION NOTE

Tomatoes are a treasure trove of good-for-you plant compounds, including vitamins C and E, beta-carotene, and lycopene, a disease-fighting antioxidant that gives some varieties their brilliant red hue. High lycopene intake has been linked to lower risk for cardiovascular disease.

Spaghetti with Tomato Sauce

Hands-on time: 34 min. Total time: 55 min.

How to Peel Tomatoes Easily

Peeling tomatoes is an important first step when making tomato sauce—you want to avoid curled skins speckling your sauce. To avoid spending hours in the kitchen peeling the tomatoes by hand, follow these steps:

1. Bring a pot of water to a boil. While you're waiting for the water to boil, cut a 1-inch X in the bottom of each tomato. Place the tomatoes in the boiling water, and cook for 30 seconds to 1 minute.

2. Quickly remove each tomato with a slotted spoon, and drop it into a bowl of ice water for 1 minute to stop the cooking process.

3. Remove the tomatoes from the water, and peel back the flaps from the X; the skin will be easy to remove.

Don't doubt this sauce because it's so easy. The key is your sun-ripened garden tomato. San Marzano, Roma, or the smaller, dark-shouldered Black Plum would be ideal. Use the sauce on fresh, artisanal pastas for a truly special meal.

1½	pounds plum tomatoes, peeled and halved lengthwise
3	tablespoons extra-virgin olive oil, divided
2	garlic cloves, minced
2	tablespoons plus ½ teaspoon fine sea salt, divided
¼	teaspoon crushed red pepper
6	quarts water
12	ounces uncooked spaghetti
¼	cup basil leaves
6	tablespoons grated fresh Parmigiano-Reggiano cheese

1. Squeeze juice and seeds from tomato halves into a fine sieve over a bowl, reserving juices; discard seeds. Finely chop tomatoes.

2. Heat 2 tablespoons oil in a large nonstick skillet over medium heat. Add garlic to pan; cook 30 seconds or just until garlic begins to brown, stirring constantly. Add tomatoes, reserved juices, ½ teaspoon salt, and pepper. Increase heat to medium-high, and cook 15 minutes or until liquid almost evaporates, stirring occasionally.

3. Bring 6 quarts water and 2 tablespoons salt to a boil in an 8-quart pot. Add pasta to pot; stir. Cover; return to a boil. Uncover and cook 8 minutes or until pasta is almost al dente. Drain pasta in a colander over a bowl, reserving ½ cup cooking liquid.

4. Add hot pasta and reserved ½ cup cooking liquid to tomato mixture. Cook 5 minutes or until sauce is thick and pasta is al dente, tossing to combine. Remove from heat. Sprinkle with basil; toss. Place 1 cup pasta mixture on each of 6 plates. Drizzle each serving with ½ teaspoon of oil; sprinkle each with 1 tablespoon cheese. Serves 6.

CALORIES 313; FAT 9.5g (sat 2.1g, mono 5.6g, poly 1.5g); PROTEIN 10.3g; CARB 47g; FIBER 3.2g; CHOL 4mg; IRON 2.3mg; SODIUM 576mg; CALC 83mg

Arctic Char with Blistered Cherry Tomatoes

Hands-on time: 15 min.   Total time: 15 min.

Highlight two champions of summer: wild arctic char and pints of sunny sweet cherry tomatoes. Wild arctic char from the northern seas is available for only a few weeks in late summer, when the ice has melted enough for the local fishermen to reach them. It is a sought-after delicacy, and one that will cost you. Fresh is well worth the splurge when you can find it. Farmed char is a smart, sustainable option, or substitute fresh wild salmon. Sun Gold, Green Grape, Black Cherry, and Gold Nugget tomatoes are perfect choices to grow for this recipe.

3   tablespoons extra-virgin olive oil, divided
4   (6-ounce) arctic char fillets
¾   teaspoon coarse salt, divided
½   teaspoon black pepper, divided
4   garlic cloves, halved
3   pints multicolored cherry tomatoes
¼   cup thinly sliced fresh basil
2   shallots, thinly sliced

1. Preheat oven to 400°.

2. Heat a large ovenproof skillet over high heat. Add 1 tablespoon oil to pan; swirl to coat. Sprinkle fillets with ½ teaspoon salt and ¼ teaspoon pepper. Add fillets, flesh sides down, to pan, and sauté 2 minutes. Place pan in oven; bake at 400° for 3 minutes or until desired degree of doneness.

3. Heat a large cast-iron skillet over medium heat. Add 2 tablespoons oil to pan; swirl to coat. Add garlic, and cook 2 minutes or until lightly browned, stirring occasionally. Increase heat to medium-high. Add tomatoes to pan; sauté 2 minutes or until skins blister, stirring frequently. Remove pan from heat. Sprinkle tomato mixture with ¼ teaspoon salt, ¼ teaspoon pepper, basil, and shallots; toss to combine. Serve with fish. Serves 4 (serving size: 1 fillet and about ¾ cup tomato mixture).

CALORIES 380; FAT 20.4g (sat 3.8g, mono 11.7g, poly 3.6g); PROTEIN 31.4g; CARB 20g; FIBER 2.9g; CHOL 65mg; IRON 2mg; SODIUM 514mg; CALC 49mg

WINTER SQUASH

Butternut squash, acorn squash, spaghetti squash, and pumpkins rarely have a pristine appearance. But as they cook, they become sweet and rich on the palate, while holding a gorgeous autumn hue.

SEASON: Summer and fall are harvest times for winter squash, but they store so well that they're available almost year-round.

CHOOSING: Winter squash should have a hard rind and feel heavy. The stem and rind should be undamaged.

STORING: The ideal storage place would be one that is not as cold as a refrigerator, but not as warm as a heated house. A cool pantry or cabinet or an unheated garage or basement that stays in the 50s is ideal.

GROWING: Although you grow them at the same time as summer squash, winter squash is named because of its harder skin that makes it capable of long winter storage. The vigorous vines do best planted in full sun on hills—small mounds in the garden where a hole has been dug and then backfilled with a mixture of compost and the existing soil. Space the hills about 8 feet apart; the vines need room to ramble.

After all danger of frost has passed in spring, push about five seeds into each hill, water well, and after a week or two, thin the seedlings to two plants. Since the vines will cover a lot of ground, cover the bed with mulch to keep down weeds while protecting the developing fruits from rot. It takes about 80 to 100 days for them to be ready for harvest. You'll know they're ready when the rind is so hard that you can't puncture it with your thumbnail. Depending on the length of your growing season, you may want to eat the first batch of squash and plant a second round for storing over the winter.

Roasted Butternut Squash Risotto with Sugared Walnuts

Hands-on time: 63 min.   Total time: 1 hr. 18 min.

½ cup coarsely chopped walnuts
1 tablespoon butter, melted
1 teaspoon brown sugar
⅛ teaspoon freshly ground black pepper
2 cups (½-inch) cubed peeled butternut squash
1 tablespoon olive oil
2 teaspoons minced fresh garlic
4 cups fat-free, lower-sodium chicken broth
½ cup water
1 ounce pancetta, finely chopped (about ¼ cup)

1 cup finely chopped onion
1¼ cups uncooked Arborio rice
½ cup chardonnay
2 tablespoons finely chopped fresh lemon thyme or 1½ tablespoons thyme plus ½ teaspoon grated lemon rind
¼ teaspoon salt
¼ teaspoon freshly ground black pepper
1 ounce shaved fresh Parmigiano-Reggiano cheese (about ¼ cup)

This is a hearty side that can work as a main entrée or as a vegetarian dish, if you omit the pancetta and substitute vegetable broth.

Seeds of Winter

Make sure to save the seeds to season with cumin, cayenne, or salt and roast for several minutes until they pop and crisp. These roasted seeds are great atop salads or eaten out of hand. Avoid putting them in your compost pile; these mature seeds may take root and thrive.

1. Preheat oven to 400°.
2. Arrange nuts in a single layer on a jelly-roll pan. Bake at 400° for 5 minutes or until toasted, stirring twice. Place nuts in a bowl. Drizzle butter over warm nuts; sprinkle with sugar and ⅛ teaspoon pepper. Toss well to coat.
3. Combine squash and 1 tablespoon oil, tossing to coat. Arrange squash in a single layer on jelly-roll pan. Bake at 400° for 15 minutes or until squash is just tender. Remove from pan; stir in garlic. Set aside.
4. Bring broth and ½ cup water to a simmer in a saucepan (do not boil). Keep warm over low heat.
5. Heat a large saucepan over medium heat. Add pancetta to saucepan; cook 5 minutes or until browned, stirring frequently. Add onion; cook 3 minutes or until tender, stirring occasionally. Add rice; cook 2 minutes, stirring constantly. Add wine; cook 1 minute or until liquid is nearly absorbed, stirring constantly. Add broth mixture, ½ cup at a time, stirring constantly until each portion of broth is absorbed before adding the next (about 20 minutes total). Stir in squash, thyme, ¼ teaspoon salt, and ¼ teaspoon pepper. Top with cheese and nuts. Serves 8 (serving size: about ⅔ cup risotto, 1½ teaspoons cheese, and 1 tablespoon nuts).

CALORIES 259; FAT 10.7g (sat 2.7g, mono 2.6g, poly 3.8g); PROTEIN 7.5g; CARB 35.5g; FIBER 3.9g; CHOL 9mg; IRON 1.3mg; SODIUM 397mg; CALC 95mg

Indian-Spiced Roasted Squash Soup

Hands-on time: 15 min.   Total time: 63 min.

Roast acorn and butternut squash to deepen their flavors and caramelize them into sweetness. Contrast that with the spices, top with yogurt and honey, and enjoy a rich, warm winter soup. Roast the seeds for added crunch.

1	cup chopped yellow onion	2	cups water
8	ounces chopped carrot	1	teaspoon Madras curry powder
4	garlic cloves, peeled	½	teaspoon garam masala
1	(1-pound) butternut squash, peeled and cut into ½-inch cubes	¼	teaspoon ground red pepper
1	(8-ounce) acorn squash, quartered	2	(14-ounce) cans fat-free, lower-sodium chicken broth
1	tablespoon olive oil	¼	teaspoon kosher salt
½	teaspoon black pepper	6	tablespoons Greek yogurt
		6	teaspoons honey

1. Preheat oven to 500°.

2. Arrange first 5 ingredients on a jelly-roll pan. Drizzle with oil; sprinkle with black pepper. Toss. Bake at 500° for 30 minutes or until vegetables are tender, turning once. Cool 10 minutes. Peel acorn squash; discard skin.

3. Place vegetable mixture, 2 cups water, curry powder, garam masala, and red pepper in a food processor; pulse to desired consistency. Scrape mixture into a large saucepan over medium heat. Stir in broth; bring to a boil. Cook 10 minutes, stirring occasionally; stir in salt. Combine yogurt and honey, stirring well. Serve with soup. Serves 6 (serving size: 1 cup soup and 4 teaspoons yogurt mixture).

CALORIES 143; FAT 3.1g (sat 0.7g, mono 1.8g, poly 0.4g); PROTEIN 4.8g; CARB 27g; FIBER 4.4g; CHOL 1mg; IRON 1.5mg; SODIUM 343mg; CALC 98mg

Spaghetti Squash with Tomato-Basil Sauce

Hands-on time: 18 min.   Total time: 1 hr. 20 min.

Pasta sauce from scratch and "pasta" from a squash? You bet! Bring the kids in to see the spaghetti strings emerge from baked squash. Add sausage or ground beef for a filling main entrée.

1 (3-pound) spaghetti squash	¼ teaspoon salt
Cooking spray	½ cup chopped fresh basil, divided
1 tablespoon olive oil	
2 garlic cloves, minced	6 tablespoons shredded fresh pecorino Romano cheese
3½ cups diced, peeled fresh tomatoes	

1. Preheat oven to 350°.

2. Cut squash in half lengthwise. Scoop out seeds; discard. Place squash halves, cut sides down, on a baking sheet coated with cooking spray. Bake at 350° for 1 hour or until tender.

3. While squash cooks, heat a medium saucepan over medium heat. Add oil to pan; swirl to coat. Add garlic; cook 3 minutes, stirring occasionally. Add tomatoes and salt; bring to a simmer. Cook 15 minutes or until thick. Remove from heat; stir in ⅓ cup basil.

4. Let squash stand at room temperature 10 minutes or until cool enough to handle. Scrape inside of squash with a fork to remove spaghetti-like strands to measure about 5 cups. Divide squash evenly among 6 plates, and top each serving with about ⅓ cup sauce and 1 tablespoon cheese. Top evenly with remaining basil. Serves 6.

CALORIES 120; FAT 4.8g (sat 1.8g, mono 1.7g, poly 0.7g); PROTEIN 4.1g; CARB 17g; FIBER 4g; CHOL 4mg; IRON 1.1mg; SODIUM 252mg; CALC 148mg

NUTRITION NOTE

These dependable vegetables deliver a good dose of potassium, beta-carotene, and other phytonutrients and antioxidants—compounds that help fortify cells against damage that can lead to disease.

HERBS

Whether used by the pinch or by the bunch, fresh herbs infuse any dish with unparalleled aromas and flavors.

BASIL

Basil is a fragrant culinary superstar that makes frequent appearances in sauces, sandwiches, soups, and salads.

SEASON: Spring through fall

CHOOSING: Basil is delicate and bruises easily, so look for stems that aren't wilted and don't have dark spots. The ideal would be basil stems that don't have a flower bud or have just a small one. Avoid those with long flower stalks and seeds.

STORING: For gardeners, the best way to keep basil fresh is to cut just what you need when you need it. If you are buying basil or bringing it inside from the garden to have on hand, store it by placing it in a vase of water on your kitchen counter—after giving the stem a fresh cut—for up to a week. Be sure to change the water every few days. If it's wilted, place a produce bag loosely over it until it revives. Do not cut or pinch leaves from the stems until you are ready to use them.

GROWING: Basil is easy to grow, and there are many types, such as sweet, lemon, and cinnamon basil, in varying sizes, shapes, and colors. Since basil can be killed by the slightest frost, plant seeds or transplants in spring after the soil has warmed—the same time you plant tomatoes—in full sun in a compost-enriched soil. Harvest all summer long. Containers are a great place to grow basil. Although the plant may look a little lonely at first, put only one plant in a 12- to 14-inch-wide container. Even the small-leaved types will fill the container by midsummer.

Little flowers begin to form at the tips of basil stems. These aren't edible and slow down the growth of the yummy leaves. Snip them off while they are small, or simply use your basil often.

Spicy Basil-Beef Salad

Hands-on time: 16 min.   Total time: 30 min.

Go for a variety of basil, such as Purple Ruffles, Red Rubin, cinnamon, Thai, or lemon, to fully appreciate this salad. Also, mix up the colors and flavors with a variety of sun-ripened heirloom tomatoes. If Genovese basil is all you can find at the market, it will work fine—but use this as motivation to grow many more varieties in your own herb garden.

1 tablespoon canola oil

12 ounces hanger steak, trimmed

½ teaspoon freshly ground black pepper

¼ teaspoon kosher salt

3 tablespoons lower-sodium soy sauce

2 tablespoons rice vinegar

2 tablespoons minced fresh lemongrass

1 tablespoon dark sesame oil

2 teaspoons fish sauce

2 teaspoons sambal oelek (ground fresh chile paste)

1½ cups loosely packed basil leaves

1 cup thinly sliced English cucumber

3 large ripe heirloom tomatoes, cut into wedges

2 medium shallots, thinly sliced

1. Preheat oven to 425°.

2. Heat a large ovenproof stainless-steel skillet over medium-high heat. Add canola oil to pan; swirl to coat. Sprinkle both sides of steak evenly with black pepper and salt. Add steak to pan; cook 5 minutes or until browned. Turn steak over. Bake at 425° for 8 minutes or until a thermometer inserted into thickest portion of steak registers 135° or until desired degree of doneness. Remove steak from pan; let stand 10 minutes. Slice across grain.

3. Combine soy sauce and next 5 ingredients (through sambal) in a small bowl, stirring well. Combine basil and remaining ingredients in a large bowl. Drizzle dressing over basil mixture; toss gently. Divide salad evenly among 4 plates; divide beef evenly among salads. Serves 4.

CALORIES 226; FAT 11.9g (sat 2.5g, mono 5.5g, poly 2.7g); PROTEIN 17g; CARB 14.6g; FIBER 2g; CHOL 22mg; IRON 1.2mg; SODIUM 585mg; CALC 49mg

Classic Pesto

Hands-on time: 9 min.   Total time: 9 min.

Beyond Basic Pesto

Classic pesto is made with sweet Genovese basil and is the very essence of summer when served on pasta topped with heirloom tomatoes. Venture outside the basics, though, and experiment with other leafy herbs such as mint, arugula, or parsley, and swap walnuts or pecans for pine nuts. You can also try substituting a tablespoon or two of mint for sweet basil when making pesto. It adds a clean, bright note that your guests won't be able to guess.

No garden-to-table cookbook—and no gardener—should be without a great pesto recipe. Enjoy it fresh all summer long, and then freeze large batches to store for use in the colder months. Thanks to the olive oil, pesto retains its bright color when frozen. Just drop a tablespoon of pesto into each section of an ice-cube tray, and freeze. Transfer the frozen cubes to a heavy-duty zip-top plastic bag.

2   tablespoons coarsely chopped walnuts or pine nuts
2   garlic cloves, peeled
3   tablespoons extra-virgin olive oil
4   cups basil leaves (about 4 ounces)
2   ounces grated fresh Parmesan cheese (about ½ cup)
¼   teaspoon salt

1. Drop nuts and garlic through food chute with food processor on; process until minced. Add oil; pulse 3 times. Add basil, cheese, and salt; process until finely minced, scraping sides of bowl once. Serves 12 (serving size: 1 tablespoon).

CALORIES 58; FAT 5.3g (sat 1.3g, mono 3g, poly 0.8g); PROTEIN 2.1g; CARB 0.9g; FIBER 0.6g; CHOL 3mg; IRON 0.5mg; SODIUM 125mg; CALC 72mg

Purple Basil Lemonade

Hands-on time: 8 min.
Total time: 8 min.

Basil is a delicious herb to muddle in beverages, as there are so many varieties with which to experiment. Purple basil creates a party-pleasing pink tone. If you don't have a mortar and pestle, process the basil, sugar, and about ¼ cup of the water in a food processor or blender.

4　cups water
½　cup fresh lemon juice
½　cup loosely packed purple basil
　　leaves (about ¼ ounce)
6　tablespoons sugar
4　cups ice
4　purple basil sprigs

1. Combine 4 cups water and juice in a large bowl. Place ½ cup basil and sugar in a mortar; pound with pestle until a paste forms. Add sugar mixture to juice mixture; stir until sugar dissolves. Strain mixture through a sieve over a bowl; discard solids. Place 1 cup ice in each of 4 glasses. Pour about 1 cup lemonade into each glass; garnish each serving with 1 basil sprig. Serves 4.

CALORIES 82; FAT 0g; PROTEIN 0.3g; CARB 21.6g; FIBER 0.4g; CHOL 0mg; IRON 0.2mg; SODIUM 5mg; CALC 16mg

CHIVES

*Their delicate onion flavor and edible lavender blossoms
are two reasons chives are a perennial favorite.*

SEASON: Spring and summer

CHOOSING: Look for healthy green leaves with no signs of yellow or brown.

STORING: Use chives fresh from the garden or market, storing any extra in a produce bag in the vegetable bin of your refrigerator. Thinly slice the narrow leaves for maximum flavor impact. When cooking, toss them in at the end, as heat destroys their flavor. Fresh chives should remain usable for about a week. For longer storage, cut them into short sections using kitchen shears, and place in a heavy-duty zip-top plastic bag in the freezer.

GROWING: Chives are small, perennial onions that remain green and usable all season. They go dormant after a hard freeze but return each season as the weather warms, growing about 12 inches tall with tubular, grass-like leaves. Single, wispy seedlings will grow into clumps in a couple of years, so space them out to avoid over-crowding. Chives make an excellent border for a garden bed, or they can be grown in a 4- to 6-inch pot if only a few are needed. Start with either seeds or transplants, and select a site with full sun and rich soil.

Just after the leaves appear, edible lavender-pink flowers emerge like puffballs. Enjoy them in the garden, or use them in the kitchen for herbal vinaigrettes or mixed in fresh with salad greens. Remove the browned flower stalks after they fade.

When cutting chives, select a few leaves on the edge of a clump. Snip them off near the soil, even if you do not need the entire leaf. This encourages new growth and prevents the accumulation of little brown-edged stumps. Add compost around your chives each spring, or give them a boost with a timed-release fertilizer.

Crispy Herbed Shrimp with Chive Aioli

Hands-on time: 31 min.   Total time: 31 min.

This dish is full of flavor-rich, fresh herbs in the breading and aioli. Chives are the standout in the aioli and many sauces because they lend a light onion flavor that isn't overpowering. Keep a pot of them near your kitchen door, and move it to a windowsill in winter; you'll find that snippets of chives go well atop many dishes year-round.

3/4   cup panko (Japanese breadcrumbs), divided

1   tablespoon chopped fresh parsley

2   teaspoons chopped fresh thyme

1/8   teaspoon crushed red pepper

2   tablespoons cornstarch

2   large egg whites, lightly beaten

1 1/2   pounds large shrimp, peeled and deveined

1/4   teaspoon salt

1/4   teaspoon freshly ground black pepper

2   tablespoons olive oil, divided

1/2   cup 2% reduced-fat Greek yogurt

1/4   cup canola mayonnaise

3   tablespoons chopped fresh chives

1   tablespoon fresh lemon juice

1/4   teaspoon ground red pepper

1. Place 1/4 cup panko, parsley, thyme, and crushed red pepper in a mini food processor; pulse to combine. Combine herb mixture with 1/2 cup panko in a shallow dish. Place cornstarch and egg whites in separate shallow dishes. Sprinkle shrimp with salt and black pepper. Dredge half of shrimp in cornstarch, shaking off excess; dip in egg whites. Dredge shrimp in panko mixture; press to adhere. Repeat procedure with remaining shrimp.

2. Heat a large nonstick skillet over medium-high heat. Add 1 tablespoon oil to pan; swirl to coat. Add half of shrimp to pan; cook 3 minutes on each side or until done. Repeat with remaining oil and shrimp.

3. Combine yogurt and remaining ingredients in a small bowl. Serve with shrimp. Serves 4 (serving size: about 5 shrimp and 2 tablespoons sauce).

CALORIES 430; FAT 21.7g (sat 2.9g, mono 11.4g, poly 4.9g); PROTEIN 41.3g; CARB 14.8g; FIBER 0.7g; CHOL 265mg; IRON 4.4mg; SODIUM 583mg; CALC 115mg

Parmesan Corn Muffins

Hands-on time: 15 min. Total time: 28 min.

How to Make Corn Muffins

The trick with corn muffins is the cornmeal-to-flour ratio; you need just enough of the former to hearty-up the texture and enough flour and leavening to avoid doorstop density. Flour lends tender structure.

1. Combine the wet ingredients. In a separate bowl, mix the dry ingredients together, and make a well in the center.

2. Add the wet ingredients to the dry ingredients, and stir just until combined. Over-mixing can create tough muffins.

3. Divide the batter evenly into muffin cups coated with cooking spray, filling each cup about two-thirds full. An ice-cream scoop is great for even portioning.

Cheese and chives are a can't-miss combo in corn bread recipes, but this one takes the cake. Simmer a pot of speckled butterpeas or cranberry beans in summer to serve alongside. Freeze any extra muffins for future harvest dinners. Splurge on quality Parmigiano-Reggiano.

1¼ cups nonfat buttermilk
¼ cup olive oil
1 large egg
4.5 ounces all-purpose flour (about 1 cup)
¾ cup yellow cornmeal
1 tablespoon sugar
2 teaspoons baking powder
¼ teaspoon baking soda
¼ teaspoon salt
⅛ teaspoon ground red pepper
3 ounces grated fresh Parmigiano-Reggiano cheese (about ¾ cup), divided
3 tablespoons finely chopped fresh chives, divided
Cooking spray

1. Preheat oven to 400°.
2. Combine first 3 ingredients in a medium bowl.
3. Weigh or lightly spoon flour into a dry measuring cup; level with a knife. Combine flour and next 6 ingredients (through red pepper) in a bowl, stirring well with a whisk. Make a well in center of flour mixture. Add buttermilk mixture; stir just until moist.
4. Stir in 2 ounces cheese (about ½ cup) and 2 tablespoons chives. Spoon batter into 12 muffin cups coated with cooking spray. Sprinkle muffins evenly with 1 ounce cheese and 1 tablespoon chives.
5. Bake at 400° for 13 minutes or until a wooden pick inserted in center comes out with moist crumbs clinging. Remove muffins from pan; cool on a wire rack. Serves 12 (serving size: 1 muffin).

CALORIES 164; FAT 7.1g (sat 1.8g, mono 1.8g, poly 3.5g); PROTEIN 0.7g; CARB 18.5g; FIBER 0.7g; CHOL 20mg; IRON 1mg; SODIUM 300mg; CALC 177mg

Beef Tenderloin with Horseradish-Chive Sauce

Hands-on time: 13 min.   Total time: 48 min.

Beef tenderloin looks sophisticated but is an easy dinner party main dish. The lean beef pairs well with a coating of black pepper and a side of zesty horseradish and chive sauce.

1	(2-pound) beef tenderloin, trimmed	2	tablespoons chopped fresh chives
1	tablespoon olive oil	3	tablespoons prepared horseradish
1½	teaspoons coarsely ground black pepper	1	teaspoon fresh lemon juice
¾	teaspoon kosher salt	1	teaspoon Dijon mustard
⅔	cup light sour cream	⅛	teaspoon kosher salt

1. Preheat oven to 450°.

2. Heat a large skillet over medium-high heat. Rub beef with oil; coat on all sides with pepper and ¾ teaspoon salt. Add beef to pan; cook 3 minutes, browning on all sides.

3. Place beef on a broiler pan. Bake at 450° for 25 minutes or until a thermometer registers 125°. Remove from oven; let stand 10 minutes before slicing.

4. Combine sour cream and remaining ingredients; serve with beef. Serves 8 (serving size: 3 ounces beef and about 1½ tablespoons sauce).

CALORIES 210; FAT 10.1g (sat 4.1g, mono 3.9g, poly 0.5g); PROTEIN 25.7g; CARB 2.4g; FIBER 0.3g; CHOL 67mg; IRON 1.7mg; SODIUM 310mg; CALC 21mg

CILANTRO

This pungent herb has a distinctive flavor with a faint undertone of anise.

SEASON: A cool-season herb for fall and early spring, it is available year-round in some climates.

CHOOSING: Cilantro is usually sold in bunches. It looks a lot like flat-leaf parsley, so be sure you read the label, and look for the thinner, brighter green leaves of cilantro. Or just smell it—the pungent, sharp, medicinal scent is hard to mistake—and avoid bunches that are wilted or have mushy leaves.

STORING: Place fresh bunches of cilantro in a produce bag in the vegetable bin of your refrigerator. It will last up to a week. If cutting from your garden, snip as needed.

GROWING: Cilantro is an annual that prefers the cool season. For most gardens, early fall is the time to plant. If the climate is mild, it will be green and growing all winter, but hard, prolonged freezes will kill cilantro. If that happens, replant in early spring.

Start cilantro from seeds or transplants, planting in full sun and soil that is well-drained and enriched with compost. Growing your own cilantro is twice as nice as buying, because you can continually harvest the fresh leaves and, later, gather the seed heads, known as coriander. When the weather heats up and coriander bolts into bloom, don't despair. Just wait until the flowers turn to green seeds and then to a dried brown form. Put cut stems in a paper bag to collect the seeds easily. Store coriander seeds in a small airtight jar or container. Seeds that fall into the garden will grow again in the fall or following spring. Once cilantro blooms and produces seeds, the plant dies, and you can pull it up to make room for something else. If you minimize mulching, plants will grow again in fall.

Pork Posole

Hands-on time: 25 min.   Total time: 1 hr. 35 min.

This is a rainy-day, warm-your-insides kind of meal. The peppery radish slices are a must, as are wedges of lime and a sprinkling of fresh cilantro. It's also convenient that you have most of a beer (preferably a locally brewed, nutty ale) left to drink with it!

1	tablespoon olive oil	1/2	cup beer
12	ounces boneless pork shoulder, trimmed and cut into 1/2-inch pieces	2	cups fat-free, lower-sodium chicken broth
1	cup chopped onion	1/2	cup salsa verde
4	garlic cloves, minced	1	(28-ounce) can hominy, drained
1 1/2	teaspoons ground cumin	1/4	cup cilantro leaves
1/2	teaspoon ground red pepper	4	radishes, sliced
		4	lime wedges

1. Heat a Dutch oven over medium-high heat. Add oil to pan; swirl to coat. Add pork; sauté 5 minutes, turning to brown on all sides. Remove pork from pan. Add onion; sauté 4 minutes, stirring occasionally. Add garlic; sauté 1 minute, stirring constantly. Return pork to pan; stir in cumin and pepper. Add beer; bring to a boil. Cook until liquid almost evaporates (about 9 minutes).
2. Add broth, salsa, and hominy, and bring to a boil. Cover, reduce heat, and simmer 1 hour and 10 minutes or until pork is very tender, stirring occasionally. Ladle 1 1/2 cups soup into each of 4 bowls. Top each serving with 1 tablespoon cilantro and 1 sliced radish. Serve with lime wedges. Serves 4.

CALORIES 245; FAT 8g (sat 1.6g, mono 4g, poly 1.2g); PROTEIN 12.7g; CARB 29.8g; FIBER 5.5g; CHOL 29mg; IRON 2.8mg; SODIUM 631mg; CALC 60mg

Herb Revival

If you find that your fresh herbs have gone limp during storage, you can revive them by trimming a half inch off the stems and placing them in ice water for a couple of hours. Wash herbs just before using, and then pat dry with a paper towel.

Ancho Chicken Tacos with Cilantro Slaw and Avocado Cream

Hands-on time: 20 min.   Total time: 20 min.

Fresh cilantro is a natural topping for most any taco, but this crunchy slaw becomes the star of the dish. Finely grate green cabbage to toss with green onions and cilantro in a lime dressing for a zingy topping. Finish with a squeeze of lime. See page 11 for tips on warming and toasting tortillas.

1	pound skinless, boneless chicken breast, cut into ¼-inch strips	¼	cup light sour cream
		2	tablespoons 1% low-fat milk
¾	teaspoon ancho chile powder	½	ripe peeled avocado, diced
½	teaspoon garlic salt	2	cups finely grated green cabbage
¼	teaspoon ground cumin	½	cup thinly sliced green onions
	Cooking spray	¼	cup chopped fresh cilantro
⅛	teaspoon grated lime rind	1	tablespoon canola oil
2	tablespoons fresh lime juice, divided	¼	teaspoon salt
		8	(6-inch) corn tortillas

1. Heat a large skillet over high heat. Sprinkle chicken evenly with chile powder, garlic salt, and cumin. Coat pan with cooking spray. Add chicken to pan; cook 4 minutes, stirring frequently. Remove chicken from pan.

2. Place rind, 1 tablespoon juice, and next 3 ingredients (through avocado) in a blender or food processor; process until smooth.

3. Combine 1 tablespoon juice, cabbage, onions, cilantro, oil, and salt, tossing to coat.

4. Heat tortillas according to package directions. Divide chicken mixture evenly among tortillas. Top each tortilla with about 1 tablespoon avocado mixture and ¼ cup slaw. Serves 4 (serving size: 2 tacos).

CALORIES 319; FAT 11.6g (sat 2.3g, mono 5.5g, poly 2.4g); PROTEIN 30g; CARB 25.3g; FIBER 5.1g; CHOL 72mg; IRON 1.3mg; SODIUM 385mg; CALC 80mg

Lamb Chops and Cilantro Relish

Hands-on time: 23 min. Total time: 39 min.

This is a restaurant-grade meal with the finest point of dining—quick prep. The added pride of harvesting fresh herbs and peppers from the garden or purchasing from local farmers makes the relish even better. Serve with a simple side of fresh lima beans tossed with grape tomatoes and sliced kalamata olives.

1   teaspoon extra-virgin olive oil
½   teaspoon grated lemon rind
¼   teaspoon ground cumin
Cooking spray
1   (1½-pound) French-cut rack of
     lamb (8 ribs), trimmed
¼   teaspoon kosher salt
¼   teaspoon black pepper
1   cup finely chopped red onion
1   jalapeño pepper, seeded and
     finely chopped
¾   cup chopped fresh cilantro
1   tablespoon fresh lemon juice
2   teaspoons extra-virgin olive oil
¼   teaspoon kosher salt

1. Preheat oven to 400°.
2. Combine first 3 ingredients in a small bowl.
3. Heat a large ovenproof skillet over medium-high heat. Coat pan with cooking spray. Sprinkle lamb with ¼ teaspoon salt and black pepper. Add lamb to pan; cook 2 minutes on each side. Spread oil mixture over lamb; place pan in oven. Bake at 400° for 15 minutes or until a thermometer registers 138°. Remove lamb from pan; let stand 8 minutes. Cut into chops.
4. Heat a skillet over medium-high heat. Coat pan with cooking spray. Add onion and jalapeño to pan; sauté 5 minutes. Combine onion mixture, cilantro, and remaining ingredients in a bowl. Serve relish with lamb. Serves 4 (serving size: 2 chops and 3 tablespoons relish).

CALORIES 225; FAT 13.2g (sat 4.7g, mono 6.4g, poly 0.7g); PROTEIN 21g; CARB 4.5g; FIBER 0.9g; CHOL 66mg; IRON 1.6mg; SODIUM 310mg; CALC 25mg

DILL

*The feathery leaves lend a distinctive sweet flavor
that transforms any dish it touches.*

SEASON: Summer through fall

CHOOSING: Bunches of feathery dill foliage, also called dill weed, should be bright green and fragrant with no signs of wilting. Dill can look a lot like the darker, glossier fennel foliage, so check carefully to be sure which one you're buying.

STORING: Wrap fresh dill in a moist paper towel, and place it in a plastic produce bag in the vegetable bin of your refrigerator. Dill seeds should be gathered when brown by cutting whole stalks and placing them in an open paper bag. When dry, they'll fall easily from the stalks and can be stored for use in the kitchen or later in the garden.

GROWING: Dill enjoys cooler weather, so plant in early fall or early spring unless you're in a locale where summers are mild, in which case you can replant dill monthly for a continuous supply. Choose a sunny, well-drained bed with loose, rich soil. Sow seeds directly into prepared garden beds, or set out young transplants.

Once the plants have grown into rosettes big enough to spare a leaf, cut the large outer leaves as needed, allowing the plant to continue growing from the center. A full-sized leaf looks like a feathery branch measuring 6 to 10 inches long. The blooms will ultimately produce brown, flavorful seeds. If allowed to drop into the garden, the seeds will sprout again, sometimes months later, for an ongoing supply of fresh dill. Like butterflies? Plant extra for the caterpillars to feast upon before they grace your garden as butterflies.

Persian Rice-Stuffed Zucchini with Pistachios and Dill

Hands-on time: 34 min. Total time: 56 min.

6 medium zucchini (6 ounces each)
3/4 teaspoon kosher salt, divided
3/8 teaspoon freshly ground black pepper, divided
3 tablespoons olive oil, divided
3/4 cup jasmine rice
6 cardamom pods
1 (3-inch) cinnamon stick
1/2 teaspoon ground cumin
1/8 teaspoon ground red pepper
1 1/4 cups water
8 dried apricots, coarsely chopped (about 1/3 cup)
1/2 teaspoon grated orange rind
2 tablespoons fresh lemon juice
2 tablespoons fresh orange juice
1/3 cup chopped shelled dry-roasted, unsalted pistachios
1/4 cup chopped fresh dill
1/4 cup chopped fresh flat-leaf parsley
2 ounces goat cheese, crumbled (about 1/4 cup)
1 (15-ounce) can no-salt-added chickpeas (garbanzo beans), rinsed and drained

Sweet and savory, this recipe makes the most of an abundance of zucchini with a medley of spices, fruits, and herbs. Use 1½ cups cooked, shelled fresh chickpeas (garbanzo beans) in place of canned if you can find them. Don't skip the broiling step for the crispest finish.

1. Preheat oven to 375°.
2. Cut zucchini in half lengthwise; scoop out pulp, leaving a 1/4-inch-thick shell. Chop pulp. Place zucchini halves, cut sides up, on a baking sheet lined with parchment paper; sprinkle with 1/4 teaspoon salt and 1/8 teaspoon black pepper. Bake at 375° for 15 minutes or until tender.
3. Heat a medium saucepan over medium heat. Add 1 tablespoon oil to pan; swirl to coat. Add rice, cardamom, and cinnamon; cook 5 minutes or until rice is opaque, stirring frequently. Add 1/4 teaspoon salt, cumin, red pepper, and 1 1/4 cups water. Bring to a boil; cover, reduce heat, and simmer 12 minutes. Remove from heat; stir in apricots. Cover and let stand 10 minutes; discard cardamom and cinnamon. Spoon rice mixture into a large bowl; cool slightly.
4. Combine 2 tablespoons oil, 1/4 teaspoon salt, 1/4 teaspoon black pepper, orange rind, and juices in a small bowl, stirring with a whisk. Add dressing, reserved zucchini pulp, pistachios, and remaining ingredients to rice mixture; toss well to combine.
5. Preheat broiler.
6. Spoon about 1/4 cup rice mixture into each zucchini shell. Broil 6 minutes or until lightly browned. Serves 6 (serving size: 2 stuffed zucchini halves).

CALORIES 265; FAT 12.7g (sat 2.8g, mono 7.1g, poly 1.9g); PROTEIN 9.2g; CARB 31.6g; FIBER 5.6g; CHOL 4mg; IRON 2.2mg; SODIUM 309mg; CALC 81mg

Tzatziki Chicken Salad

Hands-on time: 16 min.   Total time: 16 min.

This Greek yogurt–based sauce with fresh cucumber, onions, and dill (an essential part of classic tzatziki sauce) gives traditional chicken salad a face-lift.

- ²/₃ cup plain 2% reduced-fat Greek yogurt
- ¼ cup finely chopped red onion
- 1 tablespoon fresh lemon juice
- 2 teaspoons chopped fresh dill
- ³/₈ teaspoon kosher salt
- ¼ teaspoon freshly ground black pepper
- 1 cucumber, seeded and shredded
- 1 garlic clove, minced
- 2 cups shredded skinless, boneless rotisserie chicken breast
- 3 ounces multigrain pita chips

1. Combine first 8 ingredients in a medium bowl, stirring with a whisk. Add chicken; toss to coat. Serve with pita chips. Serves 4 (serving size: about ²/₃ cup salad and ½ cup chips).

CALORIES 230; FAT 7.5g (sat 1.5g, mono 1.4g, poly 2.1g); PROTEIN 23g; CARB 18.7g; FIBER 2.1g; CHOL 53mg; IRON 1mg; SODIUM 569mg; CALC 60mg

Tomato-Dill Couscous

Hands-on time: 9 min.   Total time: 17 min.

This easy side will be an instant hit with your family. Cook just a few minutes on the stove, and throw in snips of fresh dill, a handful of Sun Gold or Sweet 100 cherry tomatoes, and chopped red onion.

- 1 tablespoon olive oil
- 1 cup uncooked couscous
- 1 cup plus 2 tablespoons fat-free, lower-sodium chicken broth
- ⅛ teaspoon salt
- ½ cup quartered cherry tomatoes
- ¼ cup finely chopped red onion
- 2 tablespoons chopped fresh dill

1. Heat a small saucepan over medium-high heat. Add olive oil to pan; swirl to coat. Stir in couscous; sauté 1 minute. Add chicken broth and salt; bring to a boil. Cover, remove from heat, and let stand 5 minutes. Fluff with a fork. Stir in tomatoes, onion, and dill. Serves 4 (serving size: ³/₄ cup).

CALORIES 201; FAT 3.7g (sat 0.5g, mono 2.5g, poly 0.5g); PROTEIN 6g; CARB 35.2g; FIBER 2.6g; CHOL 0mg; IRON 0.6mg; SODIUM 149mg; CALC 15mg

Tzatziki Chicken Salad

MINT

Bursting with fragrance and flavor, mint is a versatile herb, adding sprightly, fresh coolness to sweet and savory dishes.

SEASON: Spring

CHOOSING: Look for stems of healthy, bright green, crisp leaves that show no signs of wilting or browning.

STORING: Place freshly cut stems of mint from the farmers' market or your garden in a vase of water on the kitchen counter for up to several days. Mint from the supermarket has been cut for several days, so place it in a plastic produce bag in the vegetable bin of the refrigerator.

GROWING: Mint is a perennial herb, remaining year after year. It will go dormant when exposed to freezing temperatures, and then sprout again in the spring.

Known for its aggressive runners, mint should be planted where it can be contained or where it can fill several square yards of space. There are many varieties—peppermint, spearmint, apple mint, chocolate mint, and orange mint are only a few. Choose one that suits your taste buds.

Set a plant or runner, with roots attached, in full sun to light shade in rich, well-drained soil. Once established, mint should be cut frequently to encourage new growth for an ongoing supply of flavorful leaves. A bed that's bordered by concrete, such as between your sidewalk and your foundation, is an excellent place to grow and contain mint. If the patch grows too large, use a shovel to cut the runners and pull out the ones that have become aggressive.

Mint can also be grown in a large pot measuring at least 12 to 14 inches across. Note: If the pot is placed on soil, rather than concrete, mint will escape through the drainage hole of the pot and take root in the garden.

Mint Gremolata Zucchini with Sea Salt

Hands-on time: 20 min. Total time: 20 min.

2 teaspoons extra-virgin olive oil
¼ teaspoon coarse sea salt
¼ teaspoon freshly ground black pepper
2 medium zucchini, cut diagonally into ½-inch-thick slices

¼ cup finely chopped fresh flat-leaf parsley
¼ cup finely chopped fresh mint
1½ tablespoons grated lemon rind
1 tablespoon olive oil
2 garlic cloves, minced

1. Preheat a grill pan over medium-high heat. Combine first 4 ingredients in a bowl. Arrange zucchini in a single layer in pan; grill 4 minutes, turning after 2 minutes.
2. Combine parsley and next 4 ingredients in a small bowl. Divide zucchini evenly among 4 plates; top evenly with gremolata. Serves 4 (serving size: about 4 slices).

CALORIES 72; FAT 5.9g (sat 0.8g, mono 4.1g, poly 0.7g); PROTEIN 1.5g; CARB 4.7g; FIBER 1.6g; CHOL 0mg; IRON 0.8mg; SODIUM 133mg; CALC 30mg

Grilled zucchini is great with olive oil and sea salt, but take the extra step and serve with this mint, parsley, and lemon gremolata. Mint and zucchini are a smart pairing in recipes, too, since both are such prolific producers in the garden.

Greek Lamb Chops and Mint Yogurt Sauce

Hands-on time: 16 min. Total time: 20 min.

2 tablespoons fresh lemon juice
2 teaspoons chopped fresh oregano
3 garlic cloves, minced and divided
8 (4-ounce) lamb loin chops, trimmed
³⁄₈ teaspoon kosher salt, divided

¼ teaspoon freshly ground black pepper
2 teaspoons canola oil
½ cup plain fat-free yogurt
1 tablespoon chopped fresh mint
½ teaspoon fresh lemon juice

1. Combine 2 tablespoons juice, oregano, and 2 minced garlic cloves in a small bowl. Sprinkle lamb with ¼ teaspoon salt and pepper; rub with oregano mixture. Heat a large skillet over high heat. Add oil to pan; swirl to coat. Add lamb; cook 3 minutes on each side or until desired degree of doneness. Let stand 5 minutes.
2. Combine yogurt, ⅛ teaspoon salt, mint, ½ teaspoon juice, and 1 garlic clove. Serve sauce with lamb. Serves 4 (serving size: 2 lamb chops and 2 tablespoons sauce).

CALORIES 347; FAT 14.1g (sat 4.9g, mono 6.2g, poly 1.3g); PROTEIN 48.2g; CARB 3.9g; FIBER 0.1g; CHOL 147mg; IRON 4.5mg; SODIUM 347mg; CALC 86mg

Freezing Fresh Mint

Simply rinse the leaves, pat dry, and freeze in a heavy-duty zip-top plastic bag. The leaves will darken once frozen, but the color change doesn't affect flavor. Later, pull out what you need, and return the rest to the freezer. You may prefer to freeze whole or chopped mint leaves in ice-cube trays with water, which preserves the green color. After they're frozen, remove the cubes from the trays and store in a heavy-duty zip-top plastic bag. Add these minty ice cubes to drinks, or thaw, drain, and use in recipes.

Fresh Mint Ice Cream

Hands-on time: 12 min. Total time: 2 hr. 44 min.

Mint is decidedly one of the most refreshing flavors, doubly so in ice-cream form. The trick to getting your preferred mint flavor is in choosing spearmint or peppermint. Sweet mint, also labeled as spearmint, tastes sweeter when muddled for recipes, while peppermint has a faint menthol flavor. Or try some of the flavored varieties like chocolate, apple, or citrusy orange mint.

2	cups 2% reduced-fat milk		Dash of salt
1	cup half-and-half	2	large egg yolks
1	cup mint sprigs (about 1 ounce)		Small mint leaves (optional)
¾	cup sugar		

1. Combine milk, half-and-half, and mint sprigs in a medium, heavy saucepan over medium-high heat. Heat milk mixture to 180° or until tiny bubbles form around edge (do not boil). Remove from heat; cover and let stand 10 minutes.
2. Pour milk mixture through a fine sieve over a bowl, pressing slightly with a wooden spoon; discard solids. Return liquid to pan.
3. Place sugar, salt, and egg yolks in a bowl; stir with a whisk until pale. Gradually add half of hot milk mixture to egg mixture, stirring constantly with a whisk. Pour egg yolk mixture into pan with remaining milk mixture; cook over medium-low heat until a thermometer registers 160° (about 2 minutes), stirring constantly. Place pan in a large ice-filled bowl until custard cools completely, stirring occasionally. Pour mixture into the freezer can of an ice-cream freezer; freeze according to manufacturer's instructions. Spoon ice cream into a freezer-safe container; cover and freeze 1 hour or until firm. Garnish with mint leaves, if desired. Serves 6 (serving size: about ½ cup).

CALORIES 207; FAT 7.6g (sat 4.4g, mono 2.4g, poly 0.5g); PROTEIN 4.8g; CARB 30.8g; FIBER 0g; CHOL 89mg; IRON 0.2mg; SODIUM 84mg; CALC 148mg

How to Make Light Ice Cream

Using full-fat half-and-half helps maintain a rich creaminess.

1. Scald the milk by heating it to 180°. This is an important step; it infuses the custard with the flavor of fresh mint. Let the mint steep in the hot milk mixture. Don't add sugar to the milk before heating, as sugar can cause the milk to curdle when hot.

2. Slowly add the hot milk mixture to the egg mixture, stirring constantly. This process, known as tempering, slowly heats the yolks without "scrambling" them.

3. Chilling the custard ensures it will freeze quickly and more smoothly. In fact, you'll get the best results if you make the custard up to a day ahead and refrigerate it overnight or until it's thoroughly chilled.

4. If you're using an old-fashioned churn, add about ½ cup salt over every 4 cups ice. Any salt will do the trick, but the smaller the grains, the faster the custard will freeze.

OREGANO

Warm, aromatic oregano offers a bold, gutsy bite.

SEASON: Spring through fall

CHOOSING: Look for fresh, green oregano that isn't bruised or wilted.

STORING: Keep cut oregano in a plastic produce bag in the vegetable bin of your refrigerator, or store in the freezer.

GROWING: Oregano is a perennial herb in all except the coldest areas of the United States, where it can be grown as an annual. In warm areas, it can be evergreen. No matter where you live, it is a flavorful, easy-to-grow kitchen staple.

There are many types of oregano, but the most common plants for sale are grown from seeds. Flavorful Spanish and Greek oregano are good options if you can find them. Ornamental forms such as golden oregano are lovely decorative plants in the garden but are not what you need in the kitchen. Set plants in a sunny bed with rich, well-drained soil. Although oregano is drought-tolerant, an established plant will be more productive when watered about once a week.

The aromatic, dime-sized leaves grow on stems that can reach as long as 3 feet. The stems are likely to droop, especially as flower buds begin to form, which signals that the foliage is at its peak flavor. This is also the ideal time to cut the plant back to 6 to 8 inches—do so once or twice each growing season to keep it full and thriving. Fertilize with timed-release granules or a liquid fertilizer as needed to maintain healthy growth.

Wild Rice with Bell Pepper and Fennel

Hands-on time: 16 min.   Total time: 16 min.

1   (8.5-ounce) package precooked wild rice
1½   tablespoons olive oil
½   cup diced yellow bell pepper
½   cup diced fennel bulb
1½   teaspoons chopped fresh oregano
½   teaspoon freshly ground black pepper
¼   teaspoon salt

1. Prepare rice according to package directions.
2. Heat a large nonstick skillet over medium heat. Add oil to pan; swirl to coat. Add bell pepper and fennel; cook 8 minutes or until tender, stirring frequently. Stir in rice, oregano, black pepper, and salt; cook 1 minute. Serves 4 (serving size: about ¾ cup).

CALORIES 116; FAT 5.4g (sat 0.7g, mono 3.7g, poly 0.7g); PROTEIN 2.8g; CARB 15g; FIBER 1.9g; CHOL 0mg; IRON 0.6mg; SODIUM 156mg; CALC 12mg

Three-Bean Salad

Hands-on time: 40 min.   Total time: 1 hr. 20 min.

1   medium-sized red bell pepper
¾   cup frozen shelled edamame (green soybeans), thawed
8   ounces haricots verts, trimmed
1½   cups cooked, shelled fresh chickpeas (garbanzo beans)
½   teaspoon kosher salt
½   teaspoon black pepper
¼   cup minced shallots
3   tablespoons fresh parsley leaves
1½   tablespoons oregano leaves
2   tablespoons fresh lemon juice
1   tablespoon Dijon mustard
1   tablespoon extra-virgin olive oil

Fresh oregano has a more intense flavor than dried and complements roasted vegetables well. The three beans are done in a flash. Mix it all together for a crisp, seasonal salad with a snappy shallot vinaigrette. Don't underestimate this green garden salad; it offers bold flavor and a healthy dose of protein.

1. Preheat broiler.
2. Cut bell pepper in half lengthwise; discard seeds and membranes. Place halves, skin sides up, on a foil-lined baking sheet; flatten. Broil 10 minutes or until blackened. Place in a paper bag; fold to close tightly. Let stand 10 minutes. Peel and chop. Cook edamame and haricots verts in boiling water 4 minutes. Rinse with cold water; drain.
3. Combine bell pepper, edamame mixture, chickpeas, salt, and black pepper in a bowl. Combine shallots and remaining ingredients, stirring well with a whisk. Drizzle dressing over bean mixture; toss. Serves 6 (serving size: about ⅔ cup).

CALORIES 255; FAT 6.2g (sat 0.6g, mono 2.3g, poly 1.6g); PROTEIN 12.8g; CARB 38.8g; FIBER 11.5g; CHOL 0mg; IRON 4.2mg; SODIUM 245mg; CALC 90mg

Oregano and Lime Roasted Chicken Breasts

Hands-on time: 20 min. Total time: 4 hr. 45 min.

Drying Fresh Oregano

Oregano keeps its flavor when dried, so you can air-dry cut stems in an air-conditioned or dehumidified room. Hang them or spread them out on a clean cloth. Avoid heat as a means of drying because the herb's flavorful oils will be lost. When they are crisp, strip the leaves from the stems and store them in a plastic bag or glass jar away from sunlight. The freezer is an ideal storage space if you have room, particularly in humid areas where the leaves may not get sufficiently dry.

Need a way to refresh regular chicken? Season bone-in chicken breasts with fresh oregano and lime. Make sure you keep the skin on, as a highlight is the crispy bite of skin with tequila-lime sauce. Garnish with fresh oregano leaves.

Chicken:
1 tablespoon chopped fresh oregano
2 teaspoons grated lime rind
1 teaspoon ground cumin
2 teaspoons minced garlic
¼ teaspoon freshly ground black pepper
4 bone-in, skin-on chicken breast halves (about 3 pounds)
2 teaspoons olive oil
½ teaspoon salt

Sauce:
1 tablespoon all-purpose flour
¼ teaspoon ground cumin
1 cup fat-free, lower-sodium chicken broth
1 tablespoon tequila
½ teaspoon fresh lime juice

1. To prepare chicken, combine first 5 ingredients in a small bowl. Loosen skin from breast halves by inserting fingers, gently pushing between skin and meat. Rub oregano mixture evenly under loosened skin of each breast half. Arrange chicken breasts in a shallow dish; cover and refrigerate at least 4 hours.
2. Preheat oven to 375°.
3. Heat a large ovenproof skillet over medium-high heat. Add oil to pan; swirl to coat. Sprinkle chicken with salt. Add chicken to pan, skin sides down; cook 5 minutes or until browned. Turn chicken over, and transfer to oven. Bake at 375° for 25 minutes or until chicken is done. Remove chicken from pan, reserving 1½ tablespoons drippings; set chicken aside, and keep warm.
4. To prepare sauce, heat reserved drippings in pan over medium-high heat. Add flour and ¼ teaspoon cumin to pan, and cook 30 seconds, stirring constantly with a whisk. Add chicken broth, tequila, and lime juice, scraping pan to loosen browned bits. Bring to a boil, and cook until reduced to about ⅔ cup (about 2 minutes), stirring occasionally. Serve with chicken. Serves 4 (serving size: 1 breast half and about 2½ tablespoons sauce).

CALORIES 446; FAT 18.8g (sat 4.9g, mono 8.1g, poly 3.8g); PROTEIN 60.2g; CARB 2.9g; FIBER 0.7g; CHOL 167mg; IRON 2.6mg; SODIUM 534mg; CALC 46mg

PARSLEY

With its mild, grassy flavor, parsley is a fresh accent to almost any savory dish.

SEASON: Spring through fall

CHOOSING: Select a bunch that's bright green and free of bruising, decay, and blemishes.

STORING: To be sure parsley stays perky and hydrated during storage, cut half an inch off the ends of the stems using kitchen shears. Plunge the cut ends into a glass of water for about an hour; remove, and place the entire bunch in a plastic produce bag to prevent wilting. Unlike produce that must be kept in the vegetable bin (which is a little warmer and more humid than the shelves), parsley lasts longer if kept in the coolest section of your refrigerator. When treated properly, parsley lasts about a week in the refrigerator.

GROWING: Parsley is a biennial, so it grows one season, and then blooms the next, and must be planted every year. Its season varies from place to place: In temperate areas, plant in the spring so it will thrive all summer and fall. Where winter is mild, it will remain green year-round, but it won't continue to grow through light freezes and can die during severe winter weather. In tropical areas with hot summers, such as Florida, parsley should be planted in fall for harvest all winter.

Choose between two familiar favorites, curly and flat-leaf parsley. Curly parsley is well suited for garnishing for a burst of color. Flat-leaf parsley, often called Italian parsley, has a wonderful flavor and stands up better to heat, ideal for various culinary uses.

Set transplants or sow seeds in sunny, well-drained, moist soil, either in the garden or in a pot. Container-grown parsley needs a pot deep enough to accommodate its 6- to 10-inch taproot. With the aid of a timed-release fertilizer or a monthly liquid fertilizer, each plant can grow a foot across, lush with delicious foliage.

Cheesy Meat Loaf Minis

Hands-on time: 15 min.   Total time: 40 min.

Toss your "meh" meat loaf thoughts aside and try this cheesy comfort-food classic. Made with fresh parsley, white cheddar, and ground sirloin, these mini loaves taste more indulgent than they actually are. Gear up for a new go-to family favorite.

1   ounce fresh breadcrumbs (about ½ cup)
Cooking spray
1   cup chopped onion
2   garlic cloves, chopped
3   ounces white cheddar cheese, diced (about ¾ cup)
½   cup ketchup, divided
¼   cup chopped fresh parsley
2   tablespoons grated fresh Parmesan cheese

1   tablespoon prepared horseradish
1   tablespoon Dijon mustard
¾   teaspoon dried oregano
¼   teaspoon salt
¼   teaspoon freshly ground black pepper
1½ pounds ground sirloin
1   large egg, lightly beaten

1. Preheat oven to 425°.

2. Heat a skillet over medium-high heat. Add breadcrumbs; cook 3 minutes or until toasted, stirring frequently.

3. While breadcrumbs cook, heat a large skillet over medium-high heat. Coat pan with cooking spray. Add onion and garlic; sauté 3 minutes. Combine onion mixture, breadcrumbs, cheddar cheese, ¼ cup ketchup, and remaining ingredients. Shape into 6 (4 x 2-inch) loaves on a broiler pan coated with cooking spray; spread 2 teaspoons ketchup over each. Bake at 425° for 25 minutes or until done. Serves 6 (serving size: 1 meat loaf).

CALORIES 254; FAT 11.4g (sat 5.8g, mono 3.8g, poly 0.9g); PROTEIN 28.3g; CARB 11.1g; FIBER 0.9g; CHOL 112mg; IRON 2.6mg; SODIUM 607mg; CALC 150mg

NUTRITION NOTE

Packed with vitamins C and K, ¼ cup of fresh parsley also offers a dose of folate, a vitamin essential for pregnant women to help prevent neural tube defects.

Quinoa and
Parsley Salad

Quinoa and Parsley Salad

Hands-on time: 10 min. Total time: 34 min.

1	cup water	1	tablespoon olive oil
½	cup uncooked quinoa	1	tablespoon honey
¾	cup parsley leaves	¼	teaspoon salt
½	cup thinly sliced celery	¼	teaspoon freshly ground black
½	cup thinly sliced green onions		pepper
½	cup finely chopped dried	¼	cup unsalted pumpkinseed
	apricots		kernels, toasted
3	tablespoons fresh lemon juice		

1. Bring 1 cup water and quinoa to a boil in a medium saucepan. Cover, reduce heat, and simmer 20 minutes or until liquid is absorbed. Spoon into a bowl; fluff with a fork. Add parsley, celery, onions, and apricots.

2. Combine lemon juice and next 4 ingredients (through black pepper) in a small bowl, stirring with a whisk. Add to quinoa mixture, and toss well. Top with pumpkinseeds. Serves 4 (serving size: about ⅔ cup).

CALORIES 238; FAT 8.6g (sat 1.3g, mono 4.3g, poly 2.8g); PROTEIN 5.9g; CARB 35.1g; FIBER 3.6g; CHOL 0mg; IRON 4.6mg; SODIUM 172mg; CALC 47mg

Avoid the clichéd stem of curly-leaf lurking on the side of the plate, and bring the brightness of flat-leaf parsley to center stage. This dish is a nice change from a traditional green lettuce salad, as it is fresh *and* filling. Celery and toasted pumpkinseeds add crunch, while dried apricots lend a soft, sweet touch.

Chimichurri

Hands-on time: 10 min. Total time: 10 min.

1	cup flat-leaf parsley leaves	2	tablespoons fresh lime juice
1	cup cilantro leaves	2	tablespoons extra-virgin olive
¼	cup oregano leaves		oil
2	garlic cloves	¼	teaspoon salt
½	teaspoon grated lime rind	¼	teaspoon crushed red pepper

1. Place first 4 ingredients in a food processor; process until finely chopped. Add lime rind and remaining ingredients to herb mixture; process until herbs are very finely chopped and mixture is well combined. Serves 4 (serving size: 2 tablespoons).

Note: Use the freshest, most pristine herbs you can find for the best flavor. Stick with the leaves, and try not to incorporate the thick stems, which can taste bitter.

CALORIES 79; FAT 7.2g (sat 1g, mono 5g, poly 0.9g); PROTEIN 0.9g; CARB 4.2g; FIBER 1.9g; CHOL 0mg; IRON 2.4mg; SODIUM 155mg; CALC 73mg

If someone asked what the color green tastes like, chimichurri might very well be an answer. The parsley and cilantro create a bright, fresh, and tart sauce with a touch of spicy heat from the red pepper flakes. A classic condiment for meat, it is extremely versatile. Try it with grilled steak, chicken, or fish; roasted lamb; roasted new potatoes, fingerling potatoes, or baby carrots; sandwiches as a dipping sauce; grilled bread; or raw oysters on the half shell.

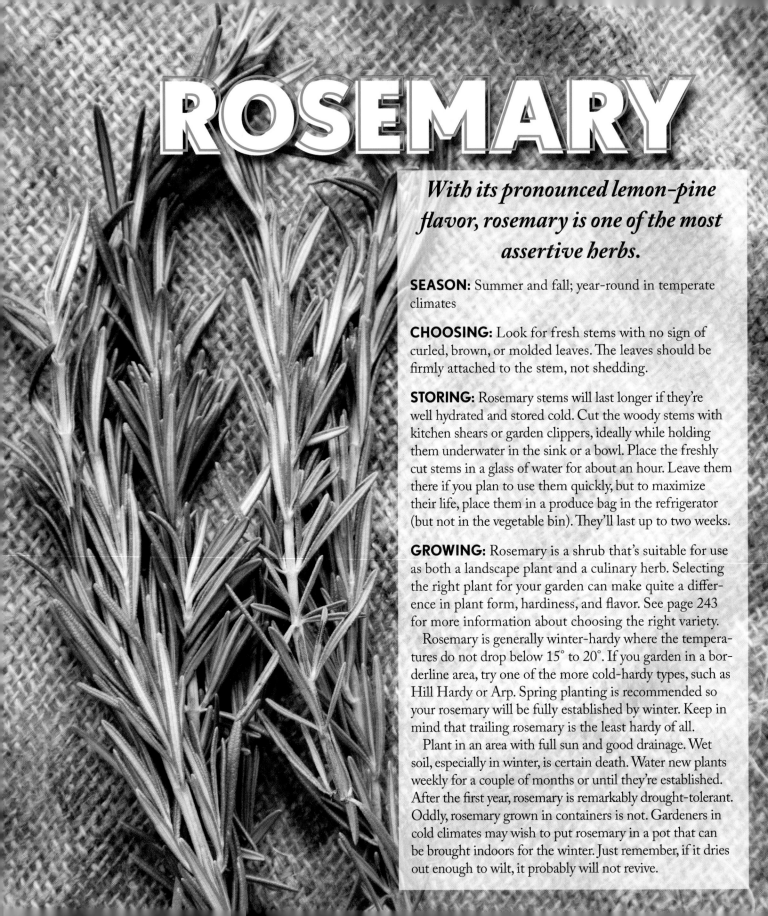

ROSEMARY

With its pronounced lemon–pine flavor, rosemary is one of the most assertive herbs.

SEASON: Summer and fall; year-round in temperate climates

CHOOSING: Look for fresh stems with no sign of curled, brown, or molded leaves. The leaves should be firmly attached to the stem, not shedding.

STORING: Rosemary stems will last longer if they're well hydrated and stored cold. Cut the woody stems with kitchen shears or garden clippers, ideally while holding them underwater in the sink or a bowl. Place the freshly cut stems in a glass of water for about an hour. Leave them there if you plan to use them quickly, but to maximize their life, place them in a produce bag in the refrigerator (but not in the vegetable bin). They'll last up to two weeks.

GROWING: Rosemary is a shrub that's suitable for use as both a landscape plant and a culinary herb. Selecting the right plant for your garden can make quite a difference in plant form, hardiness, and flavor. See page 243 for more information about choosing the right variety.

Rosemary is generally winter-hardy where the temperatures do not drop below 15° to 20°. If you garden in a borderline area, try one of the more cold-hardy types, such as Hill Hardy or Arp. Spring planting is recommended so your rosemary will be fully established by winter. Keep in mind that trailing rosemary is the least hardy of all.

Plant in an area with full sun and good drainage. Wet soil, especially in winter, is certain death. Water new plants weekly for a couple of months or until they're established. After the first year, rosemary is remarkably drought-tolerant. Oddly, rosemary grown in containers is not. Gardeners in cold climates may wish to put rosemary in a pot that can be brought indoors for the winter. Just remember, if it dries out enough to wilt, it probably will not revive.

Lemon-Rosemary Olive Oil Cake

Hands-on time: 15 min.   Total time: 1 hr. 45 min.

Intrigued? Try it! This Mediterranean-inspired cake, infused with the clean, evergreen essence of rosemary and the brightness of lemon, features olive oil to keep it moist. You can prepare it up to two weeks ahead and freeze, unglazed. Top the thawed cake with lemon glaze and a sprig of rosemary before serving.

Cooking spray
2   tablespoons all-purpose flour
13.5 ounces all-purpose flour (about 3 cups)
1½   tablespoons finely chopped fresh rosemary
2   teaspoons baking powder
½   teaspoon baking soda
½   teaspoon salt
1½   cups granulated sugar
½   cup olive oil
½   cup fat-free milk
2   teaspoons grated lemon rind
¼   cup fresh lemon juice
½   teaspoon vanilla extract
¼   teaspoon lemon extract
3   large eggs
1   cup powdered sugar
1   tablespoon fresh lemon juice
Rosemary sprig (optional)

1. Preheat oven to 350°.

2. Coat a 10-inch tube pan with cooking spray; dust with 2 tablespoons flour. Weigh or lightly spoon 13.5 ounces flour (about 3 cups) into dry measuring cups; level with a knife. Combine flour and next 4 ingredients (through salt) in a large bowl.

3. Place granulated sugar and next 7 ingredients (through eggs) in a medium bowl; beat with a mixer at low speed 2 minutes or until smooth. Add to flour mixture; beat until blended.

4. Pour batter into prepared pan. Bake at 350° for 45 minutes or until a wooden pick inserted in center comes out clean. Cool in pan 15 minutes on a wire rack. Remove from pan. Cool completely on wire rack. Combine powdered sugar and 1 tablespoon lemon juice, stirring until smooth. Drizzle sugar mixture over cake. Garnish with rosemary sprig, if desired. Serves 16 (serving size: 1 slice).

CALORIES 265; FAT 7.9g (sat 1.3g, mono 5.3g, poly 0.9g); PROTEIN 3.9g; CARB 45.1g; FIBER 0.7g; CHOL 40mg; IRON 1.3mg; SODIUM 211mg; CALC 20mg

Choosing the Right Rosemary

Seedlings labeled simply "rosemary" can be quite nice. However, named varieties have predictable habits and size, so they may be more desirable for specific applications. Upright rosemary can grow 4 to 6 feet tall; cultivars include Collingwood Ingram, Gorizia, Logee Blue, Majorca Pink, Tuscan Blue, and Sissinghurst White, with the color referring to the late-winter and spring flowers. In addition to the upright form, a trailing (prostrate) form will cascade over a wall or grow low to the ground. Look for prostrate rosemary or named varieties, such as Huntington Carpet, Lockwood de Forest, Pink Cascade, and Shimmering Stars. For a milder-flavored variety, try the upright Tuscan Blue.

Honey-Almond Focaccia with Rosemary

Hands-on time: 17 min.   Total time: 1 hr. 42 min.

Infusing the olive oil and almonds with rosemary's woodsy flavor gives this sweet and salty focaccia an irresistible earthiness. Use fresh rosemary, not dried.

½ cup sliced almonds	1 package dry yeast
½ cup olive oil	14.7 ounces all-purpose flour (about 3¼ cups), divided
1 tablespoon chopped fresh rosemary	1 teaspoon salt
⅛ teaspoon salt	1 large egg yolk
⅛ teaspoon crushed red pepper	2 tablespoons olive oil, divided
1 cup warm 1% low-fat milk (100° to 110°)	3 tablespoons powdered sugar
	1½ teaspoons honey
1½ teaspoons granulated sugar	1 large egg white

1. Combine first 3 ingredients in a small saucepan; bring to a boil over medium-high heat. Cook 1 minute or until golden. Drain nut mixture through a fine sieve into a bowl, reserving oil. Toss nuts with ⅛ teaspoon salt and red pepper in a bowl.
2. Combine milk, granulated sugar, and yeast in a large bowl; let stand 5 minutes or until bubbly. Weigh or lightly spoon flour into dry measuring cups; level with a knife. Add reserved oil, 5.7 ounces flour (about 1¼ cups), 1 teaspoon salt, and egg yolk to yeast mixture; beat with a mixer at low speed until combined. Gradually add 9 ounces flour (about 2 cups) to oil mixture; beat at low speed until a soft, elastic dough forms (about 3 minutes). Press dough into a jelly-roll pan coated with 1½ tablespoons oil. Cover with plastic wrap; let rise in a warm place (85°), free from drafts, 40 minutes or until almost doubled in size.
3. Preheat oven to 350°.
4. Press dough gently with fingertips. Combine 1½ teaspoons oil, powdered sugar, honey, and egg white in a small bowl, stirring with a whisk until smooth. Gently brush dough with half of egg white mixture. Bake at 350° for 20 minutes. Remove pan from oven. Brush top of bread with remaining egg white mixture; sprinkle with almonds. Bake an additional 10 minutes or until golden brown. Remove from pan; cool 10 minutes on a wire rack. Serves 24 (serving size: 1 [2½-inch square] piece).

CALORIES 137; FAT 7.1g (sat 1g, mono 4.9g, poly 0.9g); PROTEIN 2.9g; CARB 15.5g; FIBER 0.8g; CHOL 8mg; IRON 1mg; SODIUM 119mg; CALC 21mg

Rosemary-Dijon Crusted Standing Rib Roast

Hands-on time: 15 min. Total time: 3 hr. 5 min.

Rosemary is a strong, pungent herb that does well with heavy, rich beef dishes, and this rosemary-Dijon combination smells heavenly. Getting the perfect crust on the roast is important. Serve with roasted potatoes to soak up the juices and a lighter side, such as steamed green beans, or pair it with a medley of grilled vegetables.

1	(5-pound) standing rib roast, trimmed
1	teaspoon salt
1	teaspoon freshly ground black pepper
5	garlic cloves
1/4	cup Dijon mustard
1 1/2	tablespoons chopped fresh thyme
1	tablespoon chopped fresh rosemary
1	tablespoon extra-virgin olive oil
	Cooking spray
1 1/2	cups fat-free, lower-sodium beef broth
2/3	cup pinot noir

1. Let beef stand 1 hour at room temperature. Sprinkle beef evenly with salt and pepper.

2. Preheat oven to 400°.

3. Place garlic in a mini food processor; pulse until finely chopped. Add Dijon, thyme, rosemary, and oil; pulse to combine. Rub Dijon mixture evenly over beef. Place roast on the rack of a roasting pan coated with cooking spray; place rack in pan. Bake at 400° for 30 minutes. Reduce oven temperature to 350° (do not remove roast from oven); bake at 350° for 30 minutes. Add broth to pan. Bake 30 minutes or until a thermometer registers 135° or until desired degree of doneness. Remove roast from oven, and let stand 20 minutes before slicing.

4. Heat roasting pan over medium-high heat; bring broth mixture to a boil, scraping pan to loosen browned bits. Stir in wine; boil 6 minutes or until reduced to 2/3 cup (about 6 minutes). Serve with beef. Serves 12 (serving size: about 3 ounces beef and about 2 1/2 teaspoons sauce).

CALORIES 255; FAT 15.4g (sat 5.7g, mono 6.7g, poly 0.7g); PROTEIN 23g; CARB 1.9g; FIBER 0.1g; CHOL 107mg; IRON 1.6mg; SODIUM 417mg; CALC 20mg

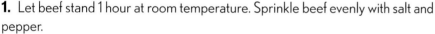

Rosemary Skewers

Grilling fresh garden vegetables on a rosemary skewer infuses a smoky, herbal flavor. Make your own by cutting 8-inch stems that are stronger and "woodier." Holding the leafy end in one hand, strip the leaves by pulling down between forefinger and thumb. Save the leaves for another use. Soak skewers in water for an hour before grilling veggie, shrimp, chicken, or steak kebabs. Small ones make for a great appetizer presentation, too.

THYME

Fragrant thyme flourishes in kitchen gardens and rock gardens.
Consider planting several varieties if you have the space.

SEASON: Spring through fall

CHOOSING: Sold in little bundles of stems with the small leaves attached, thyme should appear fresh, not wilted. It is normal for some types to be gray, but yellowed or shedding leaves indicate the bunch is past its prime.

STORING: Place freshly cut thyme in a plastic produce bag in the refrigerator, preferably not in the vegetable bin.

GROWING: Remarkably easy to grow and versatile in the garden, thyme can be tucked into corners, planted between stones, or set on the front edge of a flower or vegetable bed.

Dozens of varieties are available, but those interested in the best culinary thymes have only a handful of choices. Those best for flavor, as well as ease of use, are the low-growing, shrubby ones known as English, French, lemon, or winter thyme. The sturdier stems and small, flavorful leaves make it easy to strip the leaves from the cut stems by holding the tip of the stem between the thumb and forefinger of one hand, and then sliding the thumb and forefinger of the other hand down the stem, raking off the leaves.

The creeping thyme varieties are remarkable as landscape plants, as well as container plants. However, they are not as easy to harvest because the tender stem tends to break as the leaves are stripped. With a little patience, both cook and gardener will be pleased with these mat-forming perennials.

Give thyme full sun, or even partial shade in hot climates. It enjoys moist, rich soil, and is remarkably drought-tolerant once established. Well-drained soil is a must; the roots will rot in soggy ground. After severe winters, a little pruning is needed to remove dead stems and encourage new growth. As with most herbs, regular snipping during the growing season improves the plant.

Roast Pork Tenderloin with Thyme-Scented Plums

Hands-on time: 22 min. Total time: 53 min.

Use either common thyme or lemon thyme for the plums broiled in honey. Pork pairs well with fresh plums, or try it with fresh peaches.

2½ tablespoons olive oil, divided
1   (1-pound) pork tenderloin, trimmed
¾   teaspoon kosher salt, divided
½   teaspoon freshly ground black pepper, divided

1   pound small, ripe plums, quartered and pitted (about 6)
2   tablespoons honey
1   garlic clove, minced
2   teaspoons chopped fresh thyme
Thyme sprigs (optional)

1. Preheat oven to 500°.

2. Heat a large ovenproof skillet over medium-high heat. Add 1½ tablespoons olive oil to pan; swirl to coat. Sprinkle pork with ½ teaspoon salt and ¼ teaspoon black pepper. Add pork to pan; cook 4 minutes, turning to brown on all sides. Place pan in oven. Bake at 500° for 15 minutes or until a thermometer registers 145°. Remove pork from pan. Let stand 10 minutes; slice crosswise into 12 slices.

3. Preheat broiler.

4. Without cleaning pan, arrange plums, cut sides up, in pan. Combine 1 tablespoon oil, honey, and garlic, stirring well; brush plums evenly with honey mixture. Sprinkle with ¼ teaspoon salt and ¼ teaspoon pepper. Broil plums 6 minutes or until lightly charred; sprinkle with chopped thyme. Serve with pork. Garnish with thyme sprigs, if desired. Serves 4 (serving size: 3 ounces pork and 6 plum quarters).

CALORIES 285; FAT 10.9g (sat 2g, mono 7.1g, poly 1.3g); PROTEIN 24.6g; CARB 23.4g; FIBER 1.7g; CHOL 74mg; IRON 1.6mg; SODIUM 421mg; CALC 11mg

Dijon, Thyme, and Pine Nut Broccoli

Hands-on time: 9 min.   Total time: 13 min.

Banish the tired, plain broccoli routine for one that heightens the flavor with thyme and Dijon mustard. Thyme is a key herb in vinaigrettes, and it works well in this lemony mustard dressing, too.

12   ounces broccoli florets (5 cups)
1   tablespoon minced shallots
2   tablespoons extra-virgin olive oil
1   tablespoon fresh lemon juice
1   tablespoon Dijon mustard
2   teaspoons chopped fresh thyme
2   tablespoons toasted pine nuts

1. Arrange broccoli in a steamer. Steam, covered, 4 minutes or until crisp-tender. Place broccoli in a large bowl.
2. Combine shallots, olive oil, lemon juice, mustard, and thyme in a bowl, stirring with a whisk. Add broccoli and pine nuts to oil mixture; toss. Serves 6 (serving size: ²/₃ cup).

CALORIES 79; FAT 6.6g (sat 0.8g, mono 3.8g, poly 1.5g); PROTEIN 2.1g; CARB 4.4g; FIBER 1.9g; CHOL 0mg; IRON 0.8mg; SODIUM 76mg; CALC 30mg

Thyme Corn Bread

Hands-on time: 9 min.   Total time: 39 min.

Folding in fresh thyme and corn-off-the-cob makes this classic bread a good companion for soups, stews, or poultry entrées. For the most intense flavor in the tiny leaves, harvest the thyme just before it begins to flower.

4.5   ounces all-purpose flour (about 1 cup)
³/₄   cup yellow cornmeal
1   tablespoon sugar
1   teaspoon baking soda
½   teaspoon salt
³/₄   cup low-fat buttermilk
2   tablespoons canola oil
1   large egg
½   cup fresh corn kernels (about 1 ear)
1½   tablespoons fresh thyme leaves
Cooking spray

1. Preheat oven to 350°.
2. Weigh or lightly spoon flour into a dry measuring cup; level with a knife. Combine flour and next 4 ingredients (through salt) in a bowl. Make a well in center of mixture. Combine buttermilk, oil, and egg in a bowl; stir in corn and thyme. Add buttermilk mixture to flour mixture; stir just until moist.
3. Spoon batter into an 8-inch square metal baking pan lightly coated with cooking spray. Bake at 350° for 25 minutes or until corn bread is lightly browned and begins to pull away from sides of pan. Cool in pan 5 minutes on a wire rack. Serves 9 (serving size: 1 piece).

CALORIES 161; FAT 4.4g (sat 0.7g, mono 2.3g, poly 1.1g); PROTEIN 4.2g; CARB 25.5g; FIBER 0.9g; CHOL 25mg; IRON 1.1mg; SODIUM 299mg; CALC 39mg

Thyme Corn Bread

GARDENING GUIDE

This how-to guide gives you the basics on starting your garden, whether you have backyard space to spare or a small spot ready for containers.

WHY GARDEN?

Those who have tasted a summer tomato sun-sweetened on the vine or a crisp cucumber plucked from under the leaves that nourished it know the intense flavor of fresh-picked produce is unrivaled by anything found in a supermarket.

Perhaps our taste buds detect what our eyes cannot. Truly fresh produce is more nourishing and deeply satisfying to the senses. The nature of the American food system means the fruit, vegetables, and herbs found in grocery stores have often been grown hundreds of miles from our kitchens and packed, shipped, distributed, and displayed, all while being refrigerated—a process that can wreak havoc on the flavor and nutrients of delicate plants.

When food is flown or trucked to your local store, days pass between harvest and your table. Even the most perfect specimen will begin to decline before you bring it home—it loses moisture and vitamins and begins to metabolize its own reserves. Some foods, like sweet corn or snap peas, begin to transform altogether directly after picking (converting sugar to starch and losing sweetness and flavor). Although our remarkable food-distribution system provides a diverse selection of foods year-round, cost and quality are inevitably compromised.

Only a few generations ago, most of the food on the dinner table had been growing in a garden only hours before it was served. While it would be a full-time job these days to feed your family this way, it feels surprisingly good to grow some of the staples on your grocery list.

Taste: A New World of Flavors

One perk of gardening is the exposure to new varieties you may not have seen or tried before. Seed catalogs and garden centers offer seemingly endless options in varying colors and shapes, often with charming historical names. Thousands of varieties of tomatoes are at your fingertips, versus the simple red, round tomato in supermarkets. A tomato grower who supplies a large market needs to grow varieties that ripen all at once for a more economical harvest that can survive shipping in good condition, while a home gardener can select tomatoes for flavor, extended harvest, and color. The same is true for many other crops.

Cost: Get More for Less

If you buy in bulk and clip coupons for a variety of packaged foods, gardening may not cut the cost of your regular grocery bill. But if you love to buy fresh produce—especially organic—you can confidently reduce your monthly expenditures. Cost efficiency is an age-old reason to grow your own food since seeds, sun, and nature's soil are not expensive. However, like any hobby, gardening can get pricey if you choose to purchase lots of equipment or gardening gadgets.

Learning: An Outdoor Classroom

Backyard gardens teach children about the origin of food, creating a powerful connection to the dinner plate that's simply magical. Kids can help plant, water, weed, and harvest produce, and after spending time caring for the plants, they'll be more apt to eat the fruits of their labor. This same magic has an effect on adults, too. When you toss a homegrown salad together, cook a pot of greens, or serve a stir-fried medley of vegetables, you have a deeper appreciation of its amazing path to your plate.

Health: Yours, Your Children's, and the Planet's

When a family gardens, their diet is more diverse and inherently healthier, packed with vitamins, minerals, and antioxidants. Food in its purest, freshest form is not only the tastiest way to enjoy it but also the most beneficial nutritionally.

When you grow your own food, you know what goes into it: how it's fertilized, what pesticides are used, and overall care. If you grow organically, you can eat organically. Not only is that beneficial for you, but also fewer chemicals and less distance traveled to get the food on your plate make for a smaller carbon footprint.

Exercise is another bonus. Anyone who says that gardening is not aerobic has never raked leaves or shoveled compost.

Keep Your Garden in Shape

- **Work in moderation.** Though it is easy to excitedly begin big and bold, don't overdo it. Set achievable goals that don't tax your muscles or your time to the point of pain. Like exercise, gardening has no finish line. One season leads to the next. The idea is to enjoy the journey and gather your rewards along the way.
- **Challenge your mind and your body.** If you are intellectually engaged in the garden, you're more likely to be fulfilled by it. Each season is different. Try new varieties. Research the history on how a vegetable came to be in America today. Lay out new garden plans each year. Research a pest or problem and figure out how to deal with it. Then take comfort in the fact that you'll never know it all. Whether it's your first season or your fortieth, there will always be something new to grow, learn, and do.
- **Adapt your garden to your life.** If you have difficulty bending, plant in raised beds or containers. If you have sore joints, choose tools with large, padded handles. If there are tasks that are difficult for you, such as turning the soil or bringing home a quantity of mulch, get help, and then do the work that you can enjoy.
- **Be optimistic.** Try a new plant or variety each season. If a plant dies or doesn't grow as it should this season, there's always next year. Research, learn, and look forward to applying the lesson the next time.
- **Be creative.** Vegetable gardens are particularly fun because they are replanted often, sometimes three or more times each year. Think of fun ways to make a trellis for tomatoes and cucumbers, arrange your veggies in an ornamental pattern, and mix in flowers with your vegetables to use as table decorations or garnishes.
- **Be social.** Gardeners learn from one another. Sign up for a gardening class. Volunteer at a local botanical garden. Rent a plot in a community garden. Visit other gardeners and invite them to visit you. Get online to share and learn; many social media sites are fantastic resources for virtually visiting any garden or sharing recipes.
- **Relax.** Time spent weeding or doing other mindless chores is a great time to work out frustration, daydream, and problem-solve. Many gardeners find that working with their hands frees their minds.

BACKYARD GARDENING

Selecting a Site

Fruit, vegetables, and herbs almost universally require the energy of the sun to be productive, so it's important to select a site that receives a minimum of six hours of sun each day, preferably eight hours. If your garden is close to a structure, such as your house, choose a spot on the west or south side, provided tall trees or an adjacent house or building does not shade the site in the afternoon.

Deep soil and good drainage are also crucial. If your sunny spot has compacted soil or the land is low and apt to be wet for days after a rain, consider building raised beds. The ideal size is 4 feet wide so the middle is easily reachable from both sides. Beds that are 4 x 4 or 4 x 8 feet are the most manageable; they can be built from stock lumber, work in a variety of patterns, and allow for neat and tidy configurations.

The height can range from 10 to 12 inches of mounded soil with no permanent edging to several feet tall—high enough to provide seating on the edge or easy access from a wheelchair.

The soil for a raised bed can be bagged garden soil or a mix of local topsoil and organic matter. Ask your garden center for brand or supplier recommendations. Many municipalities encourage composting by collecting organic matter and selling finished compost to residents at low or no cost—a great additive for large beds. Before filling, be sure to remove turf, loosen the soil beneath the raised bed, and amend it with organic matter so deep-rooted plants can benefit. Building and filling raised beds is heavy work in the beginning, but gardening will be easier in the long run.

Water supply is also essential. If there's not a spigot nearby, call the plumber before you do anything else. Consider collecting rainwater runoff in rain barrels at your downspouts, too.

Soil Testing

A soil test is the smart way to assess your soil's pH and any nutrient deficiencies. The results will help you determine what types of amendments or fertilizers are needed and how to apply them in the correct amounts. You can have your soil tested by a private lab or through a kit obtained from your local garden center or Cooperative Extension office (www.csrees.usda.gov/Extension).

Getting Started

Once you decide where to grow, it's finally time to break ground. Preparing the soil is essential to success. Mark off the space for your garden using spray paint or stakes and string. If there is grass, it's best to remove it or kill it rather than turning it into the soil—it'll be a constant weed-producing nuisance. If the area is large, consider renting a sod cutter and transplanting the turf to another part of your property. Otherwise, cover the area with a plastic drop cloth or sheet, weigh down the edges with boards, bricks, or stones, and then wait. The heat generated by the sun will kill the lawn in two to four weeks, depending on the time of year. Take caution: Before choosing a chemical solution to kill your lawn, read the herbicide label carefully. You don't want to apply any product not labeled for use with food crops.

For an in-ground garden: Once the grass is gone, the next step is loosening the soil. Assuming you have average topsoil that is 4 to 6 inches thick, cover the area with at least a 2-inch layer of organic material, such as homemade compost, municipal compost, rotted sawdust, bagged garden soil, aged manure, or whatever is affordable and available where you live. Turn it in using a rototiller or a garden fork, depending on the size of the plot. If you already know the garden's layout, till just the beds and simply cover the paths with mulch to save you time and energy.

For a raised-bed garden: If you are building above the soil in raised beds, you'll still need to remove turf. It is possible to grow atop concrete; read online to find construction plans. Prefab raised-bed kits make for easy installation.

CONTAINER GARDENING

Getting Started

If you don't have much land—or your only direct sunlight falls on a paved surface such as a driveway, porch, patio, or deck—plant in containers. Select large pots or a grouping of pots in different sizes so you can grow a variety of fruit, vegetables, and herbs. You'll be surprised how productive they can be. What you lack in surface area you make up in soil depth. Roots grow deep in a pot, while they tend to grow horizontally in a garden. Follow these tips to get the most from your container garden:

- Select a good potting soil for optimum plant growth. For best results, don't use soil from your garden. Purchase potting soils from recognizable brands or those recommended by your local garden center. Look for a potting mix, rather than a bagged product labeled "garden soil." Avoid those that are dense and heavy when wet. If in doubt, try small bags of different kinds. You'll find your favorite pretty quickly, based on plant growth.
- Do not overfill your pots. Leave about an inch of the rim above the soil so that water is forced to drain down through the potting mix, rather than spilling over the edge. The soil warms quickly in a container, so gardeners may find containers helpful in getting an early start for a few plants.
- Ensure proper drainage. Use pots with drainage holes or drill sizable ones.

What's the Right Size?

If in doubt, use a larger container than you think you'll need. You can always add more plants later, but don't underestimate how large these tiny seedlings can grow.

Hanging basket: strawberries, parsley, thyme

6-inch pot: lettuce, spinach, chives

8- to 12-inch pot: strawberries, beets, carrots, lettuce, radishes, spinach, chives, dill, parsley, sage, thyme

14-inch pot: arugula (3 plants), cabbage and collards (1 plant), spinach and loose-leaf lettuce (3 to 4 plants), all herbs

18-inch pot: low-bush or dwarf blueberries, strawberries, broccoli, cauliflower, large cabbage, small eggplant, all greens (in multiples), small peppers, determinate tomatoes

24-inch pot: small citrus, melons, artichokes, cucumbers, large peppers, pumpkins, summer squash, indeterminate tomatoes, cherry tomatoes, various combinations of vegetables and herbs

See our suggestions for plant combinations starting on page 266.

Choosing the Right Container

Containers are available in a variety of materials to suit your space and aesthetic. Pot feet (or any piece of brick or stone) raise a container off the surface below so as not to block the drainage hole. This also preserves surfaces like wooden decks that may rot under constant moisture.

- Terra-cotta pots are traditional and look great, but they dry quickly due to evaporation from the sides of the pot. Also, if you have freezing temperatures in your area during winter, the pots need to be stored in a dry place. The moisture that is absorbed into the terra-cotta will freeze and crack the pot.
- Glazed ceramic pots come in a variety of colors, sizes, and shapes for design-conscious gardeners. They survive mild freezes, but where the soil freezes, it may crack the pot as it expands.
- Resin or plastic pots have the advantage of being lightweight and durable. Nice ones can be costly, but they'll last for years.
- Wooden pots or whiskey barrels are favorites of gardeners everywhere because of their generous size and rustic appearance. You can grow mixed plantings in a container this size.
- Concrete pots are an excellent choice, as long as you don't like to rearrange your container garden very often. They can be extremely heavy, but they're durable. It's a good idea to place the empty pot where you want it permanently, fill it with potting mix, and then plant.
- Fiberglass pots resemble stone, wood, terra-cotta, or any material the maker wants to replicate. They're lightweight and durable, albeit costly.

PLANNING

Choosing What to Plant

Deciding what to plant depends on the season, your site, and of course, your taste buds. Here are a few things to keep in mind:

- **Cost.** Growing the highest-value fruit, vegetables, and herbs can be a smart way to save on your grocery bill. Bell peppers and heirloom tomatoes, particularly if you buy organic, can be costly, so consider planting those in your summer garden. Likewise, leaf lettuce and mesclun blends can be harvested repeatedly by picking the outer, mature leaves and leaving the plant in the ground to continue growing. With any luck, you'll be able to strike salad greens off your grocery list for half the year.

- **Quality.** Sometimes you can't buy the same standard of produce that you can get from the garden. If small, tender okra is nowhere to be found in the grocery store and your growing season is long and hot enough, then grow your own.

- **Convenience.** If basil is an herb you love and often purchase, you may want to include it in your garden or grow it in a container so that you always have fresh leaves on hand to add to a sandwich or mix into a salad. Lettuce, cilantro, and dill all have an extended season in the spring and fall garden, but they spoil quickly in the refrigerator.

Knowing When to Plant

Once you know what you'd like to grow, the question is when to grow it. Most vegetables and herbs fall into one of three groups, and sometimes the group changes depending on where you live.

Season	Vegetables & Fruits	Herbs
warm-season crops	artichokes, beans, corn, cucumbers, okra, peppers, squash (summer and winter), sweet potatoes, tomatoes	basil
cool-season crops	arugula, beets, broccoli, Brussels sprouts, cabbage, carrots, cauliflower, fennel, greens, leeks, lettuce, onions, snow or sugar snap peas, potatoes, spinach	cilantro, dill, parsley
perennial crops	all fruits, except strawberries, which are usually replanted every few years	chives, mint, oregano, rosemary, thyme

Exceptions: In areas such as South Florida, where summers are steamy, even heat-loving plants can become stressed or diseased. Many warm-season crops are grown along with cool-season crops during the frost-free winter days or during the shoulder seasons of spring and fall.

Research Your Frost Date

Frost dates for spring and fall are the most important dates on a gardener's calendar, as they are the benchmarks for planting. Years of weather records have resulted in fairly accurate predictions of when to expect the last killing freeze in spring and the first killing frost in fall in areas around the country. Consult the chart on the National Oceanic and Atmospheric Administration's website (cdo.ncdc.noaa.gov/climatenormals/clim20supp1/states) to find the spring and fall dates for your area.

In addition to the plant profiles throughout this book, you'll find planting instructions (i.e., "plant in spring two to four weeks before the last expected frost") on seed packets and plant labels. It's important to note that a light freeze will not kill cool-season crops. Even lettuce can withstand temperatures in the mid- to high 20s. However, warm-season plants, such as basil and squash, will show damage from the slightest 32° frost.

Seeds vs. Transplants

Most vegetables and herbs can be grown from either seeds or transplants, while most fruit mentioned in this book (except melons) must be grown from transplants.

When the season is short, vegetable and herb transplants have the advantage because you get a jump start on the growing season with a healthy, sizable plant. If you don't have space to start your own seedlings indoors, it's often easier and more successful to buy transplants. For beginning gardeners, it's best to start with mostly transplants and mix in seeds as you learn.

If the season is appropriate, seeds are always a good idea. They're simply more economical. A seed packet might produce 50 lettuce plants for the cost of one cell pack of six transplants. Some items, such as carrots or radishes, must be grown from seeds.

Availability will also dictate what you choose because your local garden center might not carry the particular variety you want to grow. You'll need to plant seeds directly in garden soil or grow your own transplants by sowing seeds indoors in containers prior to planting outside.

GARDEN DESIGNS

Space is at a premium for many gardeners, but with careful planning you can have a fruitful garden no matter the size. Here you'll find plans for all seasons to give you some ideas for your garden.

Beds The plans shared over the next few pages were designed for 4 x 8–foot beds that can take you from cool to warm season. The plant combinations are flexible and meant to serve as a guide to help you get started. Follow these specifications exactly or customize your garden to suit your taste buds by planting any of the recommended substitutes.

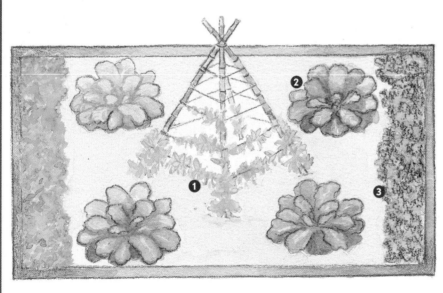

Bed 1: Cool Season

A semipermanent tepee constructed of three to four vertical stakes made of bamboo, spiral stakes, or rebar provides support for vining plants season after season. Wrap the tepee with twine to give the plants horizontal supports on which to climb.

Sugar snap peas (1): Substitute green peas or snow peas.

Collard greens (2): Substitute cabbage, broccoli, Brussels sprouts, kale, or mustard greens.

Lettuce (3): Substitute carrots, radishes, dill, parsley, or cilantro.

Bed 1: Warm Season

This bed shows a variety of plants, but if your family doesn't care for one of the vegetables or herbs shown, feel free to make substitutions.

Cherry tomatoes (1): The plant has rambling vines that bear fruit all summer. Training the vines around the tepee and not just up the legs of the support will help handle the plant's vigorous growth. You can also tame unruly vines by pruning them midsummer.

Peppers: Plant any variety you like, including serrano, cayenne (2), bell (3), habanero, jalapeño, and Thai chile. If your plants grow large, add a tomato cage for additional support.

Lemon thyme (4) and chives (5): These are perennial herbs that, once planted, will carry through from season to season unless they're transplanted to another location.

Eggplant (6) and basil (7): Plant any varieties you like.

Bed 2: Warm Season

Corn (1): Plant in a block of four rows by four rows for the best pollination.

Squash (2): Substitute crookneck, straightneck, zucchini, or pattypan squash.

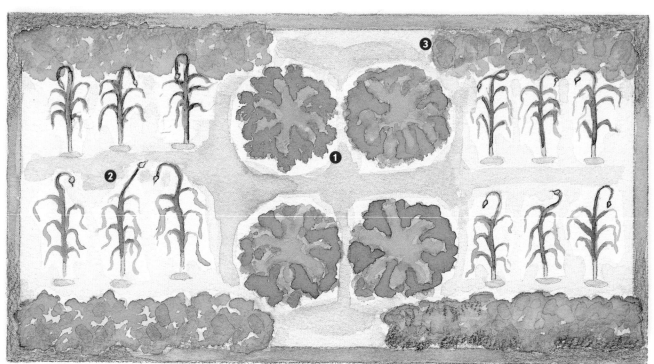

Bed 2: Cool Season

Kale (1): Substitute collards, broccoli, cauliflower, or Brussels sprouts.

Garlic (2): Substitute onions.

Arugula (3): Substitute lettuce or other salad greens. Stagger planting one corner every few weeks for a continuous harvest.

Bed 3: Cool Season

This bed features a raised diamond-shaped bed in the center, which is intended to be elevated with additional timbers to create deeper soil.

Broccoli (1): Substitute cauliflower, cabbage, kale, or collards.

Carrots (2): Substitute radishes, parsley, or arugula.

Green (3) and red (4) lettuces: Substitute leaf lettuce, romaine, or a mix of different types.

Bed 3: Warm Season

Sunflowers and pole beans (1): In the summer, plant the center section with sunflowers. After they reach 3 to 4 feet tall, sow pole bean seeds at the base of the stalks, using the sunflowers as a homegrown trellis.

Bush cucumbers (2): Substitute summer squash or bush-type watermelons.

Bed 4: Cool Season

This traditional row-type layout lends itself to a variety of options.

Cauliflower (1): Substitute cabbage, broccoli, Brussels sprouts, kale, or mustard greens.

Swiss chard: The red (2) and yellow (3) varieties shown in this design make a pretty contrast to the blue-green of the cauliflower in the center of the bed. Substitute Asian greens, such as pak choi or bok choy.

Radishes (4) and dill (5): Radishes grow quickly, which means you can replant as soon as they're harvested and get in a few plantings each season. Substitute cilantro or parsley for both the dill and the radishes, if you like.

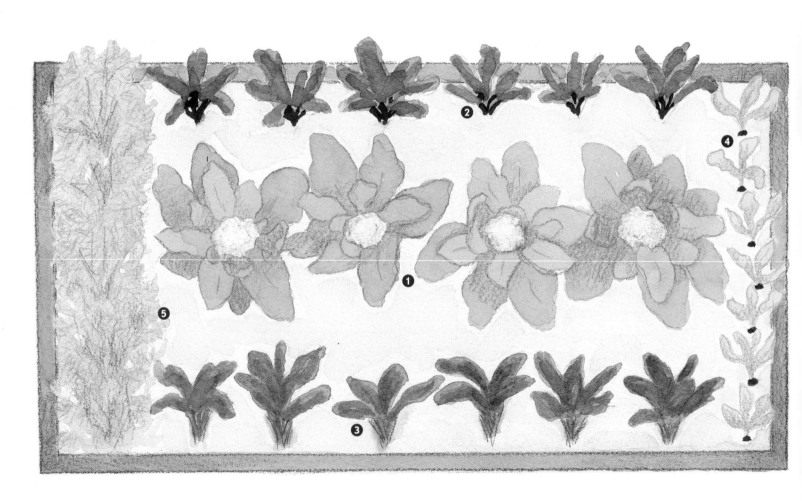

Bed 4: Warm Season

Tomatoes (1): Three tomatoes grown in cages give you an opportunity to try a few different varieties. Choose three options for variety in color and timing so you'll have tomato-y goodness all season long. Determinate varieties are recommended for these smaller tomato cages, but if you prefer indeterminate tomatoes, use two large cages that are 3 feet in diameter and 6 feet tall. They'll need to be made of sturdy wire fencing with openings large enough for you to reach through. Be sure to anchor these larger cages by tying them to rebar hammered into the soil.

Watermelon (2): Unlike the bush type, vine watermelon needs room to ramble. Plant just one, and train the vines to cover the bed rather than the path around the bed. Substitute pumpkins, winter squash, or melons.

Containers

Containers For containers, a grouping of three or more pots of differing sizes is a great way to get a variety of produce from a limited amount of space. A good base will include a large urn with lots of room for roots, accompanied by an 18- to 24-inch pot and a smaller 12- to 14-inch pot. Choose lighter-weight material for those placed on a patio or balcony, which may not be able to handle the weight of heavier containers.

Containers: Warm Season

Tomatoes (1): Plant tomatoes in a larger urn, and choose varieties bred for containers, such as Patio or Sweet 'N' Neat, which can be grown without support. You can also plant a determinate (Better Bush, Bush Early Girl, Bush Goliath) or dwarf indeterminate (Husky Cherry Red) that can be supported using a tomato cage or homemade tepee. If you have an area next to a railing or fence that gets adequate sunlight, you'll have more options because the vines can use it for support.

Zucchini (2): One plant can be quite prolific in an 18- to 24-inch pot. Substitute crookneck, straightneck, or pattypan squash.

Chives (3): Perennial herbs such as chives or thyme can remain in a small pot year-round. Substitute creeping thyme or Spicy Globe basil.

Containers: Cool Season

If the plants don't live through the winter, replant them again in early spring before the last frost.

Kale (1): Substitute cabbage, broccoli, mustard greens, cauliflower, or Brussels sprouts.

Lettuce (2): Potted lettuce won't provide endless salads, but it's ideal to supplement store-bought greens and provide enough for sandwiches.

Cilantro (3): Substitute parsley, chives, or dill.

Containers: Herbs

Potted herbs are ideal for those who'd like year-round seasoning at their door.

Rosemary (1): A large urn is perfect for a large plant like rosemary. This woody shrub is cold-tender and better suited for gardeners in warmer states, although it will tolerate temperatures in the 20s without a problem. Choose a cold-hardy variety, such as Hill Hardy and Arp, for those areas where temperatures dip into the teens. Until the rosemary grows large, creeping thyme (2) can be planted on the sunny side (south or west) of the pot to trail over the edge.

Basil (3): Plant basil in an 18- to 24-inch pot. This annual is only perennial in gardens that are frost-free. Plant any variety you'd like.

Parsley (4): Plant parsley in a small pot. Substitute chives, creeping thyme, or mint.

CARING FOR YOUR GARDEN

The best thing you can do for your garden is to closely observe its progress and take steps to correct little problems before they become big ones. These other essentials will help, too.

Water

Water is essential and is at times in short supply. To make it through the good times and bad, encourage deep rooting by having loose, porous soil and keeping your garden covered with mulch to minimize water loss through evaporation. Drip irrigation, a method of trickling water from tubes slowly and directly onto the surface of the soil, is recommended for gardeners in drought-prone areas. It's beneficial because no water is lost to evaporation or runoff.

A good rule of thumb is that gardens need about an inch of water each week. However, this measurement doesn't take into account variations in water use due to temperature, humidity, and how close plants are spaced from each other, so you may need to tweak this to fit the needs of your garden. By regular observation, most gardeners quickly figure out which plants wilt first, which is a useful indicator when you are first learning watering cycles. Ideally, you should avoid stressing the plants: Apply water before the soil dries out. Wet the soil thoroughly to encourage deep rooting, and then avoid watering again until it's needed. Overwatering can be just as detrimental as underwatering.

The same principle applies when watering containers, although container-grown plants will need water more often than in-ground plants. Be sure to water containers until you see water spill from the bottom of the pot to ensure the soil is thoroughly moist. When the weather is hot, they may need water daily. Mulch will also help conserve moisture in containers: Use small bark nuggets; they're easy to turn into the soil at season's end to enrich it further. Also, mulch herbs with small pea gravel; it protects foliage from soil splatter and is helpful in humid climates.

Fertilizer

Fertilizer is one way to supply the nutrients essential for a productive garden. The key is to use the right kind and apply it in moderation.

The most common fertilizers are made from salts of nitrogen, phosphorus, and potassium, nutrients used by plants in the largest quantity. You'll see them labeled as N-P-K: 5-10-10, 20-20-20, or similar. The three numbers are the percentages of those three nutrients in the product. Because they are salts, too much can kill your plants. Use the product in the amount recommended on the label to help your plants flourish.

Overfertilizing can also delay harvest. Plants that must bloom in order to produce their fruit (tomatoes, peppers, eggplant, squash, cucumbers, melons, beans, peas, and okra) need a balanced approach to nutrition. If they get too much nitrogen, they'll grow a lot of foliage and flowering will be delayed.

Usually a dilute liquid fertilizer is used when transplants are set in the soil, followed in a week or two by granular fertilizer or timed-release granules applied at the rate recommended on the product label. Reapply as recommended, as different products remain active in the garden for varying lengths of time.

Organic gardeners use compost and other amendments, such as kelp, fish emulsion, cottonseed, and soybean meal to enrich the soil and feed the worms and soil microbes. This plant-feeding system works quite well, and it has long-term benefits.

Mulch

Mulch is organic material that hasn't yet decomposed. It reduces evaporation, which keeps soil moist and cool. It also prevents weeds. Common choices include pine needles, tree bark from various species, wheat straw, and even newspaper and pasteboard boxes. If papers are used, be sure to cover them with another mulch or they'll blow about on windy days. Areas covered with four to five sheets of newsprint or flattened boxes are certain to be weed-free. Avoid rubber mulches that don't break down; you want mulch to decay and enrich the soil.

Pests

Pests are part of gardening and take many forms: mildew that disfigures your cucumber foliage, tomato hornworms eating every leaf from your plant, or deer feasting on blueberries. Solutions vary, too, from chemicals that require careful and knowledgeable application to traps that simply capture the problem.

One of the most common problems is the havoc hungry wildlife can wreak on your garden. Birds peck ripening fruit, opening them to invasion by bacteria and ants. To keep them at bay, drape small and medium-sized fruiting plants with bird netting, use fake snakes and owls to scare them away, hang reflective tape on the plant, or simply plant enough to share with them. Remember, some birds damage fruit, while others eat the caterpillars that are eating your plants.

Deer can also be troublesome, eating fruit and foliage and trampling your hard work. Where there is consistent damage, try repellents or use motion-activated sprinklers and lights to keep them away. If those fail, consider installing a deer fence to protect your produce.

Keep in mind that any chemical used in the garden should be considered carefully before applying since it will also affect the fruit, vegetables, and herbs you're growing and could harm the bees that pollinate the flowers. General insecticides also harm beneficial insects that deter or rid your garden of troublesome ones. There are many solutions, from organic to homemade to commercial tried-and-true. Please consult your garden center or Cooperative Extension office for guidance.

Compost

Compost is a simple way to add nutrient-rich organic matter to your soil. Whereas fertilizer feeds the plants, compost feeds the soil, promoting the health of microbes that aid in plant growth. In addition, the organic matter in compost helps clay soils become lighter and more porous, and it helps sandy soil hold more moisture. No matter what kind of soil you have, compost makes it better. You can buy compost, but homemade is best.

Getting Started

Composting may sound intimidating, but it's easy. A mounded pile of leaves, branches, and other trimmings in a corner of your yard will eventually decompose without any work required, yielding a rich soil amendment. This process can take up to a year to produce results, but can be sped up by creating optimum conditions for the helpful organisms responsible for decay. You'll need the right mix of air, water, and materials rich in nitrogen and carbon. Sound complicated? It's not.

Anything that was once a plant can be composted. Your kitchen and yard will provide plenty of material. You'll need about twice as much by volume of brown matter as green matter. Brown matter comes from trees and is high in carbon. It includes dry leaves, hay, sawdust, wood chips, and woody trimmings. Green matter is fresher, wetter, and high in nitrogen. Generally, it comes from garden and kitchen waste, such as grass, food scraps, and animal manure (but not dog or cat droppings). Avoid plants that are diseased or infested with insects, weeds with seeds, or hardy weeds that could survive composting. To speed the process, shred or chop large materials. The summer season is rife with green matter, so be sure to layer in plenty of browns to keep the compost from getting soggy. If you lack brown matter, use shredded newspaper.

Include:

Browns
- Leaves
- Twigs
- Pine needles
- Shredded newspaper or cardboard
- Straw
- Sawdust
- Cornstalks

Greens
- Fresh grass clippings and weeds
- Eggshells
- Coffee grounds
- Tea
- Fruit peels and trimmings
- Vegetable trimmings

Avoid:

- Meats
- Bones
- Dairy products

- Oils and greasy waste
- Pet droppings

Piles vs. Compost Bins

There are a number of composting options to suit your space and needs: freestanding piles; homemade structures; or plastic compost bins, tumblers, or barrels sold at garden centers.

To create an open-air pile, begin by layering materials until the pile is 3 to 5 feet tall and wide—anything larger may not allow enough air to penetrate to the center. Apply water between each layer, but don't add so much that the pile becomes soggy or saturated. Once you've finished layering, sprinkle the pile with topsoil or previously composted material, which will infuse it with the microorganisms needed to start the decomposition process. The pile will heat up in just a few days. If left unattended, the pile will decompose slowly on its own. Turning it regularly introduces oxygen to the interior, which will speed the process. As you add new scraps, completely cover them within the pile.

If you don't have room for a compost pile, you can leave one garden bed unplanted each season and bury buckets of scraps from the kitchen every day or two. The earthworms will have a feast. After two weeks you'll find little left but the eggshells, which take a bit longer to break down. Just keep it covered in mulch to keep weeds down.

If most of your compost materials come from your kitchen or if you don't have the yard space, an enclosed container is a good option and will keep animals at bay. Layer as you would in an open-air pile, and turn it regularly.

Good compost has an earthy smell. If your compost smells rotten, it's a sign there's too much water or too many greens. Turn it more often, reduce the amount of greens you add, or apply more brown ingredients to balance the pile.

Organic Gardening

If you opt to go organic in your garden, these are the common practices. Always read labels carefully. Just because they're safe for food does not mean that they won't irritate or harm you if used improperly.

- Bt, or *Bacillus thuringiensis*, is a bacterial parasite of the larvae of butterflies and moths that can be sprayed or dusted. It combats troublesome larvae, including cabbage worms, cabbage loopers, tomato hornworms, and corn earworms.
- Copper fungicide is used to prevent fungal diseases of fruit. It can also be mixed with a dormant-oil spray in winter.
- Horticultural oils include dormant-oil sprays applied to fruit trees to smother overwintering insects. Use growing-season sprays carefully, as sun can be damaging after spraying.
- Insecticidal soap kills mealybugs, aphids, spider mites, and more with no residual effects.
- Kaolin spray is used as a protective coating on fruit trees for a variety of insect pests, as well as on some garden plants, such as squash, that are vulnerable to borers. Spray before the problems arise.
- Lime sulfur spray has long been considered the least toxic treatment for fungal problems, such as brown rot on peaches and cherries.
- Neem oil comes from the seed of a tropical tree and is effective against certain insects, mites, and fungi, but it should be used with caution. Apply when bees are not working.
- Spinosad is a biological insecticide used to control pests in organic gardens. Use against fire ants in the food garden, as well as against roly-polies (pill bugs). Use sparingly in consideration of beneficial insects.
- Sulfur spray can be used as a fungicide, insecticide, and miticide. It is commonly used for powdery mildew on grapevines. It can be irritating, so wear protective clothing as recommended on the label.

Get Growing

Gardening is a simple yet rewarding way to spend time outdoors, reconnect with nature just outside your door, and have something delicious to eat. Not everything will work out like you plan, but some of it will—in fact, most of it will. If you have fun growing the greens for your salads or pears for preserves, then your hard work has been rewarded.

CONNECTING KIDS TO FRESH PRODUCE

FoodCorps, a charity supported by **Cooking Light,**
is taking the healthy-food message to American school kids.

Boston, MA

This fast-growing nonprofit organization places motivated leaders in limited-resource communities for a year of public service. Working under the direction of local partner organizations, FoodCorps service members implement a three-ingredient recipe to give all youth an enduring relationship with healthy food: teach kids what healthy food is and where it comes from, build and tend school gardens, and bring high-quality local food into public school cafeterias.

The Challenge
In the last 30 years, the percentage of American children who are overweight or obese has tripled. Diet-related disease, diminished academic performance, and a shortened life expectancy threaten the future of our kids. What we feed our children and what we teach them about food in school and in school gardens shapes how they learn, how they grow, and how long they will live.

A National Network of Partners
When it comes to the challenging and important work of improving school food, FoodCorps embraces a model of collaboration. In each of the states it serves, FoodCorps selected a lead partner organization to direct its work, collaborating with them to develop a network of local partners in the communities where service members are placed.

FoodCorps' Three Pillars

1. Knowledge: Educating young minds about food

The typical elementary student receives just 3.4 hours of nutrition education each year. FoodCorps service members work with teachers to increase the quality and quantity of nutrition education, and they make learning about food fun. They conduct hands-on cooking demonstrations and model positive lifestyle choices that motivate kids to exercise and eat well.

2. Engagement: Getting hands in the dirt in school gardens

School gardens are powerful gateways for getting kids to try new foods. They also bring parents and community members together and help them become advocates for healthier school lunches. FoodCorps service members establish or expand school garden programs, engaging students, parents, and community volunteers in the active outdoor play of growing fruits and vegetables.

3. Access: Serving healthy school food to kids

Children who know the farmer who grew their broccoli are more likely to eat it. Studies show that children participating in Farm to School programs choose to eat one more serving of fruits and vegetables per day. FoodCorps service members create relationships between school food-service directors and local farmers and help transform cafeterias into educational environments where healthy food choices are celebrated and served.

FoodCorps event in Washington, DC

Roxbury, MA

Lewiston, ME

The publisher will donate $1 from the sale of each *Pick Fresh Cookbook* to FoodCorps up to a maximum of $10,000.

Inspiring Stories From the Field

Each service member spends a year in one of the high-obesity, limited-resource communities that FoodCorps serves across the country. Here, three share their experiences:

"A ringing highlight from my first year was using ingredients right from the garden to make a salsa. A lot of the kids had no idea we could make the stuff in the jar, but better—without the high salt and fat content—and the kids absolutely loved it!"

—Norris Guscott

▲ Member: Norris Guscott
Location: Boston, MA

Norris' parents cultivated his interest in food from a young age, teaching him to eat right and lead a healthy lifestyle. Since then, he's encouraged his friends and family to do the same. In college he studied community psychology, which focuses on the problems of people in relation to their surroundings and emphasizes that helping whole communities is the path to positive changes in physical and psychological health. Norris realized that he could combine his academic knowledge with his passion for health and nutrition to make a difference.

Working in Boston, Massachusetts, Norris connects students and their families with local food resources; meets with parents, teachers, administrators, and community groups to improve the school food environment; and brings nutrition education and school gardening to high-need schools.

▼ Member: Jessica Polledri
Location: Portland, OR

After viewing a segment on *60 Minutes* about food deserts, Jessica's life changed course. She realized that many people living in poverty don't have access to healthy foods in their local grocery stores and corner markets. Since then, Jessica has focused on improving eating habits, particularly in at-risk children in areas with a high incidence of diet-related disease. She's served with FoodCorps at Growing Gardens in Portland, Oregon, for two years. Jessica spends most of her time growing veggies, cooking with kids, and helping them discover their passion for beets, dirt, and worms.

"One of the best parts of working with kids in the garden is seeing how receptive they are to eating whole foods if they grow them themselves. My students harvested two heads of broccoli for our afternoon salad, but ate all of it before we got inside—all we had left were stumps."

—Jessica Polledri

▲ **Member: Mauricio Rosas-Alvarez**
Location: Des Moines, IA

As far back as he can remember, Mauricio Rosas-Alvarez's life has revolved around food. He comes from a big Mexican family that builds its community, values, and morals at the table.

He is a culinary and nutrition graduate of Johnson & Wales University and served two terms with FoodCorps in Des Moines, Iowa, where he has taught the Pick-a-Better-Snack curriculum in three schools. He also develops and implements two garden- and cooking-focused after-school programs, develops and tends school gardens for the Des Moines Public School District, and identifies procurement opportunities for classrooms and cafeterias. He served as coordinator of the agricultural appreciation aspect of the Culinary Arts Program and as the chef recruiter for the Let's Move Chefs to Schools event.

Get Involved!

FoodCorps is always looking for friends to:

- Support their work through sponsorships and donations
- Volunteer alongside service members in the field
- Tweet about them and connect with them on Facebook to spread the word
- Connect with their community to stay informed

To get involved, go to www.foodcorps.org/get-involved

"One of the highlights from my first year was helping a particular middle-school student realize that she loved garlic. When I first introduced it, she raved about garlic powder, but hated 'real garlic.' On a different day, we roasted some garlic for a recipe and when it came time to use it, it was all gone. I looked around to see where it went and found her huge smile saying, 'I love roasted garlic.'"

—Mauricio Rosas-Alvarez

Nutritional Analysis

How to Use It and Why

Glance at the end of any *Cooking Light* recipe, and you'll see how committed we are to helping you make the best of today's light cooking. With chefs, registered dietitians, home economists, and a computer system that analyzes every ingredient we use, *Cooking Light* gives you authoritative dietary detail like no other magazine. We go to such lengths so you can see how our recipes fit into your healthful eating plan. If you're trying to lose weight, the calorie and fat figures will probably help most. But if you're keeping a close eye on the sodium, cholesterol, and saturated fat in your diet, we provide those numbers, too. And because many women don't get enough iron or calcium, we can help there, as well. Finally, there's a fiber analysis for those of us who don't get enough roughage.

Here's a helpful guide to put our nutritional analysis numbers into perspective. Remember, one size doesn't fit all, so take your lifestyle, age, and circumstances into consideration when determining your nutrition needs. For example, pregnant or breast-feeding women need more protein, calories, and calcium. And women older than 50 need 1,200mg of calcium daily, 200mg more than the amount recommended for younger women.

In Our Nutritional Analysis, We Use These Abbreviations

sat	saturated fat	CARB	carbohydrates	g	gram
mono	monounsaturated fat	CHOL	cholesterol	mg	milligram
poly	polyunsaturated fat	CALC	calcium		

Daily Nutrition Guide

	Women ages 25 to 50	Women over 50	Men ages 24 to 50	Men over 50
Calories	2,000	2,000 or less	2,700	2,500
Protein	50g	50g or less	63g	60g
Fat	65g or less	65g or less	88g or less	83g or less
Saturated Fat	20g or less	20g or less	27g or less	25g or less
Carbohydrates	304g	304g	410g	375g
Fiber	25g to 35g	25g to 35g	25g to 35g	25g to 35g
Cholesterol	300mg or less	300mg or less	300mg or less	300mg or less
Iron	18mg	8mg	8mg	8mg
Sodium	2,300mg or less	1,500mg or less	2,300mg or less	1,500mg or less
Calcium	1,000mg	1,200mg	1,000mg	1,000mg

The nutritional values used in our calculations either come from The Food Processor, Version 10.4 (ESHA Research), or are provided by food manufacturers.

Metric Equivalents

The information in the following charts is provided to help cooks outside the United States successfully use the recipes in this book. All equivalents are approximate.

Cooking/Oven Temperatures

	Fahrenheit	Celsius	Gas Mark
Freeze Water	32° F	0° C	
Room Temp.	68° F	20° C	
Boil Water	212° F	100° C	
Bake	325° F	160° C	3
	350° F	180° C	4
	375° F	190° C	5
	400° F	200° C	6
	425° F	220° C	7
	450° F	230° C	8
Broil			Grill

Liquid Ingredients by Volume

¼ tsp	=						1 ml	
½ tsp	=						2 ml	
1 tsp	=						5 ml	
3 tsp	=	1 Tbsp	=	½ fl oz	=		15 ml	
2 Tbsp	=	⅛ cup	=	1 fl oz	=		30 ml	
4 Tbsp	=	¼ cup	=	2 fl oz	=		60 ml	
5⅓ Tbsp	=	⅓ cup	=	3 fl oz	=		80 ml	
8 Tbsp	=	½ cup	=	4 fl oz	=		120 ml	
10⅔ Tbsp	=	⅔ cup	=	5 fl oz	=		160 ml	
12 Tbsp	=	¾ cup	=	6 fl oz	=		180 ml	
16 Tbsp	=	1 cup	=	8 fl oz	=		240 ml	
1 pt	=	2 cups	=	16 fl oz	=		480 ml	
1 qt	=	4 cups	=	32 fl oz	=		960 ml	
				33 fl oz	=	1000 ml	=	1 l

Dry Ingredients by Weight

(To convert ounces to grams, multiply the number of ounces by 30.)

1 oz	=	¹⁄₁₆ lb	=	30 g
4 oz	=	¼ lb	=	120 g
8 oz	=	½ lb	=	240 g
12 oz	=	¾ lb	=	360 g
16 oz	=	1 lb	=	480 g

Length

(To convert inches to centimeters, multiply the number of inches by 2.5.)

1 in	=					2.5 cm	
6 in	=	½ ft		=		15 cm	
12 in	=	1 ft		=		30 cm	
36 in	=	3 ft	=	1 yd	=	90 cm	
40 in	=					100 cm	= 1m

Equivalents for Different Types of Ingredients

Standard Cup	Fine Powder (ex. flour)	Grain (ex. rice)	Granular (ex. sugar)	Liquid Solids (ex. butter)	Liquid (ex. milk)
1	140 g	150 g	190 g	200 g	240 ml
¾	105 g	113 g	143 g	150 g	180 ml
⅔	93 g	100 g	125 g	133 g	160 ml
½	70 g	75 g	95 g	100 g	120 ml
⅓	47 g	50 g	63 g	67 g	80 ml
¼	35 g	38 g	48 g	50 g	60 ml
⅛	18 g	19 g	24 g	25 g	30 ml

Subject Index

Recipe Index

C